CW00351837

Internet!
I Didn't Know You Could Do That...™
Second Edition

Alan R. Neibauer

SYBEX®

San Francisco • Paris • Düsseldorf • Soest • London

Associate Publisher: Cheryl Applewood
Contracts and Licensing Manager: Kristine O'Callaghan
Editor: Rob Siedenburg
Service Representative: Jan Fisher
Technical Editor: Dana Jones
Book Designer: Franz Baumhackl, Kate Kaminski
Graphic Illustrator: Don Waller
Electronic Publishing Specialist: Rhonda Ries
Proofreaders: Phil Hamer, Jenny Putman
Indexer: Matthew Spence
CD Technicians: Keith McNeil, Siobhan Dowling
CD Coordinator: Kara Eve Schwartz
Cover Designer: Daniel Ziegler
Cover Illustrator/Photographer: PhotoDisk

Copyright © 2000 SYBEX Inc., 1151 Marina Village Parkway, Alameda, CA 94501. World rights reserved. No part of this publication may be stored in a retrieval system, transmitted, or reproduced in any way, including but not limited to photocopy, photograph, magnetic, or other record, without the prior agreement and written permission of the publisher. First edition copyright © 2000 SYBEX Inc.

Library of Congress Card Number: 00-106232

ISBN: 0-7821-2844-0

SYBEX and the SYBEX logo are trademarks of SYBEX Inc. in the USA and other countries.

IDKYCDT and I Didn't Know You Could Do That are trademarks of SYBEX Inc.

Screen reproductions produced with FullShot 99. FullShot 99 © 1991–1999 Inbit Incorporated. All rights reserved.
FullShot is a trademark of Inbit Incorporated.

The CD interface was created using Macromedia Director, © 1994, 1997–1999 Macromedia Inc. For more information on Macromedia and Macromedia Director, visit http://www.macromedia.com.

Internet screen shot(s) using Microsoft Internet Explorer 5 reprinted by permission from Microsoft Corporation.

Trademarks: SYBEX has attempted throughout this book to distinguish proprietary trademarks from descriptive terms by following the capitalization style used by the manufacturer.

The author and publisher have made their best efforts to prepare this book, and the content is based upon final release software whenever possible. Portions of the manuscript may be based upon pre-release versions supplied by software manufacturer(s). The author and the publisher make no representation or warranties of any kind with regard to the completeness or accuracy of the contents herein and accept no liability of any kind including but not limited to performance, merchantability, fitness for any particular purpose, or any losses or damages of any kind caused or alleged to be caused directly or indirectly from this book.

Photographs and illustrations used in this book have been downloaded from publicly accessible file archives and are used in this book for news reportage purposes only to demonstrate the variety of graphics resources available via electronic access. Text and images available over the Internet may be subject to copyright and other rights owned by third parties. Online availability of text and images does not imply that they may be reused without the permission of rights holders, although the Copyright Act does permit certain unauthorized reuse as fair use under 17 U.S.C. Section 107.

Manufactured in the United States of America

10 9 8 7 6 5 4 3 2 1

Software License Agreement: Terms and Conditions

The media and/or any online materials accompanying this book that are available now or in the future contain programs and/or text files (the "Software") to be used in connection with the book. SYBEX hereby grants to you a license to use the Software, subject to the terms that follow. Your purchase, acceptance, or use of the Software will constitute your acceptance of such terms.

The Software compilation is the property of SYBEX unless otherwise indicated and is protected by copyright to SYBEX or other copyright owner(s) as indicated in the media files (the "Owner(s)"). You are hereby granted a single-user license to use the Software for your personal, noncommercial use only. You may not reproduce, sell, distribute, publish, circulate, or commercially exploit the Software, or any portion thereof, without the written consent of SYBEX and the specific copyright owner(s) of any component software included on this media.

In the event that the Software or components include specific license requirements or end-user agreements, statements of condition, disclaimers, limitations or warranties ("End-User License"), those End-User Licenses supersede the terms and conditions herein as to that particular Software component. Your purchase, acceptance, or use of the Software will constitute your acceptance of such End-User Licenses.

By purchase, use or acceptance of the Software you further agree to comply with all export laws and regulations of the United States as such laws and regulations may exist from time to time.

Software Support

Components of the supplemental Software and any offers associated with them may be supported by the specific Owner(s) of that material but they are not supported by SYBEX. Information regarding any available support may be obtained from the Owner(s) using the information provided in the appropriate read.me files or listed elsewhere on the media.

Should the manufacturer(s) or other Owner(s) cease to offer support or decline to honor any offer, SYBEX bears no responsibility. This notice concerning support for the Software is provided for your information only. SYBEX is not the agent or principal of the Owner(s), and SYBEX is in no way responsible for providing any support for the Software, nor is it liable or responsible for any support provided, or not provided, by the Owner(s).

Warranty

SYBEX warrants the enclosed media to be free of physical defects for a period of ninety (90) days after purchase. The Software is not available from SYBEX in any other form or media than that enclosed herein or posted to www.sybex.com. If you discover a defect in the media during this warranty period, you may obtain a replacement of identical format at no charge by sending the defective media, postage prepaid, with proof of purchase to:

SYBEX Inc.
Customer Service Department
1151 Marina Village Parkway
Alameda, CA 94501
(510) 523-8233
Fax: (510) 523-2373
e-mail: info@sybex.com
WEB: HTTP://WWW.SYBEX.COM

After the 90-day period, you can obtain replacement media of identical format by sending us the defective disk, proof of purchase, and a check or money order for $10, payable to SYBEX.

Disclaimer

SYBEX makes no warranty or representation, either expressed or implied, with respect to the Software or its contents, quality, performance, merchantability, or fitness for a particular purpose. In no event will SYBEX, its distributors, or dealers be liable to you or any other party for direct, indirect, special, incidental, consequential, or other damages arising out of the use of or inability to use the Software or its contents even if advised of the possibility of such damage. In the event that the Software includes an online update feature, SYBEX further disclaims any obligation to provide this feature for any specific duration other than the initial posting.

The exclusion of implied warranties is not permitted by some states. Therefore, the above exclusion may not apply to you. This warranty provides you with specific legal rights; there may be other rights that you may have that vary from state to state. The pricing of the book with the Software by SYBEX reflects the allocation of risk and limitations on liability contained in this agreement of Terms and Conditions.

Shareware Distribution

This Software may contain various programs that are distributed as shareware. Copyright laws apply to both shareware and ordinary commercial software, and the copyright Owner(s) retains all rights. If you try a shareware program and continue using it, you are expected to register it. Individual programs differ on details of trial periods, registration, and payment. Please observe the requirements stated in appropriate files.

Copy Protection

The Software in whole or in part may or may not be copy-protected or encrypted. However, in all cases, reselling or redistributing these files without authorization is expressly forbidden except as specifically provided for by the Owner(s) therein.

To Barbara

Acknowledgments

No book is really ever the effort of only one person. It took a number of people to complete this book, and to all of them I am forever grateful.

My thanks to AOL expert Laura Arendal for doing such a wonderful job with the AOL section of this book that is on the CD. Laura is the author of her own book devoted to AOL, and she was kind enough to add her expertise to this project.

My appreciation to everyone at Sybex who helped with this book, especially associate publisher Cheryl Applewood, acquisitions and developmental editor Sherry Bonelli, and associate editorial supervisor Colleen Wheeler Strand.

Thanks also to all of the folks at Publication Services for doing such a great job: project coordinator Rhonda Ries, copy editor Rob Siedenburg, proofreaders Jenny Putman and Phil Hamer, technical editor Dana Jones, and service representative Jan Fisher.

Thanks to all of the companies, Web site developers, and software developers who generously granted permission to use their Web sites as illustrations in this book and their software in the CD.

I also want to thank all of the folks who suggested topics and Web sites, including Lori Secouler, Herb Kaufman, Kenn Venit, Miriam Greenwald, Richard Modes, Bonnie Moses, Dave Olshina, Marsha Sobel, and Curtis Philips.

Finally, my deepest appreciation and love to a remarkable woman, a Xena Warrior Princess in her own time, my wife Barbara. I find it impossible to describe her, and her importance in my life, in just a few words. Honey, you're the greatest.

Contents

Introduction

The Internet is one great place to be! No matter what type of information you need, what products you want to buy, or who you want to contact, you can find what you need on the Internet. I know that from some very personal experiences.

Years ago, when my physician was treating me for the flu, I was able to diagnose a rash that I had as a symptom of Lyme disease. I was then able to get the treatment I needed. I found this information on an Internet health site.

More recently, my wife and I were able to save over $70,000. To make a long and agonizing story short, we needed to get public water installed in our house because the water from our well was tainted. The initial estimate from the local water company was just under $80,000. That's when my wife, Barbara, learned how to use the Internet. Through an e-mail campaign directed at government officials and agencies, water department officials, and consumer groups, Barbara was able to get water installed for a substantial savings.

So while the Internet can be a fun place to shop and play, it can also be a very valuable resource for you and your family.

One of the best things about the Internet is that you don't even need your own computer and Internet account to take advantage of most of the topics discussed in this book and most of the free offers and resources on the Internet. You just need access to the Internet and your own e-mail account. You can get access to the Internet for free or for very little cost. You'll find such access at local libraries and schools, Internet cafes, and other establishments that make the Internet available to the public. If you need an e-mail account to sign up for offers and other freebies, you can get a free e-mail account, as you'll learn how to do in this book. So even without your own computer and a monthly Internet charge, you can send and receive e-mail and even have your own Web page!

This book is my way of sharing some of the interesting and often unique things that you can do over the Internet. Some of the topics you'll read about in this book are not well known; others may seem familiar, but you'll learn about new features and unique approaches. It may be something you've heard can be done over the Internet but never knew exactly how to do.

How This Book Is Organized

The book is divided into parts. Each part is a collection of numbered sections that cover things to do and see on the Internet.

In "See It, Hear It, Say It," you'll learn some entertaining things. You'll learn how you can watch television, documentaries, sporting events, and classic movies on your computer screen as you work. You'll also learn how to watch people all over the world through Web cameras, and how to download music and make your own CDs. You will learn how to chat and talk to friends, relatives, and strangers online, and how to see them and let them see you if you both have inexpensive video-conferencing cameras. If you do not have cameras for real video, you'll learn how to see who you are chatting with in virtual worlds.

Searching the Unlimited Resource is all about finding things on the Internet. Since you probably already know about using search engines such as Yahoo! and Lycos, I'll show you techniques for supercharging your searches. You'll learn how to find driving directions, people, jobs, a place to live, even a date or spouse—and how to track down your family tree.

In "It's About Time," you'll learn how to keep track of your online time and keep your computer's clock on time. You'll also know what time it is at any place around the world, and you'll be able to keep track of your own time online by maintaining your schedule on the Internet.

In "News and Mail," you'll learn to access the latest news online. You'll find out what's happening right in your own town, you'll get and manage free e-mail accounts, and you'll reduce the clutter of junk e-mail. You'll also learn how to get your e-mail no matter where you are, and how to include sound and video in your e-mail messages.

Free e-mail is only the tip of the freebie iceberg on the Internet. In "More Free Stuff," you'll learn how to get free stuff of all types, including totally free Internet accounts, electronic greeting cards, and your very own voice mail and fax telephone numbers. You'll also learn how to get free software and books, make free or inexpensive long distance telephone calls, and buy postage stamps online.

In "Enhancing the Internet Experience," you'll learn secrets for speeding up surfing; after you are finished with this part, you will be able to browse more than one site at a time and browse offline. You'll also learn how to safeguard your computer from Internet hackers, how to share one phone line and one

Internet account after your computers are networked, and all about high-speed Internet access.

In "Web Sites, Free or Easy," you will learn how to grab graphics and sounds that you see online. You will also learn how to find out who owns a Web site you are interested in. You'll read about how to get your own free Web sites, how to store personal documents on the Internet, how to share photographs and files, and how to register your own Web domain.

In "Buying and Selling Online," you'll learn techniques for winning Web auctions, registering your wish list or bridal registry, and finding hard-to-locate, out-of-print books and collectibles for almost any collection. You'll also learn how to make money by selling things online—through auctions and by running your own e-commerce store.

In "Getting Help," you will find out how to get the latest device drivers for your hardware and how to upgrade Windows 98. You'll also uncover secrets for getting legal, medical, and do-it-yourself help.

Each of the numbered topics in this book is organized in about the same way. After a brief introduction, you'll find two general topics— "Here's What You Need" and "Sites and Features" (in the AOL part of the CD, the second section is called "Here's How It Works").

In the "Here's What You Need" sections, you'll find out what resources you need to take advantage of the features described in a specific numbered section. In most cases, all you need is access to the Internet. In some cases, you'll need a special piece of software—which you get on the CD-ROM that comes with this book.

In "Sites and Features," you'll learn all of the tips and techniques as well as what sites you can access on the Internet.

One word of caution. Internet sites are changing constantly. Some are just redesigned; others are taken off the Web entirely. It is very possible that some of the Web sites described and pictured in this book may not appear the same way on your screen. Some of the sites may not even be available. We'll keep you up-to-date on as many changes as possible, and show you some new, interesting, and secret Internet facts at the SYBEX Web site at www.sybex.com.

NOTE Web site addresses are shown in this book without the `http://` prefix because most Web browsers let you enter site names without it. You can enter `www.sybex.com` in your Web browser's location or address box and press Enter to go to `http://www.sybex.com`, or enter `gldss7.cr.usgs.gov` to go to `http://gldss7.cr.usgs.gov`.

If you have a favorite Web site that you'd like to share with other readers, drop me a note at `alan@neibauer.net`.

What Is on the CD?

Many of the secrets and techniques you'll learn about in this book involve a software program, so look for this icon:

This icon means that the program described in the book is on the CD packaged with the book. The CD contains valuable programs that will enhance your Internet experience.

Some of the programs are freeware, which means you can use the program as long as you want for no charge. Other programs are shareware. You can use these programs, but you're asked to pay a small fee if you like the program and want to continue using it after the trial period has ended. In some cases, you can use the program only for a certain number of days before it expires. You'll have to register and pay for the program to continue using it.

You'll find complete information about each program when you install it, and you'll find a list of the programs that are on the CD in the Readme file on the CD.

N O T E Once again, it is important to remember that these products are being changed and updated regularly. Although we have tried to put the most recent version of the software on the CD, it is very possible that there will be a more recent version of some of this software available when you get this book. Please check the URLs that are provided for the most up-to-date information.

Downloading Software

Almost all of the programs on the CD are also available for downloading from the Internet. Downloading means that you transfer a copy of the program from the Internet to your computer. The location on the Internet where you can download the program and get more information will be listed in the text and on the Readme document on the CD.

You do not need to download a copy of a program if you see the CD icon in the text. But sometimes you'll find a more recent or improved version of the program on the appropriate Web site. If you find a program that you really like and intend to use frequently, check out the Web site for the latest version.

In this book you will also learn about programs that are not included on the CD. You may want to download and try out these programs as well. Somewhere on the Web site you'll see a link for downloading the file. Its name and position will vary with every program and with every Web site. When you click the link, your Web browser will usually display a message asking whether you want to open the file or save the file on your disk. Always choose the Save option. You may then see a dialog box in which you select the location to place the file and provide it with a name. There will always be a default name given, so don't change that, but you might want to make a note of the location to which the file will be saved, or you may even want to select a new location. The dialog box is much like the Save As dialog box you find with most Windows applications.

Unzipping Files

Files that you'll find on the CD or for download are either executable programs or ZIP files.

Some of the products on the CD will be executable programs with .EXE extensions. To install or run these programs, double-click the EXE file. The program will either begin running immediately, or you will be guided through the steps of a setup and installation program.

Many of the files you download from the Internet, however, are Zip files with the .ZIP extension. Because program files can be quite large and actually require a number of individual files, they are compressed, or shrunken, and saved in a special reduced format, called a Zip file. You can download a Zip file in much less time than it would take to download it in its uncompressed format.

 To install or run a program that is in a Zip file, you have to first unzip it. This decompresses, or expands, the files to their actual, full size. In order to unzip a Zip file, you'll need a special program called WinZip that you'll find on the CD with this book. Run the program WinZip80 from the CD to install WinZip on your computer. When you download a Zip file from the Internet, just double-click the file's Zip icon. In the box that appears, click I Agree to start WinZip and see a list of the items in the archived Zip file. Click the Extract button on the WinZip toolbar, choose the location where you want to place the files in the box that appears, and then click Extract.

Internet Tool Pack

In addition to WinZip, which you'll need to unzip some programs, you'll also find some other programs on the CD for general Internet surfing:

 Internet Explorer 5   A complete Web browser for surfing the Internet.

 Webroot's Window Washer   Lets you delete extraneous files that are added to your hard disk during Internet browsing and everyday computing tasks.

ClipCache   Lets you copy multiple items into the Windows clipboard, which you'll find useful for copying Web site addresses, graphics, or other items of interest on the Internet.

 Adobe Acrobat   A utility for reading specially formatted files that you frequently find on the Internet.

Bonus Section on CD Exclusively for AOL Users

On the CD-ROM, you'll find a bonus section, "What You Didn't Know You Could Do with AOL," designed just for America Online members. Here you'll find out how to supercharge and enhance your AOL experience in ways you never thought possible. This bonus section, by the way, was written by Laura Arendal, an expert on squeezing the most out of AOL.

An Internet Potpourri

There are an unfathomable number of places to go on the Internet for help of all kinds. We've touched on some of them in this book, but you will certainly find thousands of additional sites on your own, and you will also get recommendations from friends and relatives. You'll see Internet sites in company advertisements and hear them in television and radio announcements. You can find, buy, and sell just about everything.

In addition to the sites in this book, here are a few that have been recommended to me by interested observers:

◆ To find weird, exotic, stupid, and just plain fun stuff there is on the Internet, go to www.whattheheck.com.

◆ For interesting short films and movie parodies (such as *Saving Ryan's Privates*) go to www.atomfilms.com.

◆ To learn the truth about urban legends, such as "A stranger stole my kidney," check out www.snopes.com.

◆ To see what any Web site looks like in the dialect of **rednecks,
jive, Cockney, Elmer Fudd, a Swedish Chef, or Pig Latin,** go to
`rinkworks.com/dialect`.

◆ For online gambling, try `www.gamingclub.com` or `www.gambling.com`.

◆ For earthquake information try `gldss7.cr.usgs.gov`.

◆ To track airlines in flight go to `www.thetrip.com/usertools/
flighttracking`.

◆ To find out the time of high and low tides visit `tbone.biol.sc.edu/
tide/sitesel.html`.

◆ To buy cars go to `www.autobytel.com`, `www.carpoint.msn.com`,
`www.autovantage.com`, `www.autoweb.com`, or `www.kbb.com`.

◆ Finally, when you want to make some (hopefully) **very long range**
plans, the last Web site you may want to visit is
`www.funeralsoftware.com`.

See It, Hear It, Say It

Through the Internet, you can get sights and sounds from around the world. You can listen to music, watch television and video, and create your own personal collection of music to play at your convenience. You can even watch real people do real things via video cameras placed at interesting locations. You can view these videos from your computer through the Web 24 hours a day. You can also enjoy chatting with friends and strangers over the Internet. You can even talk in real time—just as if you were on the telephone—and see them on your screen and let them see you, if you have the necessary hardware. If you do not have a camera attached to your computer, you can take part in three-dimensional virtual chats that make you feel as if you were speaking in person.

1   Mix Learning with Pleasure

This is something you'll really love—it's one of my favorites. If you feel guilty about it, just tell people it's educational and beneficial, similar to the way playing games improves hand-eye coordination. It actually *is* educational. But the real reason you'll like this one is because it is just so much fun.

Watch Live News, TV, and the Classics of Hollywood

You can watch old movies and live television right on your computer screen. You can view documentaries and news (that's the educational part), watch sports programs, and listen to music and live on-air radio. Beats the heck out of watching the Windows screen saver when you're bored at work.

Here's What You Need

The quality of a movie or TV broadcast image on your screen depends on your screen resolution, the number of colors, and the speed of your Internet connection. As a general rule of thumb, the higher the resolution and the faster the connection, the better the image. You can change your screen resolution using the Display applet in the Windows Control Panel. You'll also need a working sound card. The quality of the video will be determined by the quality of your video card and the amount of memory it contains.

Windows Media Player and RealPlayer

Next, you'll need to have both Windows Media Player and a program called RealPlayer installed on your system. That's no problem because both are free (a version of RealPlayer is on the CD with this book, making acquiring it even easier!). No special hardware is required. Why both programs? When you run a music or video file on the Internet, it automatically accesses one of these programs (most Web sites that display video files contain links to download Windows Media Player or RealPlayer). You might have your choice of which to use, but often the Web site just tries to run one of them automatically. Having both programs installed means you'll be able to view and hear almost anything.

If you do not have the necessary program installed when you try to view a multimedia file, you'll be asked if you want to download the file to your computer anyway. If you get this message, just say No—the file won't do you much good without the program installed, and video files can be extremely large and time-consuming to download. Make a note of the site you visited for the file, install both Windows Media Player and RealPlayer (you'll learn how to do this later in this section), and then try again.

Both RealPlayer and Windows Media Player use a "streaming" sort of routine. This means that you don't have to wait until the entire movie or sound file is downloaded to your computer to view or listen to it. The show begins as soon as a portion of the file is downloaded, and then continues playing as more comes in. If Internet traffic is busy, however, you may notice some delay between pieces of the file transmission.

To see if you have Windows Media Player, follow these steps:

1. Try Start ➤ Programs ➤ Accessories ➤ Entertainment ➤ Windows Media Player.

2. If that is not an option, try Start ➤ Find ➤ Files or Folders.

3. Make sure that the Look in field is set at C, type **MPLAYER2.EXE**, and click Find Now.

4. Double-click MPLAYER2 if it is listed in the window.

Compare the program on your screen with the one shown in Figure 1.1.

FIGURE 1.1   Windows Media Player

If the program does appear, select Help ➢ Check for Player Upgrade. Windows dials into your Internet Service Provider (ISP), connects to the appropriate site, and sees whether you have the most recent version. Just follow the instructions on screen if you need to download a newer release.

If the program is not already installed, or if it does not appear anything like the one shown here, navigate to www.microsoft.com/windows/ mediaplayer/default.asp, and download it for free.

To see if you have RealPlayer installed and ready, follow these steps:

1. Start ➢ Programs ➢ Real ➢ RealPlayer. (The program name, RealPlayer, is followed by the version number.)

2. If that is not an option, click Start ➢ Find ➢ Files or Folders.

3. Type **REALPLAY.EXE** and click Find Now.

4. Double-click RealPlayer if it is listed in the window.

Compare it to the one shown in Figure 1.2.

If the program does appear, click Help ➢ Check for Update to dial into your ISP, connect to the appropriate site, and see whether you have the most recent version. Just follow the instructions on screen if you need to download a newer release.

If the program is not already installed, or if it does not appear anything like the one shown here, you'll find it on the CD with this book. You can also purchase a more powerful version at www.realplayer.com.

FIGURE 1.2 RealPlayer

While there are important differences between the free and paid versions of the program, start out with the free one to make sure you like it.

QuickTime

While you're downloading software, it might also help to have Apple Computer, Inc.'s QuickTime player installed on your system. There are some video files that are designed solely for that format, and they cannot be viewed on the other players. The QuickTime viewer is also free for downloading from www.apple.com/quicktime. To download the player, you'll need to enter your e-mail address and select a format—either for the Macintosh or for Windows.

What you actually download is an installation program that is about 700KB. You then run that program to reconnect to the Internet in order to download the QuickTime viewer itself. You can choose from three flavors of the viewer—Minimum, Full, and Custom. It is best to choose Full to be able to play the widest variety of movies.

Sites and Features

Once you are armed with both RealPlayer and Windows Media Player, you can use them to access interesting video sites and to display some great entertaining or educational videos. The following descriptions cover some of these sites in more detail.

Howdy Partner

To get to old westerns navigate to www.westerns.com and click the first screen. From this page, you can either choose to watch the week's featured movie, or click any of the links on the left.

Clicking Theater displays a catalog of available films. When you select the film you want to watch, you'll see details about it as shown in Figure 1.3. Click the graphic of the film to start viewing it. Windows Media Player will begin, and the movie will download for viewing.

What's great about Westerns.com is the number of films available. Some of the films are even available on old-fashioned videocassette; you can order these online from Westerns.com.

NOTE If you are interested in the cowboys of old, also check out www.cowboypal.com.

Live TV

AmericaOne.com is a family-oriented television network. This site provides all of its programming live on the Internet as well. Some of their programming consists of old films and television shows—and those wonderful action serials that brought us old folks into the Saturday matinee each week. The content is reminiscent of the material available on

FIGURE 1.3   Click the graphic to run the film.

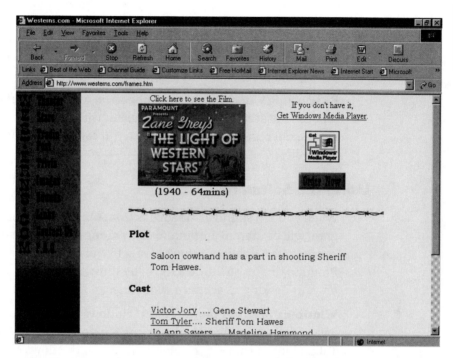

Westerns.com, but AmericaOne.com also offers plenty of children's programming and many educational shows. For a program schedule, navigate to `www.americaone.com` and click TV Schedule.

When you get to AmericaOne.com, click the animated graphic that says Click Here Watch Us On The Web. To start viewing the television broadcast, click the speed of your connection under the large television screen in the Web site. Whatever channel is broadcasting currently will appear in a Windows Media Player window.

NOTE If you like television theme songs, you can listen to hundreds of them, old and new, and see scenes from the shows at `www.tvjukebox.net`.

Take Your Choice

To access all sorts of films, television shows, and radio—both live and on demand—navigate to broadcast.com. This site offers the widest variety of broadcasts in several areas. Usually, one special item is featured. You can also scan through items in a variety of categories.

By selecting Video (one of the categories), you can access the site's Video on Demand area. You'll need to register with Broadcast.com to access the videos, but registration is free. Here you can choose from its archive of video files.

Using the Software

When you run sound or video files from the Internet, the appropriate program will be started automatically (as long as you have it installed). You can also start either Windows Media Player or RealPlayer from the Start ➤ Programs menu on the desktop or by shortcuts that you may have for them on your desktop to access a wide range of files and features.

Windows Media Player   Start Windows Media Player from the desktop using Programs ➤ Accessories ➤ Entertainment ➤ Windows Media Player. Take a look at some of the highlights of the Windows Media Player.

The Favorites Menu   Offers you the option of choosing from a number of preset channels—it lists many Web sites where you can find sound and video files—and you can add your own favorite sites for quick access. You can also click What's On Now to access the Microsoft Web events site: `windowsmedia.com/default.asp`. This is a great site to go to for a wide variety of video and music files. Choose from a list of audio and video headlines or from these categories:

The File Menu   Lets you open files on your disk.

The View Menu   Lets you change the size of the window or display videos full screen.

The Play Menu   Lets you play, stop, and move through sounds and videos.

The Go Menu   Lets you go backward and forward through visited sites; it also directs you to interesting sites containing links to media files.

The Help Menu   Gives you information about how to use Windows Media Player and how to check for program upgrades.

The controls for playing files are shown here:

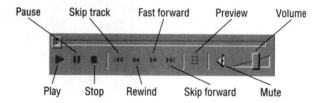

RealPlayer   Start RealPlayer using Start ➤ Programs ➤ Real ➤ RealPlayer (which will be followed by its version number) or by selecting any RealPlayer file on the Internet. Some of the most useful portions of this program are described below.

The Stations Menu   Provides access to a number of popular radio stations and other music sites, organized into categories.

The Channels Menu   Lets you access Web sites from which you can choose music or video files, or watch live television broadcasts.

The Favorites Menu   Works like Internet Explorer Favorites, except it already has present stations.

The Text Box Search   Search for files using the snap.com service by entering a keyword in the text box at the bottom of the window, then click Search.

The Control Panel   Lists preset channels. You can use it as an alternative to the menus at the top of the RealPlayer screen, or you can search for files based on keywords. The Control Panel is located along the left of the window. Click the channel you want to play, or scroll using the up and down arrows:

Internet Explorer Radio Toolbar   If you have Internet Explorer 5, you can also select and listen to live radio broadcasts using the Radio Toolbar:

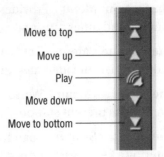

If the bar is not already displayed when you start Internet Explorer, right-click the toolbar already shown, and select Radio from the menu that appears.

To use this feature and select a radio station, click Radio Stations on the toolbar and choose Radio Station Guide from the menu. The browser will access a Web site from which you can choose a station to listen to. Stations you select will later be listed in the Radio Stations menu for your convenience.

Your Own Radio Station

If you like an eclectic mix of music, or cannot find a station that suits your listening tastes, you can create your own station at www.radio.sonicnet.com, shown in Figure 1.4. The site contains a list of stations designed by featured personalities, as well as a station directory by format.

FIGURE 1.4   **Create your own station at Radio.SonicNet.**

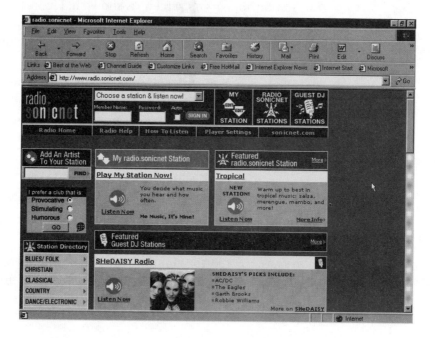

To create your own station, click Create My Station Now and then click Sign Up. Then complete the simple registration form to become a member of the service (for free), and to access a form where you describe your musical preferences.

Select the types of music you like and then click Continue. For each music type, you then select how often you want to hear it, in a range from *Never* to *A Lot*. Once you've completed the form, click Done to return to the

Radio.SonicNet home page. Click Play My Station Now. Finally, click the button that represents your connection speed to open your radio station and start the music.

NOTE   Once you are a member, enter your member name and password on the home page; click Sign in. Click Play My Station to start listening to your music. Click Edit My Station to change your music preference or the frequency with which selected types of music are played.

Your station appears on screen, as shown in Figure 1.5. It shows your station name along with information about the track currently being played. Buttons in the window let you edit your station, list other stations maintained on Radio.SonicNet, and change stations.

Radio.SonicNet automatically chooses either Windows Media Player or RealPlayer to play music, depending on which is on your system and set as the default. To specify which program to use, click the Player Settings button on the Radio.SonicNet home page and make your choice in the dialog box that appears.

Imagine the Opportunities

I've listed here just a few of the sites where you can access audio and video files—there are plenty of others.

At www.spinner.com, for example, you can download the free SpinnerPlus software. When you run the program, it connects to the Spinner Web site and lets you select a channel of music to listen to. Here are some other sites where you can access music, video, and live television:

- ◆ www.cdnow.com
- ◆ www.film.com
- ◆ www.musicnet.com
- ◆ www.hollywoodandvine.com

FIGURE 1.5   Your station at Radio.SonicNet

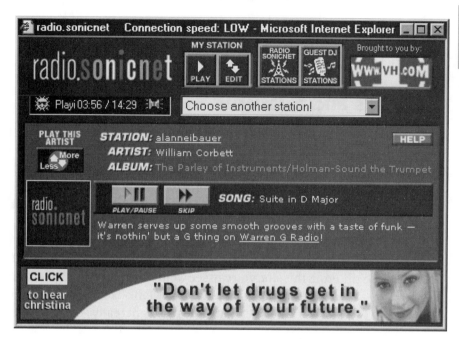

2 Discover Real-Time Video

Do you want to feel like a secret agent spying on the enemy, or are you just curious about what's going on in other parts of the world? You can watch real people doing real things and view some of nature's bounty, live on the Web.

View Real Life around the World

Web cameras (AKA Webcams) are cameras placed at various locations around the world that broadcast their images on the Internet. Most of the cameras are on 24/7—24 hours a day, seven days a week—so you can always find something to watch.

Here's What You Need

You'll need access to the Internet. You should also have the RealPlayer and Microsoft Media Player programs installed if you want to see live video rather than still pictures.

Sites and Features

You may not find all Webcams very interesting to look at. Depending on the visibility provided by the weather, or the time of day, you could be looking at a deserted street in Paris or the clouds hanging over Mount Fuji. But most of the cams are worth looking at periodically just for curiosity's sake. Some may be aimed at locations you are familiar with or plan to visit. Others may be broadcasting a beautiful natural scene or just the world of plain folks as they pass by the camera lens. There's one site, for example, www.electrolux.com/node230.asp, filmed from the inside of a refrigerator. From this site, you can see what the fruits and vegetables see when the door closes, and what we nonedibles look like when the door opens. This finally answers the question "Does the light really go off when you close the door?"

NOTE   The vast majority of Web cameras are free, but a few charge a fee. You'll have to register and give credit card information to access those sites, which are usually for adult audiences only.

There are a lot of Web cameras in people's homes, offices, and dorm rooms. Tune in to see what these folks are doing, or not doing, at any time. The cameras are all over the world, so don't be surprised if you can peek at life in Peking, admire a scene from Amsterdam, or just watch cats play in Katmandu. The text on the screen may be in a language you don't understand, but you can always just look at the pictures.

The majority of the cameras offer still photographs, so you'll see the most recent picture taken. The pictures are updated at regular intervals, so you can click your browser's Refresh or Reload button as often as you want to see the most recent shot. Some cameras are updated every second or so, others less frequently.

Many of the sites also give you the option of watching a real video scene. If you have Windows Media Player and RealPlayer installed, click the link to start watching the live action in front of the camera.

You can do a search for Webcam or Web cameras, but the best place to start is at www.Camcity.com. When you get to the site, you'll see a graphic with several sections:

Webcam resource   Displays links to several categories of Webcams.

Resource center   Displays links to Webcams and information for and about Webcam developers, as well as several featured cams from around the world.

Camcity North   Displays a virtual town from which you can access Webcams by their type and placement. By pointing to the map of the town, you can select cams located in neighborhoods, outdoors, downtown, underground, and in resorts.

Arcade   Links you to the online store of Surveyor Corporation for Webcam supplies.

Spotlight   Displays featured sites and Web events.

Once you decide on an option, use the buttons that appear at the top of the screen to select that option:

Home   Returns to the initial Camcity home page.

CamcityMap   Displays the Camcity North map of links.

Spotlight Events   Displays featured sites and Web events

Add a Cam   Lets you submit a Webcam to be listed in Camcity.

Top 10 Cams   Features currently popular Webcams.

Search   Lets you search for a Webcam using keywords.

Resource Center   Displays links to Webcams and information for and about Webcam developers, as well as several featured cams from around the world.

Contact Us   Lets you send email to Camcity.

Click the icon of a star at the top of the Camcity page to access a list of the top ten Web cameras, some of which are listed in Figure 2.1. You'll see a link for each of the top ten sites, its current number of hits from Camcity, and a brief description. Click on a link to display the site, along with the

FIGURE 2.1   Sample of Camcity's top 10 sites

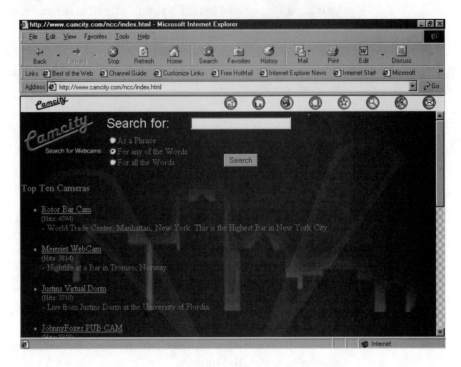

amount of time between updates, and a link to additional information about it.

One of the most popular Webcams, Camcity, is entitled *Here and Now—Real Life. Real Time.* You can access this site directly from www.hereandnow.net/webcast.html.

At Here and Now, you can access seven live cameras with full motion video and sound in an apartment where six college friends volunteered to have their lives exposed to the world, so you can tune in any time of the day to see what's going on. You may see and hear one or more of the six watching television, sleeping on the sofa, or candidly discussing some aspect of their life.

Another collection of Webcams is at www.allcam.com. The site groups cameras into these categories:

◆ Business

◆ Culture

- Education
- Entertainment
- Living
- News & Media
- People
- Science & Health
- Sports
- Travel

Click a category and then a subcategory from the list that appears to see sample screens and a link to individual Webcams. Take your time and go through the categories and subcategories. You'll be able to watch a wide variety of animals at play, and see what's happening at locations from Times Square in New York to oasis watering holes in Africa.

For another list of popular sites, go to www.excite.com. Once there, click Entertainment. From the Entertainment screen, click Humor and then click Web Cameras. You'll see a list that includes specific sites and Web camera directories—click Get More Web Sites for the complete list. Along with many other sites, you can choose to see

- The view from the top of Mount Fuji in Japan at www.sunplus.com/fuji.
- The view from the top of Pike's Peak in the United States at www.pikespeakcam.com.
- Scenes at the Kennedy Space Center at www.ambitweb.com/nasacams/nasacams.html.

You can also choose to see a list of Animal Cams featuring cows, cats, dogs, fish, rhinos, orangutans, lions, tigers, bears, and other animal friends.

Another great site for Web cameras is www.earthcam.com, which also groups cameras into a variety of categories. Click a category, or one of the links under a category, to see additional options.

From the EarthCam home page, you can also select one of the Metro cams listing major cities in the United States. Click a city link to search for a camera in that location.

Many of the Web's major search engines also give you direct links to Webcams. To access interesting sites from Yahoo, for example, go to http://dir.yahoo.com/Computers and then click the Internet link. At the new screen, click Devices Connected to the Internet. From this screen, you can click the Web Cams link to see a list of links to various sites in over 20 categories.

Working with Webcams

Webcams can be great entertainment, and even a learning experience, but the technology that creates Webcams is still new and, in a lot of ways, experimental.

Not only do you need the proper programs installed (such as Windows Media Player and RealPlayer), but your computer's settings can play a major part in your Web camera enjoyment. For example, the slower your Internet connection, the more time it takes to download and start displaying video. Real-time video might appear jumpy, with some long pauses between scenes as more information is downloaded.

You might want to try various display settings to see which one gives you the fastest and smoothest pictures. Through the Display Properties dialog box, for example, you can set the number of colors and the resolution of your screen. To open the Display Properties dialog box, right-click a blank area of the desktop, choose Properties from the shortcut menu, and click the Settings tab.

The options on Webcam sites also vary greatly. On some sites, you can choose to use either Windows Media Player or RealPlayer; you can also specify the speed of your connection. Even if you connect at 56K, the video quality can be jumpy; try connecting again by selecting a slow connection speed from the Webcam site.

Keep in mind that Webcam video takes up a lot of resources, both on the Internet and on your computer. If you can't seem to get acceptable performance, try reconnecting at a later time when the Webcam site, and your ISP, might be less busy.

3 Dance to the Music, for Free!

Free music and complete CDs are available on the Internet. Listen to music while you work, or download it for easy listening at any other time.

Download and Listen to Music—Create Your Own CDs

If you have a CD recorder, you can even make your own custom CD with all of your favorite tracks! If you don't have a CD recorder, you can save music for playback on your hard disk, zip disk, or other high-speed storage device.

Here's What You Need

Until recently, sound and music files were transmitted through the Internet in a variety of formats (such as WAV and MIDI). Full-length music files could be quite large, however, and often did not have the clarity of the original sounds.

A new music format has been developed that changes all that. With Moving Pictures Experts Group (MPEG) Audio Level 3 (known as MP3), music can be compressed by a factor of 12 and still retain its CD quality. In theory, using MP3, a complete CD can be downloaded over the Internet in about five minutes. In practice, with a 56K modem, you can get about one minute of music or several minutes of an audio book in three to five minutes. You can then play the music from your computer's hard drive or transfer it to a handheld device that you can take with you.

If you have a CD recorder, you can download or copy music tracks to your computer, and then make your own CD. The process takes a few steps, but it's worth it to be the life of the party.

NOTE Diamond Multimedia markets the Rio, a portable device that connects to your computer's printer port to download and play music that you've received over the Internet. For more information, go to www.diamondmm.com.

In addition to your Internet connection, you'll need a program that plays music in the MP3 format. The most recent versions of Windows Media Player and RealPlayer play MP3 files, so you can use the version of RealPlayer on the CD with this book. You'll also find the program MP3 CD Maker on the CD; this program plays MP3 music and lets you record MP3 files on your recordable CD.

You might have heard or read stories about illegal downloading of music with MP3. Actually, MP3 is just a music format. You may use it legally to listen to music if the song's owner has given permission for it to be downloaded and played. Sites such as www.mp3.com provide only legal music for downloading and listening. However, a new format has come along recently to help protect the rights of musical artists. The format, known as Liquid Audio, adds a special code to music so only the person who purchases it can play it.

Let's look at how you can get free music and then we will look at some other programs for playing it.

Sites and Features

There are a growing number of sites where you can find MP3 files. However, the majority of MP3 music on the Internet is not free. Music is protected by copyright, and the music industry is using MP3 as a way to sell music. You can purchase individual tracks or complete CDs, download the music, and then play it at your convenience. You can also purchase CDs and have them delivered to your home. Still, there are thousands of MP3 files that are free, especially from newer recording artists who are trying to get exposure.

There are about a zillion places to find MP3 music and information, including the following sites:

◆ www.mp3.com

◆ www.mp3now.com

◆ www.free-mp3-downloads.com/

◆ www.mp3-music-4-free.com/

Let's take a look at two of the sites in a little more detail.

MP3.com

To download MP3 software and music, and to learn all about MP3, navigate to www.mp3.com, a site that offers hundreds of thousands of free music files in a wide variety of categories. On this home page, there are links that take you to informative pages about MP3 music, as well as links to browse for free music by genre. The site also contains links to top songs, featured artists, MP3 software and hardware, and top news stories from the music industry.

When you choose a genre of music, you'll see a page similar to the one in Figure 3.1. You can then select a sub-category, choose a selection from the charts, , or display a list of items such as New Songs, Featured Songs, and Top CDs.

FIGURE 3.1   **Selecting MP3 tracks**

Selecting a specific item displays the details as shown here:

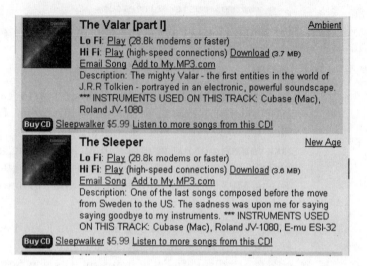

Click Play for the speed of your connection to listen to the featured song, or click Download to download the song to your computer. Once the file is downloaded, it will be played automatically if you have Windows Media Player or another MP3 player program installed. Click Song Story to find out the background of the song, or click Email Song to send a link to the song to a friend. The Add to My.MP3.com link lets you build a play list of songs that you can store online. You'll have to register as an MP3.com member, but registration is free.

MP3now.com

If you're looking for MP3 music links and information, navigate to www.mp3now.com. The options on the site's home page, shown in Figure 3.2, give you access to a variety of music sources, software, hardware, and news.

Much of the music you find through MP3now.com is not free, but can be purchased and downloaded, or ordered to be delivered to your door. By clicking the link MP3 Downloads, however, you can access a selection of categories that lead to music for free downloading. Just click the title you're interested in to download and play.

FIGURE 3.2 MP3now.com

On some pages at the site, you'll find a handy search feature to locate additional titles:

Your Own Jukebox

In addition to Windows Media Player and RealPlayer, there are lots of programs for playing MP3 music. Much of it is distributed as shareware, which you can download over the Internet. The programs not only play MP3 and other music files, but they let you create your own jukebox with music stored on your hard disk played in any order you like. Just be aware that music files can be quite large and take up a lot of hard disk space.

The most popular of these programs is WINAMP, a shareware program that supports most of the common audio file formats, including MP3, WAV, MOD, XM, IT, S3M, VOC, CDDA, WMA, and MIDI. You can download WINAMP from `www.winamp.com`.

NOTE See "Making Your Own CDs" later in this section to learn how to use MP3 CD Maker to play MP3 files on your computer.

When you first install WINAMP, you'll see the options shown in Figure 3.3. You can select to automatically play audio CDs that you insert in your CD-ROM drive and where WINAMP icons are placed. You can also select to make WINAMP the default player for all music and audio files, rather than Windows Media Player. If you make it the default player, the program will start when you choose to play an MP3 file from the Internet or when you double-click an MP3 file in Windows.

FIGURE 3.3 Setting up WINAMP

The WINAMP console is shown in Figure 3.4. It consists of the Main Window, Equalizer, Playlist Editor, and Mini Browser.

FIGURE 3.4 Running WINAMP

Main window ——

Equalizer ——

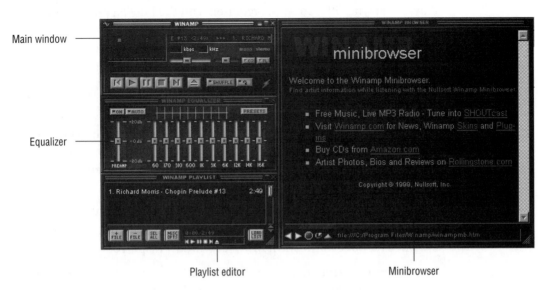

Playlist editor   Minibrowser

Use the buttons in the Main Window to play, stop, pause, and fast forward and reverse the current title. Right-click a button to see its function and an alternate keystroke combination.

Most of the buttons perform more than one function, depending on how you click them, as shown in Table 3.1. Above the buttons are controls for the volume and balance, and for the Equalizer and Playlist Editor. Information about the item on the top of the list, or the one playing, appears under the WINAMP title bar.

TABLE 3.1 Functions of WINAMP Buttons

Button	Click	Ctrl+Click	Shift+Click
Previous	Previous	Start of list	Rewind
Play	Play	Open Location	Open File
Pause	Pause		
Stop	Stop		Fadeout
Next	Next	End Of List	Fast Forward
Open	Open File	Open Location	Open Directory

The WINAMP Equalizer has sliders for controlling the range of the music; Playlist lists the titles to be played. Items on the Playlist play in order, one after the other. To add additional songs to the Playlist, you can drag the file's icon to the Playlist window, or click the + File button to choose the file from the Open dialog box. Use the –File button to delete a file.

To control other aspects of WINAMP, right-click the Main Window, Equalizer, or Playlist to display the shortcut menu.

You can choose which parts of the console to display, click Playback to control how files are played, and click Visualization to fine-tune how the Equalizer and other elements appear. Use the Options menu to change other aspects.

Use the Mini Browser to access MP3 sources from within WINAMP. By clicking a link in the mini browser, you can connect to the Internet and see the Internet page in the Mini Browser window displayed.

One interesting and fun aspect of WINAMP is the ability to change its appearance using *skins*. A *skin* is a special file that you can download from the Internet to personalize the console's appearance. Figure 3.5 shows how WINAMP looks with an alternate skin.

FIGURE 3.5   Alternate WINAMP skin

Here's how to use skins.

1. Download a skin from the Internet. There are plenty of places to find skins, including the sites listed here:

◆ www.customize.org (this site contains skins for other products as well, not just WINAMP skins.)

◆ www.1001winampskins.com

◆ www.infonet.ee/arthemes/winamp/skins.htm

◆ www.winamp-skins.com

2. Place the skin in the Program Files/WinAmp/Skins folder. If a skin is downloaded as a zip file, do not unzip it; just move the entire file to the folder.

3. Start WINAMP.

4. Press ALT+S to open the Skin Browser window.

5. Click the skin to use. From the Skin Browser window, you can also choose to download skins from the Internet, or change the folder where your skins are located.

6. Click Close.

Of course, WINAMP isn't the only program you can use to create your own jukebox. Here are three popular programs available for downloading:

◆ DJ Jukebox at www.Gammadyne.com

◆ RealJukebox at www.real.com/products/realjukebox/index.html

◆ MusicMatch jukebox at www.musicmatch.com.

DJ Jukebox, for example, lets you create a play list as well as organize your MP3 files. It allows you to rate each of your songs and then use the rating to determine how often tracks are played. In fact, there are two rating modes—personal and party—that can be used to create different play lists, based on the occasion. If you are on a local area network, you can even control the media player from another computer. You'll find a copy of DJ Jukebox on the CD.

Making Your Own CDs

If you have a CD recorder, you can make your own CDs from your favorite tracks. The trick, and it really isn't complicated, is to put your MP3 music into the industry-standard WAV format. This process is called *encoding*, which is the opposite of decoding (converting a WAV file to MP3 format).

If you download an MP3 file from the Internet, you can convert the file into WAV by using a type of program called an *encoder*. The encoder reads the MP3 data and creates a WAV file. You can then save the WAV file to your CD, using the recording software that came with the CD recorder. For a list of encoders that you can download, go to MP3.com's page at `http://software.mp3.com/software/featured/windows/encoder/`.

Your homemade CDs aren't limited to MP3 files that you download. You can also take tracks off of your favorite audio CDs and save them on your own CD or to your hard drive. This is the job of a *ripper*. A ripper is a program that extracts an audio CD track into your computer as a high-quality WAV file on your hard disk. You then burn the WAV file to your recordable CD.

For a list of rippers that you can download, go to MP3.com's page at `http://software.mp3.com/software/featured/windows/ripper/`.

 As an example of making your own CDs, we'll look at the program MP3 CD Maker from ZY2000. You'll find a demonstration copy of the program on the CD with this book, or you can download it from `www.zy2000.com`. The demo version lets you record just four MP3 tracks, but you can use it to play an unlimited number of tracks.

MP3 CD Maker, shown in Figure 3.6, automatically records MP3 files onto your CD, handling the decoding as it records. The program supports most popular CD-recording hardware.

To make a CD with MP3 CD Maker, you have to create a project list of MP3 files. To create a project list, click the Add MP3 button, then click the plus sign in the upper-left corner of the window. This will access the Open dialog box in which you can select the files you want to record. The files will then be listed in the MP3 CD Maker window. You can use the buttons along the left of the window to change the order in which they will be recorded

FIGURE 3.6 Using MP3 CD Maker

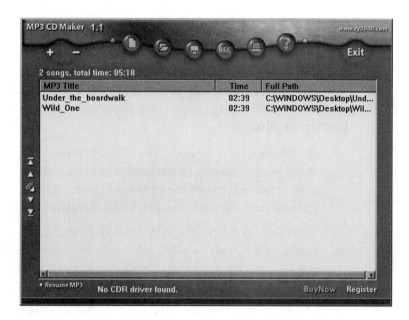

on your CD, or, after selecting a title in the main window, you can click the Play button, as shown here:

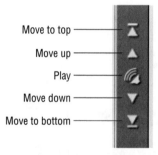

You use the buttons along the top of the window to work with the project:

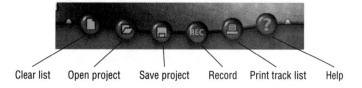

To save the project list for recording later, click Save Project, enter a project name in the box that appears, and click Save. Project files are stored with the MPJ extension. When you are ready to record the CD, click the Open Project button and double-click the name of the project.

When the list contains the tracks you want—up to 74 minutes of music— click the Record button.

Liquid Audio

Ripping tracks from your audio CDs and recording them on your own is not really legal if you give or sell the CD to someone else. Someone who should get a royalty each time the track is sold owns the music on the tracks. That's the reason there's some controversy over the MP3 format.

To allow easy purchasing and downloading of music over the Internet, how-ever, a new format called Liquid Audio has been developed. Liquid Audio has all of the convenience of MP3, but it protects the music's owners.

Each Liquid Audio file contains a digital imprint called the Genuine Music Mark that displays the artist's name and copyright information. Liquid Audio tracks cannot be played unless they contain the imprint. If you copy the track to another disk or to a writeable CD, the music is copied but not the imprint, so you can't play the song on any machine except the one you used to download it.

You can download a free Liquid Audio player, music tracks, and other Liquid Audio programs from: www.liquidaudio.com.

4 And You Thought E-Mail Was Fast!

Chats let you write messages back and forth to friends and strangers in real time. Unlike e-mail (with which you have to send mail, wait until it is re-ceived, and then await a reply), your message is visible to your chat buddies on-screen immediately so they can read and reply without delay. You'll get to communicate with folks you know, and you'll meet new groups of folks from around the world. With the proper hardware, you'll even be able to speak and listen to other folks in real time over the Internet.

Use AOL IM Even without Belonging!

Instant messaging and chat rooms are two great things AOL and similar services provide. But you don't need AOL to take advantage of both of these wonderful features. To learn more about AOL IM and AIM, check out *What You Didn't Know You Could Do with AOL* in the bonus section on the CD with the book.

Here's What You Need

All you need to chat online is access to the Internet and a free chat program. There are plenty of free programs. In this chapter, we'll look at Instant Messenger (IM) from America Online and PowWow from Tribal Voice. You'll find a copy of PowWow on the CD with the book. You'll learn how to download AOL Instant Messenger in a few minutes.

To use voice chat, in which you can speak and listen to other folks over the Internet, you'll need a sound card, speakers, and a microphone. Fortunately, most computers come with a sound card and speakers these days, so you might only need to purchase an inexpensive microphone at the local computer store.

Sites and Features

Online chats all work about the same way. The folks that provide your chat software have a big computer somewhere out there. When you want to chat with someone, you start the chat program, which connects to that big computer, to see a list of other people who are connected at the same time you are. You choose who you want to chat with and start sending messages.

All of your communications are channeled through the company's computer, so it's like having instant e-mail. In addition, with PowWow, you can have a private chat with someone. You can speak and listen using your microphone and speakers just as if you were talking on the telephone.

Because of the vast number of folks who belong to AOL, however, let's start by looking at their IM program.

AOL Instant Messenger

America Online is famous for its Instant Messenger (IM) feature. If you're an AOL member and online, you can tell when a pal who also has AOL is online. You can then send them an instant message to say "Hi. Let's talk." Your message pops up on their screen, so you can start having a private conversation by writing back and forth.

You can get the benefits of AOL IM even if you're not an AOL member. You can send and receive instant messages with your friends who are on AOL, and even with friends who belong to other ISPs. The trick is to download AOL's Instant Messaging software.

To get the program, follow these steps:

1. Connect to the Internet and navigate to http://www.aol.com.

2. Click the *AOL Instant Messenger* link or go directly to www.aol.com/aim/home.html.

3. Click the Get it Now! button.

4. Type a screen name from 3 to 16 characters in length, the AOL equivalent of a user name. AOL members and other Instant Messaging users will use this screen name to see if you are online.

5. Type a password from 4 to 16 characters in length.

6. Retype the password to confirm it.

7. Enter your e-mail address.

8. Click the Continue! button. If the screen name you've chosen is already taken, a message will appear. Click your browser's Back or Previous button and enter another screen name. You'll have to reenter your password as well.

9. Once your screen name has been accepted, you'll see a list of platforms supported by the program, including Windows 95/98/NT, Macintosh, and Windows CE.

NOTE There is also a link to Try Quick Buddy Now, a Java version of AOL Instant Messenger that runs from within your browser and which does not need to be downloaded and installed.

10. To download the software, click the platform that you are using.

11. When the software has finished downloading, disconnect from the Internet.

12. Double-click the downloaded program to install it.

Now that you're registered for AOL's IM and have the program installed on your computer, you're ready to communicate.

To start the program, open the Instant Messenger icon on your desktop. Enter your screen name, if it is not already shown, and your password. Enable the Save Password box if you don't want to enter your password each time. Enable the Auto-login box if you want to connect to IM automatically when you start Instant Messenger. Click Sign On.

The program connects to your ISP, if you are not already logged on, and to the IM system. It then opens a dialog box that will show the screen names of other people who are online. By default, any other IM users who know your e-mail address or screen name will be able to tell if you are online.

The first thing you should do is to create your buddy list. This is a list of IM users you want to chat with if they are online at the same time. Adding them to your list will automatically notify you when they go online. To do this,

1. Click the List Setup tab.

2. Click the Add Buddy button. The notation *New Buddy* appears in the list.

3. Type the screen name of the buddy. The screen name is the name AOL members use to identify themselves and which non-AOL members use to log on to Instant Messenger. Ask your buddies for their screen names in advance.

4. You can organize your buddies into groups, such as the generic Buddies, Family, and Coworkers. To place a buddy in a group, just select their name in the List Setup tab and drag it down to the group name. You can also create a new group using the Add Group icon at the bottom of the List Setup tab.

5. Click the Online tab.

You can communicate with buddies in two ways—instant message and chat.

An instant message is a one-to-one communication. If your buddy is on-line, their screen name appears in the Online tab. You'll see the total number of buddies in the list and the number of those online, and a list of your buddies that are not online, as shown here:

To send an invitation, double-click the buddy's name or click their screen name, and then click the Send Instant Message button to open the Instant Message window. Type a message and then click Send. The buddy will get a Buddy Chat Invitation message. Once the buddy responds, the IM window will open two panes: one for writing your messages and the other showing the entire conversation.

If you want to communicate with more than one buddy at a time, then open a personal chat. Here's how:

1. On the Online tab, select all of the screen names for the buddies you want in the chat room. Hold down the Ctrl key to select more than one name.

2. Click the Buddy Chat icon to open the Buddy Chat Invitation window.

3. Click Send.

You can invite a buddy to join a chat in progress. In the Chat Room window, select People from the menu bar and click Invite a Buddy in order to send an invitation.

Using Buddy Talk   Instant Messenger version 4 has the capability to voice chat. This means if you and your buddy have microphones and speakers, and are both running the latest version of IM, you can speak and listen to each other, in addition to writing messages.

To start a voice chat, click the Talk button at the bottom of the Instant Message window, or at the bottom of the Online tab. Your buddy will receive a message asking if they want to accept the voice call. If they click Accept, both of you will see the box shown here, and you can chat back and forth as on the telephone:

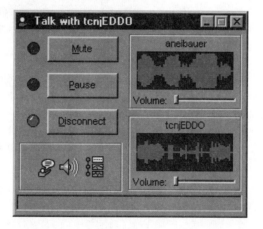

NOTE   To begin speaking, click the Push to Talk button when it appears in your Talk box.

Sending and Receiving Photos, Sounds, and Files   Instant Messenger version 4 also has the capability to transfer files, photos, and recorded sound clips between buddies.

For example, you can transfer a graphic from your computer directly into the IM box of your buddy.

Select Send IM Image from the People menu. You'll see a warning that it will create a direct connection between you and your buddy. Click Continue. Your buddy will get a message asking if they want to accept the connection—they click Accept.

The window changes to the Direct Instant Message window, and you can drag graphics onto it from your desktop that will appear on your buddy's screen. You can also click the Insert Picture button on the toolbar and browse your disk to locate the graphic to send.

In addition to a photo, you can send a recorded message up to 10 seconds long. Press the F12 key to open this box:

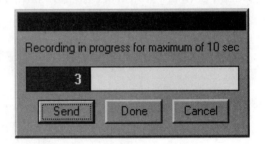

Record your message, click Done, and then click Send. Your message appears as an icon in your buddy's window, which your buddy can then double-click to play.

To save a graphic or sound file your buddy sends, right-click it and choose Save from the shortcut menu.

You can also upload files to your buddy or download files from their computer. When you install Instant Messenger, it places two folders on your hard disk: `C:/download` and `c:/filelib`. Each folder contains a subfolder with your IM screen name, such as `C:/fileib/aneibauer`. Place any files that you'd like buddies to access in the subfolder within the `C:\filelib` location. The download folder will contain files that you receive from buddies.

NOTE To send and receive files, you must turn on these options in the File Transfer tab of the Preference box.

To transfer a file to your buddy, follow these steps:

1. Start a chat with the buddy or select their name from the list of those buddies online.

2. Choose Send File to Buddy from the People menu to see the box in Figure 4.1.

FIGURE 4.1 **Sending a file to a buddy**

3. Click Browse and then locate and select the file to return to the Send File box.

4. Type a description or message (optional).

5. Click Send.

Your buddy will get a message asking if they want to accept the transfer. If they click Accept, the file is sent and stored in your buddy's download directory.

To get a file from your buddy, they must have inserted the file in their subdirectory of the `filelib` folder, and set their system to accept file requests in the Preferences dialog box.

To get a file that is on your buddy's computer, follow these steps:

1. Start a chat with the buddy or select their name from the list of those buddies that are online.

2. Select Get File from Buddy from the People menu.

3. A warning message appears, reporting that you should be careful about downloading files from strangers—click OK.

4. A list of the files in your buddy's `filelib` folder displays on your screen.

5. Select the file you want to download and click Get.

Finding Buddies   If you do not know the screen name of someone you want to chat with, you can locate them using the Find feature. There are three ways to search for an online buddy—by e-mail address, by screen name and address, and by interest.

N O T E   You'll learn how to add your own name, address, and interest to the AOL database for people to search in the section Your Buddy Profile.

1. Select People ➤ Find a Buddy.

2. Select either By E-mail Address, By Name and Address, or By Common Interest.

3. Enter the e-mail address or name and address, or select an interest, depending on the option you selected.

4. Click Next to find a screen name. If you select by interest, a list of people with that same interest in their profile will appear. Select a user from the list and click Finish.

IM Preferences   Instant Message is a very sophisticated program with lots of options. To control how the program works, click the IM icon in your system tray and select Preferences to open the box shown in Figure 4.2.

Use the tabs of the box to customize the program. The File Transfer tab, for example, lets you download files and allows buddies to request files from your computer. The Buddy Icon tab lets you assign a custom icon to each

FIGURE 4.2   **IM Preferences**

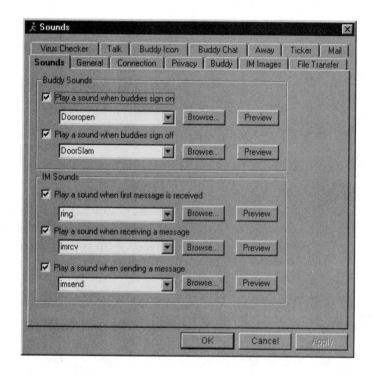

buddy. The icon then appears in your buddy window so you know who you are chatting with, as shown here:

Use the Away tab if you step away from your computer, since you won't be available to respond to IM or chat invitations. IM lets you have either of two messages, an Away message and an Idle message.

Use the idle message when you step away for a short time. It is automatically sent when you don't use your computer for 10 minutes. Here's how:

1. Click the Away tab.

2. Select the option labeled Auto Respond with Message.

3. Type the message that you want to appear.

4. Click OK.

If you plan to be away from the computer, then create an Away message using these steps:

1. Click the Away tab.

2. Select the option labeled Auto respond and insert in personal profile.

3. Type the new Away message.

4. Click Add Message.

5. Click OK.

When you go away from the computer, you have to turn on the message. Select File ➤ Away Message and then choose the message you want to use. Click I'm Back when you return to your computer.

NOTE You can block messages from certain buddies and set other options by selecting Menu ➤ Options ➤ Edit Preferences, and clicking the Controls tab.

Your Buddy Profile You can enter some information about yourself, called your profile, that other IM users can access. The profile can include your name and address, as well as up to five of your hobbies or interests. Other IM users can use the profile to locate members who share an interest.

To create or edit your profile, follow these steps:

1. Connect to IM.

2. Select My AIM ➤ My Profile.

3. Enable the check box labeled Allow People to Search for Me, if you want other IM member to find you by the information in your profile.

4. Enter the profile information and click Next.

5. Enable the option labeled I am available for chat, so other IM members can search for you based on interest.

6. Pull down a Choose Interest list and select a hobby or interest.

7. Click Next.

8. Enter any additional information that you want to appear on your profile.

9. Click Finish.

IM News and Stocks   In addition to using IM for chatting, you can run IM to keep up with news, weather, sports, and stock prices.

At the bottom of the AIM window, you'll see stock prices ticking from right to left. Click the icon to the left of the stocks to open a window in which you can change which stocks are displayed, set alerts when a stock reaches a specific level, and display additional information from AOL's financial pages.

You'll also see the Ticker scrolling news headlines along the top of your screen:

Each of the headlines is a link—click the link to open a browser window showing the full story. To display a list of all of the current headlines, click the first icon on the left of the ticker. Click the second icon to open the Ticker tab of the Preferences dialog box in which you can control the types of stories displayed, the speed of the ticker, and how often the stories are refreshed with current information.

PowWow

When you use AOL IM, you pretty much have to know with whom you want to communicate. If you want to reach a wider audience, while still being able to have private conversations, then try PowWow from Tribal Voice.

PowWow not only has a buddy feature that shows when selected people are online, but you can jump into public conversations within groups of people called communities. You can even choose to speak privately with others in your own chat room by writing messages or by speaking into your microphone and listening to your speakers or headphones.

You'll find a copy of PowWow on the CD with this book, or you can download it from www.tribalvoice.com.

When you run the program for the first time, you'll see the dialog box in Figure 4.3. Enter a screen name that you want to use to identify yourself in the

FIGURE 4.3   **Signing on to Pow Wow**

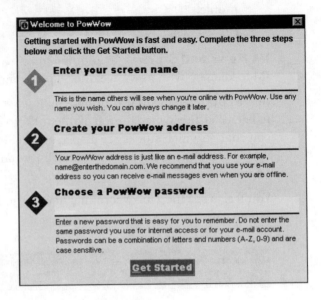

list of online members, enter your e-mail address as your PowWow address, and enter a password. Click Get Started to start the program, and dial into your ISP if you are not already online. Once connected, you'll see the PowWow window along with the CueCard window shown in Figure 4.4.

You can use the CueCards to learn how PowWow works and to select options. Just click the option that you want to select to see how to perform that task.

If you don't need the CueCards, just close the window. Disable the Show CueCards at the Startup check box to skip the cards when you next start PowWow.

The first thing you should do with PowWow is to join a community. This means seeing a list of folks already signed on and chatting. Here's how:

1. Click the Community icon.

2. Choose Online Community Guide to launch your Web browser and display a list of communities.

3. Click the one you want to join.

A list of people in the community appears in the PowWow list, and a window with their chat window opens to the right. To leave a message, just type it in the text box and click Send.

FIGURE 4.4 The PowWow and CueCard Window

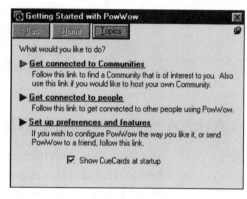

NOTE Click the Hear button to hear a computer-generated voice "speaking" the words that appear in the Chat window.

Rather than join the public discussion, you can invite one or more members to a private chat. Double-click the person's name in the list, or right-click and choose PowWow from the menu. A request for the PowWow, which they can accept or reject, is displayed on the person's screen. If they accept the invitation, the Personal Communicator window opens. You can then write messages or click the telephone icon to talk in real time. If the person is not available to respond to your request, you'll be able to leave a message for them when they return.

PowWow is a powerful chat program that offers many sophisticated features. We've just touched on the basics of PowWow here.

5 So That's What You Look Like!

For a real multimedia Internet experience, nothing beats a real-time chat in which you can actually see the folks you are chatting with. Now that videoconferencing cameras are under $100, turning your computer into a video-phone is a practicality that adds an extra boost of fun to online communications.

Audio and Video with NetMeeting

In this section we'll take a look at a handy program called Microsoft NetMeeting that lets you see the people you are talking to, and lets them see you. At a basic level, it works like a typical instant messaging or chat program, letting you type messages back and forth, and speak to and hear other folks. But NetMeeting also lets you share programs, send and receive files, work together on a graphic, and even remotely control another program over the Internet.

Here's What You Need

To use NetMeeting to send and receive written messages, all you need is the program itself. If you have version 4 or later of Microsoft Internet Explorer, NetMeeting will already be installed on your system. If NetMeeting isn't installed, you can download a free copy of it from the Microsoft Web site at this address: www.microsoft.com/windows/netmeeting/.

To speak with and listen to others over NetMeeting, you'll need a sound card, speakers, and a microphone. You don't need any special hardware if you want to see folks that you are speaking with, but to let others see you you'll need a vide-conferencing camera.

You can purchase videoconferencing cameras at computer stores and on-line. Many are available for under $100, and many plug directly into a computer's USB port. The camera will come with installation software that configures your computer for video. Once the camera is installed, NetMeeting will automatically use it for your video-conferencing.

Sites and Features

As with all online chat programs, NetMeeting works by communicating with a server. The server acts as a gigantic telephone switchboard, maintaining a directory of everyone who is logged on and ready to accept calls. There are a number of servers that handle NetMeeting communications. You and the person you want to speak with over the Internet with NetMeeting should choose the same server. You can select a default server to use when you install NetMeeting, but you can change the server at any time.

To start NetMeeting, point to Programs on the Start menu, and click Microsoft NetMeeting. The program might also be listed in the submenu that appears when you point to Internet Explorer on the Programs menu or when you point to Accessories and then point to Internet Tools.

The first time you run NetMeeting, you'll see a series of dialog boxes that help you set up the program on your system. The order and content of the boxes depend on your computer's configuration. Respond to the boxes, clicking Next after each.

NOTE Don't worry about the options you choose during the installation. You'll be able to change the setup options and fine-tune calling, audio, and video settings by selecting Options on the NetMeeting Tools menu.

The boxes let you enter this information or choose these options:

◆ Type your name, e-mail address, city, state, and country, and a brief comment about yourself that will identify you on screen to other NetMeeting users, and click Next.

◆ Choose whether you want to log on to a server whenever NetMeeting starts.

◆ Select the default server. Microsoft Corporation provides a number of servers, but they are often so busy that you may have trouble logging on. As an alternative, try ils.bytebeam.com.

◆ Select the speed and type of connection to the Internet.

◆ Confirm the devices that you have installed to record and play back sound and to display video images.

◆ Set the volume of your speakers and microphone.

Once you complete the series of dialog boxes, you'll see the NetMeeting window, shown in Figure 5.1:

FIGURE 5.1   NetMeeting

Starting a Meeting

If NetMeeting is set to automatically log on to a directory server, it will dial in to your ISP each time it's started and log on to the server. If it doesn't dial, choose Log On To from the Call menu, which is followed by the name of the server, such as ils.bytebeam.com.

To see who else is logged on to the server, and to place an Internet call, choose Directory from the Call menu. If many people are logged on, the list might take a few moments to appear while their names are downloaded. Icons next to the name indicate whether the person is not in a call, is currently speaking, or wants to be left alone. You'll also see icons indicating whether the person has voice and video capabilities.

Scroll the list to locate the person you want to speak with and double-click that person's name. The person at the computer you're calling will hear a sound like a telephone ring, and a message box will appear to ask whether the user wants to accept or ignore your call.

If the person chooses to ignore the call, a message appears on your screen reporting that the other user didn't accept your call.

When your call is accepted, the names of the people in the meeting are displayed in the NetMeeting window, and you can start communicating. If each computer has a microphone and speakers, you can each speak into the microphone to talk to one another. If your computer is equipped with a camera, the person you're talking to will also able to see you, as shown in Figure 5.2. To end the meeting, click the End Call button or choose Hang Up from the Call menu.

FIGURE 5.2   You can see who you are chatting with.

In addition to speaking to people with NetMeeting, you can open a chat window to type messages. Click the Chat button or choose Chat from the Tools menu to open the chat window. You can now type and read messages as with other chat programs.

If you want to send a private message to a particular chat participant, select the participant's name from the Send To drop-down list before clicking the Send Message button. To resume sending public messages to everyone in the chat, choose Everyone In Chat from the Send To drop-down list.

To exit a chat, close the Chat window, or choose Exit from the File menu.

Using the Whiteboard

The Whiteboard is a drawing window that you can share with others over the Internet. Whatever you draw on the Whiteboard appears on the Whiteboards of all the other participants. A NetMeeting Whiteboard is shown in Figure 5.3.

FIGURE 5.3 **NetMeeting Whiteboard**

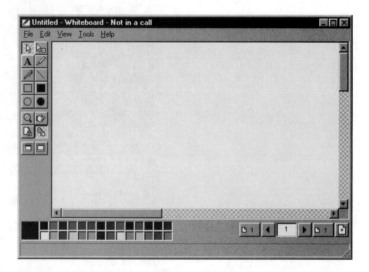

To use the Whiteboard, click the Whiteboard button, or choose Whiteboard from the Tools menu. Then draw on the Whiteboard, using tools from the Whiteboard tool palette. The tool palette contains everything you need to create and edit drawings and text on the Whiteboard.

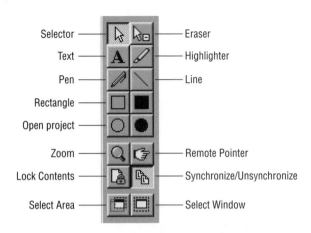

Most of the tools are designed for drawing graphics and text on the Whiteboard, highlighting, erasing, and selecting items.

Use the Zoom button (or the Zoom command on the View menu) to switch between a normal and an enlarged view. If you click Remote Pointer, a pointer appears on the screen. You can move the pointer to an area of the Whiteboard you want others to look at.

Click the Lock Contents button if you want to prevent others from changing the Whiteboard contents. Click it again to allow others to change the Whiteboard.

The Synchronize/Unsynchronize button determines whether other Whiteboard users can see the same pages you are viewing. To synchronize the pages, click the button so that it appears pressed down. If you change pages in the Whiteboard, the same page will appear to others. To unsynchronize the pages, click the button so that it appears released.

A Whiteboard can contain more than one page, just like a flipchart at a conference or in front of a class. Use the buttons at the lower-right corner of the Whiteboard window to insert a page and to switch from page to page. Choose Clear Page from the Edit menu to erase the current page, or choose Delete Page from the Edit menu to delete the page. Erasing a page removes the page's contents on the screens of all NetMeeting participants but leaves the page in place. Deleting a page actually removes it from your Whiteboard and from those of other participants as well.

Click Select Area to drag a rectangle over an area of the screen outside the Whiteboard that you want to copy to the Whiteboard. Use the Select

Window button to copy an entire window to the Whiteboard. Click Select Window and then click any window on your screen, even a partially obscured one, to copy the contents of the window to the Whiteboard.

NOTE While the Whiteboard is still displayed, print its contents by choosing Print from the File menu. Choose Save from the File menu to save the contents in a special format that you can later reopen to the Whiteboard using **Open** from the File menu.

Sharing Programs

In addition to sharing a drawing on the Whiteboard, you might want to share a software program as well. When you share a program, other persons in your chat can see the program as it appears on your screen. The person running the program is called the *owner*, and the owner can pass control of the program over to others in the chat.

So for example, you could be working on a letter in Windows Notepad. By sharing Notepad you can collaborate with others in the writing or editing process. To share a program, follow these steps:

1. Start the program you want to share, and then switch back to NetMeeting.

2. Click the Share Program button, or choose Sharing from the Tools menu.

3. Select the program you want to share, and then click Share. Other meeting participants will now be able to see exactly what you are doing with the shared program.

If you want to allow meeting participants to use the shared program, rather than just view it, click the Allow Control button in the Sharing dialog box. You can now select from these two options:

◆ Automatically Accept Requests For Control lets a meeting participant use the program without your express permission.

◆ Do Not Disturb With Requests For Control Right Now prevents requests for sharing from appearing on your screen.

When a meeting participant wants to control the program, they double-click the program window on the screen. This either takes control of the program or, if you haven't turned on automatic acceptance in the Sharing dialog box, displays a dialog box on the owner's screen asking whether you want to Reject or Accept the request.

By clicking Accept, you transfer control of the program to the participant, and you'll no longer be able to use your pointer on screen.

To regain control over the program and your cursor, and to stop any participant who is currently working with the shared program, press Esc or click the mouse button.

To stop sharing the program, click Unshare or Unshare All in the Sharing dialog box.

Sending and Receiving Files

While you're in a meeting, you can exchange files with other participants. Click the Transfer Files button or choose File Transfer from the Tools menu. In the box that appears, click Add Files to open the Choose Files To Send dialog box. Select the files you want to transfer and click Send All to send the files to everyone or, from the drop-down list of meeting participants in the File Transfer dialog box, choose the participant to whom you want the files sent and then click Send All.

When you receive a file from someone else, you see a dialog box giving you the option to close the dialog box, open the file, or delete the file.

Files that you receive are stored in the `C:\Program Files\NetMeeting\ Received Files` folder. Click the View Received Files button—the one that shows an icon of a folder—to open that folder.

Controlling a Computer Remotely

NetMeeting includes a powerful feature that lets you actually control one of the other computers on the network. For example, suppose a staff member is having trouble changing a setting in Control Panel or needs help performing some Windows task. You can take control of another person's computer from your own system and perform tasks as though you were sitting in front of the other computer.

To set up a computer to accept remote control, you have to use the Remote Desktop Sharing Wizard on that computer. Follow these steps:

1. Start NetMeeting on the computer you want to be able to control and choose Remote Desktop Sharing from the Tools menu.

2. Click Next after reading the first Remote Desktop Sharing Wizard page.

3. Type a password of at least seven characters that will allow access from the controlling computer.

4. Retype the password to confirm it, and then click Next.

5. You can now choose to password-protect a screen saver as an extra security feature. Make your choice and click Next.

6. Click Finish.

7. Close NetMeeting.

The Remote Desktop Sharing icon will appear in the computer's system tray, to the left of the clock on the Windows taskbar.

1. Right-click the Remote Desktop Sharing icon, and select Activate Remote Desktop Sharing from the shortcut menu.

2. Start NetMeeting on the computer that will be in control, and call the computer you want to share.

3. In the Place A Call dialog box that appears, select the Require Security For This Call (Data Only) check box, and then click Call to go online and connect to the other person's computer.

4. You'll be asked to type the password.

5. Type the password, and click OK.

You'll see a window that contains the other computer's desktop. You can now control the remote computer just as if you were sitting at its keyboard.

To stop sharing, right-click the Remote Desktop Sharing icon on the desktop of the computer you are sharing, and select Exit.

6 See You...Virtually

The next best thing to being there, is to be there in virtual reality. Virtual reality (VR) means using computer graphics and other techniques to simulate a real experience. In some cases, in fact, being at a place virtually is even better than being there for real.

Virtual Chats

Virtual chats let you see the people you are chatting with in a graphical way. Each person is represented by a graphic called an *avatar*. Most virtual chat sites let you select the avatar that represents you, change its expression and position, and even decorate it with props and accessories. When you type a message in the chat window, the message appears in a balloon over your avatar. This way, chat members can see who's talking, as well as the speaker's expression and body language.

Most virtual chats display the avatars over a graphic background. If you join a chat that features a beach theme, for example, the avatars appear as if they were on the beach or in the water. Other virtual chats include a more sophisticated VR background that you can walk through. You can move your avatar to visit locations within the setting and to see or interact with other chat members.

Here's What You Need

To delve into virtual reality chatting, you'll need to log on to a VR site on the Internet. Some of the sites do not require you to download or install special software; the graphics are handled by your Web browser.

In this section, we'll look at two virtual sites—Active Worlds and The Palace.

To join an Active Worlds chat, you'll need to download and install the Active Worlds Browser. You can download it from www.activeworlds.com.

You can take part in an Active Worlds chat for free as a guest. However, to access all of the Active World features, such as creating your own virtual reality, you must join Active Worlds for a $19.95 annual fee.

You can take part in a Palace virtual chat without downloading and installing any special software. The site utilizes an online environment called the Palace Viewer that displays avatars and backgrounds. For greater flexibility, however, you can also download and install a Palace User file that lets you join a chat without using your browser's interface. You can download the file at www.communities.com/downloads/client/downloads.html.

Sites and Features

Active Worlds is a good place to start because of the wide range of features and VR graphics. Download and install the Active Worlds Browser. When you run the Active Worlds Browser, it logs on to the Internet and lets you sign in with a temporary "tourist visa" by entering a name you want to use online and your email address.

The Active Worlds environment, shown in Figure 6.1, consists of worlds and teleports. A world is a virtual environment, and they are listed in the Worlds tab on the left of the Active Window program. While most worlds are open to everyone, some worlds are private and open only to selected users.

Teleports are locations within a world that you can go to, and these are listed in the Teleports tab. You can save a location as a teleport, for example, to return to it quickly at a later time. Some default teleports are listed for popular sites.

You interact in an Active World environment by chatting, moving around, and making gestures or other movements.

Use the tabs on the left of the window to change locations, get help, list other persons in the world, and send messages. Click on an item in the Worlds tab or the Teleports tab, for example, to change locations.

The virtual world itself, along with your own avatar, is shown in the middle of the screen, above the chat box. You'll see other members move within the environment, and you'll see the scenery change as you move. The right side of the window contains help information and advertisements.

FIGURE 6.1 Active World

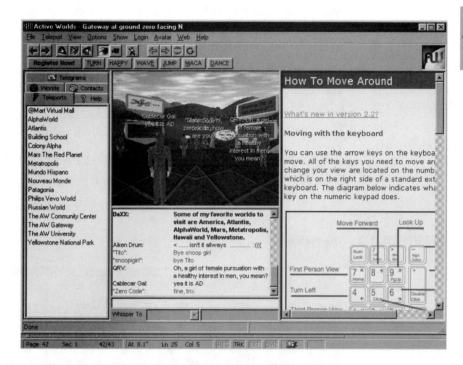

Use the toolbar to select options and the buttons below the bar to change expressions or to perform movements.

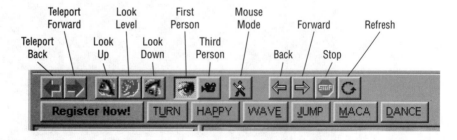

For example, click First Person if you want to see the virtual world from your own avatar's viewpoint. Click Third Person to see what your avatar looks like as it moves around the site.

To walk through the world, click the Mouse Mode button and drag your mouse. Click the mouse when you want to exit that mode to select other options.

If you join Active Worlds as a paid citizen, you can create your own custom worlds, build a contact list, and send and receive telegrams. Telegrams are short messages, up to 255 characters, that work similarly to e-mail, but between Active World citizens.

The Palace offers two ways to interact—by the Palace Browser or by the Palace User program.

When you log on to the Palace on the Internet, you'll see the window in Figure 6.2. Select the community you want to visit using any of these methods:

◆ Click a category from the top buttons, such as TV or Movies.

◆ Select one of the options as they scroll in the center of the page.

◆ Click one of the options in the large circle on the left.

FIGURE 6.2   **The Palace**

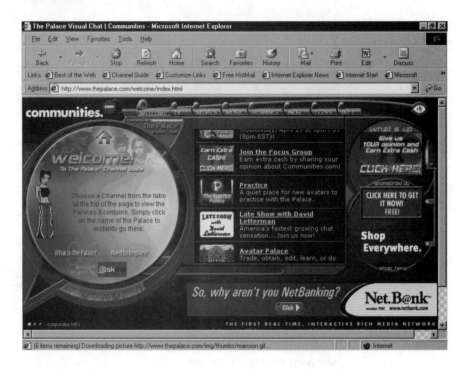

In the box that appears, enter a screen name you want to use and click Enter. The Palace Viewer window appears as in Figure 6.3.

Click the location where you want to place your avatar, type a message in the chat box, and press Enter.

FIGURE 6.3   **The Palace Viewer**

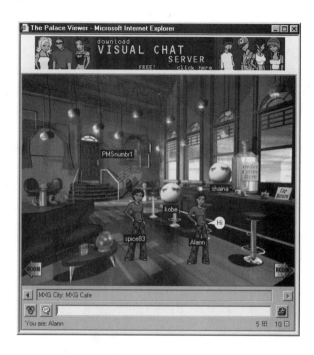

By default, your message appears with your avatar for everyone to see. You can send a private message to a particular member, or to the Palace operator, by selecting their name from the Select Who to Chat With button on the far left of the chat text box. Use the button next to that to select the shape of your chat balloon.

You can also click the Toolbar button on the right of the chat box to open this toolbar:

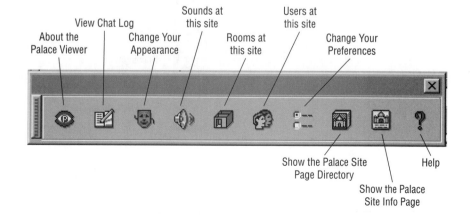

The icons at the lower right of the viewer show the number of persons in the current room and the site itself.

NOTE   To change rooms, display the toolbar, click the **Rooms at this Site** option, and click on the room you want to enter.

From the Palace Site Info page, you can select whether to view the site in your browser or by using the Palace software.

You can also access Palace chats by installing the Palace User software. Running the software lets you sign in and connect to the Internet. In addition to a viewer window that displays the virtual environment and chat, the software includes this toolbar, along with menu options for changing avatars:

- Connect to a palace
- Back
- Forward
- Normal talk balloon
- Spiky talk balloon
- Sticky talk balloon
- Thought balloon
- Log window
- Play sounds
- Guest avatars
- Drawing tools
- Show/Hide Door Outlines
- Show/Hide Names

Searching the Unlimited Resource

The Internet is truly amazing. How else could you get access to virtually the entire world when you're looking for something or someone? From the convenience of your home, school, local library, or Internet cafe, you can access this unlimited resource of people, places, and things. In this part of the book, we'll look at how to use the Internet to find things in general, and some important things in particular. Online shopping and trading will be discussed later in this book in "Buying and Selling Online".

7 Supercharge Your Searches

By using free or inexpensive utilities, you can supercharge your searches to save time and pinpoint the information you need.

Use Multiple Search Engines at One Time

There is so much information on the Internet that sometimes it is hard to find exactly what you're looking for. Rather than use one search engine at a time, you can harness the power of multiple search companies to let them all work for you at once.

Here's What You Need

 All you will need is access to the Internet and the CD that comes with this book. The CD contains a variety of programs for supercharging your searches. On the CD, you'll find these programs:

- ◆ ISearch
- ◆ Shetty Search
- ◆ Copernic 2000
- ◆ MP3 Fiend
- ◆ Search Master Demo

Sites and Features

When you're looking for specific information on the Internet, where do you go? Most ISP home pages offer a search function, and you can always go directly to one of the major search sites, some of which are listed here:

- ◆ www.yahoo.com

- ◆ www.anywho.com

- ◆ www.excite.com

- ◆ www.lycos.com

- ◆ www.snap.com

- ◆ www.iwon.com

- ◆ www.directhit.com

As an alternative to search engine hopping, you can take advantage of sites and programs that streamline the task of searching.

The program ISearch, for example, gives you a shortcut on your Windows desktop to 12 of the most popular search engines. Double-click the shortcut to open a special Web page, then just select the engine you want to use, enter a keyword or phrase to search for, and click the ISearch button. ISearch performs the search for you, so you don't have to first navigate to the search engine yourself. The ISearch installation program also gives you the option to install ISearch as the page opens automatically when you click the Web browser's search button. You can download it from www.milori.com.

If you search using one engine and still don't find what you're looking for, you have to go to another and then another search engine until you find the information you want. Rather than restrict your search to one engine, take advantage of sites and programs that automatically use several of the popular search engines at one time.

Three sites that will search a number of engines at one time are:

- ◆ www.askjeeves.com

- ◆ www.beaucoup.com

- ◆ www.profusion.com

FIGURE 7.1 Multiple searches at Beaucoup

Beaucoup, for example, shown in Figure 7.1, lets you search by keyword or by drilling-down from a list of categories. Enter a keyword or phrase and click Search for Beaucoup to use 10 different search engines. The results show a link to and description of each site found, as well as the name of the search engine used:

> **Alan Neibauer - Featured Authors** **(Excite)**
> Alan Neibauer is a veteran computer book author with several bestsellers to his credit, including the Official Guide to the Corel WordPerfect Suite and the ABCs of Windows.
> *http://mspress.microsoft.com/authors/feature/feature_neibauer.htm*

The Beaucoup site also contains links to search some specific engines, such as DirectHit, FindWhat, and AskJeeves.

Drilling-down means to start with a category and select more specific sub-categories until you locate the exact information you are searching for.

Choosing a link from the list of topics in the Beaucoup home page, for example, displays a list of related sites or search engines. Click a site in the list to visit its location and then continue searching for the information desired.

Search programs work about the same way, but they are installed on your computer. We've collected a variety of search programs for the CD that accompanies this book in order to illustrate the power and the versatility of software that can be downloaded from the Internet.

Shetty Search

This useful freeware program, shown in Figure 7.2, can be found on the CD, and downloaded from `members.aol.com/satishetty`.

FIGURE 7.2 **Running Shetty Search**

To use Shetty Search, type in the word or phrase that you're looking for, and then choose each of the search companies you'd like to use. Click the Search in All check box to use all of the companies. Then click Search.

Shetty Search dials into the Internet, if you are not already connected, and searches for your information using all of the selected sites. When the searches are complete, it opens your browser and displays the sets of results one after the other (see Figure 7.3).

FIGURE 7.3 Results using Shetty Search

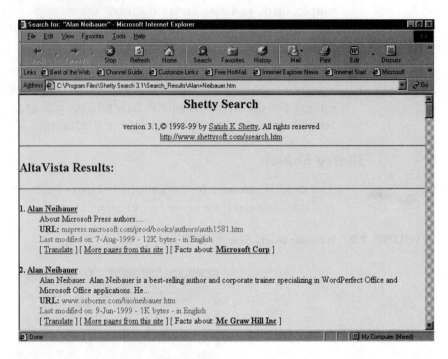

Installing Shetty Search places an icon in the system tray. Right-click the icon to open the program's window, to access a shortcut menu to search the Web, to configure the program, and to learn more about it.

Copernic 2000

To search the Web generally for information, or by category, try Copernic 2000. You'll find a copy of this program on the CD, or you can download it from www.copernic.com. Copernic 2000 not only performs a search using multiple sites, it can also download pages for offline viewing and verify that links are valid.

Copernic 2000 opens a window (see Figure 7.4) in which you select the category to search and in which your search results will later appear. Most of the categories, and some functions such as adding new categories, are not available in the free version of the program, but if you like the program enough to buy it, Copernic 2000 Plus can be purchased from the manufacturer.

FIGURE 7.4 Using Copernic 2000

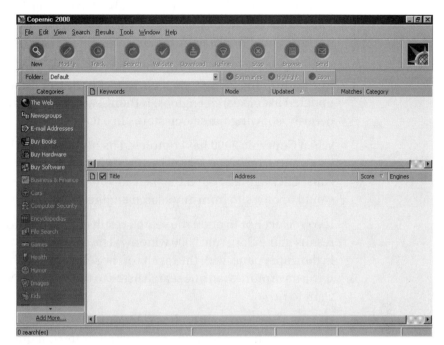

To use Copernic 2000, click The Web in the list of categories to open this dialog box:

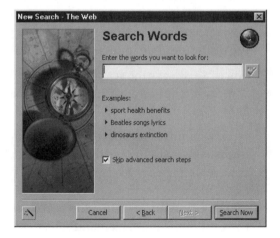

You can enter your search phase and then click Search Now, or you can turn off the check box labeled Skip Advanced Search Steps, and click Next. The advanced search steps include a couple of dialog boxes for customizing how the search is performed.

When you click Search Now, Copernic 2000 connects to the Internet. Before performing the search, it checks with the Copernic home page for an updated list of search engines. It then searches all of the engines simultaneously, showing the search status in each.

When Copernic 2000 has completed its multiple search, it asks whether you want to open the search results browser, which displays all of the results. Click a link to open the page in your browser window, just as you would open a site from any search engine.

If you select not to open the search results browser, you'll see your search results in the Copernic 2000 window. The window lists all of your searches in the upper pane, with the results of the selected search on the lower pane. If you have more than one search listed in the upper pane, click the one you want to review.

Use the check box to the left of a document title to select a document. The icons in the first column indicate whether the document is valid, invalid (no longer at the location), or has been downloaded for offline viewing. Click the Validate button, or choose Results ➤ Validate to check all or selected documents to make sure they are still available. Then to download a page for offline viewing, select it in the Copernic 2000 window and click the Download button. Double-click an item to connect to the site. To open the search results browser at any time, click the Browse button on the Copernic 2000 toolbar or choose Results ➤ Browse.

You can also save the search results on your disk for later viewing or for use with another program. Choose File ➤ Export to open the Export Search dialog box.

Enter a name for the file, then pull down the Save As Type list, choose the format you want to save the file in, and click Save. Copernic 2000 saves your search results when you exit the program. The next time you start Copernic, your previous searches will still be listed. You can still access any of the documents or refine the search as desired. To delete a search from the window, right-click it and select Delete from the shortcut menu.

Search Master

Another popular search program is Search Master. You'll find a demonstration version of the program on the CD, or you can download it from www.cosmega.com.

Run Search Master to open the window shown in Figure 7.5. The registered version of Search Master enables all of the search engines shown in its window. The demo version only accesses the engines in the top row. Enter your search phrase and click each of the search engines you want to use. Search Master is optimized for Netscape Navigator and will use that browser if it is installed on your system.

FIGURE 7.5 Using Search Master

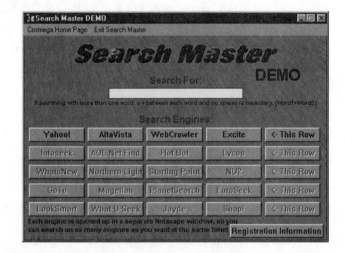

Rather than collect all of the results in one window as Copernic 2000 does, Search Master opens a separate browser window for each search engine. Open each window in turn to display the results.

MP3 Fiend

If you are interested in locating MP3 music files, then choose MP3 Fiend, a program that focuses on MP3 sites. You'll find a copy of the program on the CD, or you can download it from www.mp3fiend.com.

This program searches 11 MP3 engines simultaneously and lets you download MP3 files using the GetRight program, which is also on the CD. In fact, before running MP3 Fiend, install GetRight so you are prepared to download music files.

When you run MP3 Fiend, it first downloads the current list of search sites from the manufacturer's site and then opens the window shown in Figure 7.6. Enter a search phrase, such as song name or artist, and press Enter. The program connects to the Internet and displays the progress of its search.

FIGURE 7.6 Using MP3 Fiend

When all of the sites have been searched, click Close to display the download sites for the music files in the MP3 Fiend window, as shown in Figure 7.7. To download one of the songs, right-click it and choose either of these options:

- ◆ Download File
- ◆ Download with Utility

FIGURE 7.7   Search results in MP3 Fiend

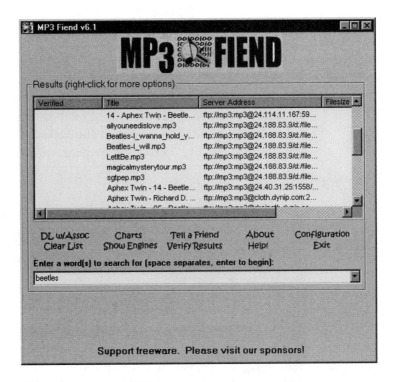

The Download File option connects to the site containing the track and attempts to download it directly. Selecting Download with Utility lets you choose one of two downloading programs—Go!Zilla and GetRight.

Turbo Start

The popular search engines are just one way to locate information on the Internet. You can also search a specific Web site for information. For example, if you're looking for information about health, you can navigate to any of thousands of health-related sites and search a specific site's own database for information.

While you'll learn about getting health, legal, and other information in later sections of this book, you can get a start by using the Turbo Start program, which you can download from www.rashminsanghvi.com/turbo.

NOTE   For Turbo Start to work correctly, it must be installed manually from the root directory of the CD-Rom, \TurboStart\setup.exe.

Turbo Start installs its basic Web page on your own hard disk. When the program is started, it launches your Web browser, quickly loads its Web page from your hard disk, and then connects to its own Internet site through your ISP. The Turbo Start page is shown in Figure 7.8.

FIGURE 7.8   **Using Turbo Start for Web searches**

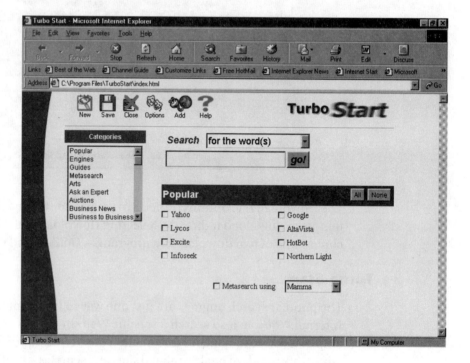

Here's how to use the page to locate specific information.

1. Select a category from the list box on the left of the screen. There are a number of options in the list; some of these include Arts, Sports, Health, Education, and MP3s and Audio.

2. When you choose a category, several search engines or sites appear to the right of the list.

3. Select the check boxes for all of the sites you wish to use for your search.

4. Enter your search words in the text box next to the Go! button.

5. Pull down the Search list and select the type of search. The options are for the word(s), for all the words, for the phrase, for the substring(s), using Boolean And, and using Boolean Or.

6. Click Go!

The searches are launched in each of the selected sites; they are then opened either in individual browser windows or in one window with a separate frame for each. If they are opened in separate windows, all of the windows are indicated on the Windows taskbar, so click each in turn to review the findings. You can specify how you want the results displayed by clicking the Options button and choosing from the dialog box that appears. You can also use the Save button to store a copy of your search criteria on your disk.

8 Real Men Look Up Directions

So maybe it's not as neat as the map on the screen in James Bond's Aston Martin, but you can get driving maps to any location off the Internet.

Find Out Where You're Going

Before heading off on that business trip or the drive to Grandma's house, get step-by-step directions from the Internet so you don't get lost. If you're headed for a vacation spot, get maps of the area around your hotel or near the popular tourist locations.

Here's What You Need

All you need is access to the Internet and a printer, if you want a hard copy of the map. A good quality ink-jet or laser printer will have the best results; a high-quality color printer would be even better!

Sites and Features

Maps on the Internet can show a specific location or provide detailed, point-to-point driving instructions. In most cases, you can easily switch from one to the other. When looking at a map of your destination, for example, there may be a button you can click to get driving instructions from your starting point.

NOTE If you want to get directions as you're driving, go to the computer store and ask for a GPS mapping program and receiver. With the kit and a laptop computer, you can see exactly where you are and where you have to go in real time.

There are lots of Web sites that offer maps. You'll probably find one that you like better than all of the others, and you will find that some may be more accurate than others. The driving directions may also be more general than specific—some tell you to turn off a major road where there is no exit, and a lot of the time you won't be able to find addresses in very new developments, within some industrial parks, or in some rural areas where only horses and cows graze. If you're city or suburban folks, then chances are the address you're looking for will be there.

Almost all of the maps let you zoom and navigate:

Zooming   Enlarges or reduces the area being shown on the screen. Zoom out when you want to see a wide geographic area, but with less detail; zoom in when you need more detail and individual street names.

Navigation   Changes the area displayed by the use of arrow buttons or compass directions. Usually the compass directions are set up so you can click the up arrow or the letter N on the compass to see what's located north of there, and so on.

Microsoft's Expedia

Microsoft's Expedia Web site is a comprehensive place to go for travel information of all types. To get a map of a location, navigate to `www.expediamaps.com`. You can choose from these options:

Find a Map   Lets you see a map showing a specific street address and locates a city or tourist attraction, such as the Eiffel Tower.

Driving Directions   Shows step-by-step locations between two cities.

My Maps and Routes   Lets you save maps and driving directions on your own page for quick reference.

Link to a Map   Lets you create a custom map to your location.

For example, to get the map to a specific address, follow these steps:

1. Click Find a Map to see these options:

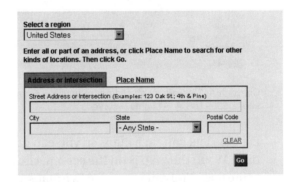

2. Select the region—Canada, Europe, Mexico, United States, World (topographic maps). The other options on the page will change based on your selection. With the United States, you can find a specific address or place. With the other regions you can only map a place name.

3. Enter as much information as possible to identify the location. You can enter either a street address or an intersection, such as Fifth and Main.

4. Click GO. Expedia displays a map as shown in Figure 8.1. You can zoom in or navigate through the map, using the Zoom Level and Map Mover sections. You can also use the Link, Print, Save, and E-mail links. If Expedia cannot find the exact location, it will display one or more similar addresses along the left of the screen. Click the address that you want to map, or click Back and try again.

FIGURE 8.1 An Expedia map

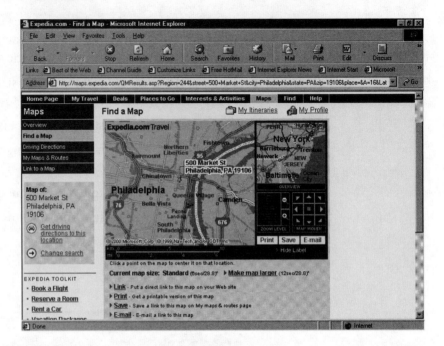

Copyright © 2000 Microsoft and/or its suppliers, One Microsoft Way, Redmond, Washington 98052-6399 U.S.A. All rights reserved.

Expedia lets you save maps so you can quickly access them again at any time. When the map is on the screen, click the Save link that is to the right of the map. You can save up to five maps and five routes. To get a list of your stored maps and routes, click the link My Maps & Routes on the left of the page, and then select the one that you want to view.

The map information is stored on your own computer, so to access a saved map, you must be using the same computer you saved the map with.

The Driving Directions option lets you specify two city names or major attractions. Enter the locations and click Go. In some cases, Expedia will ask you to refine your locations. Select the starting point and destination and then click Go to see directions such as those shown in Figure 8.2.

FIGURE 8.2   **Driving directions from Expedia**

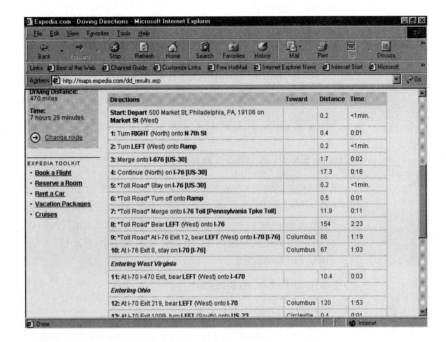

Copyright © 2000 Microsoft and/or its suppliers, One Microsoft Way, Redmond, Washington 98052-6399 U.S.A. All rights reserved.

Lycos

If you want driving directions from one address to another, rather than between cities and sites, navigate to www.lycos.com/roadmap.html. There you will be asked to fill out a form. After you are done, click Go Get It! Once the map appears, you can click a zoom level option or any of the compass directions (these appear around the map border) to navigate.

For door-to-door driving instructions, select Driving Directions from the Lycos site, or click Drive To once a map is displayed for directions to that location. In the screen that appears, enter the address from which you are starting the trip; then either enter your destination's address, or pull down the Select list to choose a site or point of interest. For example, if you need driving instructions to City Hall in Philadelphia, PA, you don't need to know the address. Pull down the Select list and choose City Halls. Then enter the city and state, and click Calculate Directions.

Select the route type, either door-to-door or city-to-city, and then one of these options:

Overview Map with Text   Shows the maps of each location with written instructions on how to get there.

Turn-by-Turn Map with Text   Shows a map for each instruction.

Text Only   Shows only the instructions without a map.

Finally, click Calculate Directions to display the driving directions.

Yahoo, Excite, and Others

All of the major search companies offer free maps and driving directions. For example, go to www.yahoo.com, click Maps, and then click Driving Directions. From www.excite.com, click Maps&Directions. Then either enter an address, or enter "from" and "to" addresses within the US to get driving directions. Then click MapIt!

Some other map sites are

◆ www3.mapsonus.com

◆ www.nationalgeographic.com/resources/ngo/maps

◆ www.mapquest.com

◆ www.mapblast.com/mapblast/start.hm

N O T E   MapBlast features the Pocket MapBlast option that lets you download maps to your PalmPilot or Windows CE hand-held device.

9 Tracking Down Lost Souls

Want to track down your first love? Do you have a phone number but can't remember who it belongs to? Wonder who lives in that house down the street? There is a world of possibilities for finding people on the Internet.

Find an Old Friend or Relative on the Internet

Imagine having the residential and business telephone books from every city in the United States on your desk. It would be an awesome job to find a person if you didn't know where they were located. But if all that information were stored electronically so you could just enter a name to search the entire country it would be much less daunting. Wait no longer; what you need is on the Internet!

Here's What You Need

The only thing you will need to use this information is access to the Internet.

Sites and Features

The amazing thing about the Internet is the vast amount of information it contains. Directory sites let you search for names, addresses, and phone numbers anywhere in the United States and around the world. If you don't know a person's name, you can also do a reverse lookup. This means you can enter a phone number to see to whom it belongs or an address to see who lives there. If you find a listing that you're interested in, you can easily look up people who live in their neighborhood. There are even e-mail listings and reverse e-mail so you can match people with their e-mail addresses.

Now you won't actually find every person in the world in online directories. Unlisted telephone numbers, corporate e-mail addresses, and very new listings won't be available. But that still leaves a couple hundred million people.

AnyWho Directories

Let's start with the site www.anywho.com, where you can search for phone numbers using the interface that AT&T maintains there.

Enter the person's last name in the Last Name text box, and the zip code or city and state, and then click Find. For more options, click Advanced Search. If you're sure of the spelling, leave the list next to the Last Name box set at Same As. You can also choose Sounds Like if you're not sure of the spelling, or you can enter just the start of the name and choose Begins With.

Instead of entering the complete first name, it's better to enter just the first letter and leave the list set at Begins With. In some cases, the listing is under the initial, and entering the full name will cause it to not be found. If you really need to enter the entire name, and you are sure that is the way it will be listed, choose Same As.

If you know the street name, city, zip code, or state, you can also enter them, but that is entirely up to you. When you're done, click Find.

If any matches are found, they will appear on-screen. If you didn't enter a state, the names are listed by state; otherwise they are listed in alphabetical order. Scan the list for the person you are interested in. To explore the entry you come up with, choose one of the following choices:

◆ Click the person's name to see the details on the listing by itself.

◆ Click their street name to get a listing of people on the same street, but not necessarily on the same block.

◆ Click the phone number to access AT&T's ClickToDial telephone conferencing facility. You can set up a conference call for up to seven people. Calls cost 15 cents per minute within the continental U.S. Find out more about ClickToDial at www.click2dial.att.com/index.html.

◆ Click Maps to see a map of the address.

◆ Click Add to Address Book to store the address in an online address book that you can maintain at the site.

◆ Click Send Cards to send an electronic or actual card, for a fee.

◆ Click Send Flowers and Gifts to send a gift to the person.

◆ Click Find Old High School Friends to look up persons who were in the same graduating class, as maintained by www.classmates.com/.

NOTE The other options on the screen let you look up businesses, do a reverse lookup of the telephone number, and look for toll-free phone numbers or Web sites.

AnyWho is not just an electronic version of the telephone book. It maintains its own listing of names and addresses. By clicking the Add Listing list on the left of the AnyWho window you can insert your name, address, e-mail address, and Web site address into their directory. You can also click Update Listing to modify your listing.

Along with name and address information, you can add a wish list to your AnyWho record. Click Wish List on the left of the screen to access a form for recording items you'd like for your birthday or any occasion. Click the Change This Listing link, and then click the Change button in the screen that appears.

When you are viewing the details page of a listing, you'll see an icon for a "vcard" next to the name. Vcards are used by some e-mail, Personal Information Managers (such as Microsoft Outlook), and personal organizers to keep more detailed records of address book listings. You can learn more about vcards at www.imc.org/pdi.

Worldwide Directories

The Internet is a worldwide phenomenon, so it should come as no surprise that you can also get telephone numbers and addresses from around the globe.

The best place to start looking for international numbers is at www.teldir.com, which bills itself as "the Internet's original and most complete index of online phone books."

This site not only lets you access telephone books in the United States, but also in these categories: North America and the Caribbean, South and Central America, Africa, Europe, Asia and the Middle East, and Australasia and the Pacific.

Click the link for the area or country that you are interested in to display additional links for specific phone books.

Reverse Lookups

A reverse lookup is just the opposite of a regular search. Instead of entering a name to find an address or telephone number, you enter a telephone number or address to locate the name and other information.

Reverse lookups are great, especially if you have a telephone number but you don't know to whom it belongs. It could be on a piece of paper you found in your pocket, part of an itemized listing on your telephone bill, or a number left on your pager or in your caller ID box.

You can also use reverse lookups to find out who lives where. Perhaps you're concerned that you cannot contact an elderly friend or relative and want to contact their neighbor. Or, perhaps you're just curious about who lives in that spooky mansion at the end of the street.

The AnyWho site provides a reverse lookup by telephone number. For more reverse options, go to `www.infospace.com/info/reverse.htm?XNavigation=ylw`.

This site lets you search by telephone number, address, or even e-mail address. There is even a reverse area code lookup that lists the geographic area covered by an area code, which is useful to know before making a long distance call.

Lookups of e-mail addresses do not catch a lot of people. Reverse lookups are more effective: you can try locating who belongs to an e-mail. If you just enter the domain, such as `@sybex.com`, you'll get a list of people at that domain who are also in the service's directory.

When All Else Fails

If you can't find the person you are looking for by using directories, there are still things you can try that might work.

- Try doing a regular Web search. Chances are your ISP offers a search box on its home page, or you can try any of the popular search engines. You never know whether the person you're looking for is famous, infamous, or has otherwise done something to get their name on the Web.

- If you know what school they graduated from, try finding the school home page and looking for an alumni list. There may even be a link to contact the alumni association.

◆ If you know the person's occupation or employer, do a business lookup. Most of the directory services let you look up a business by name, location, or category.

◆ Do you know what the person is interested in? Try looking at Internet newsgroups.

10 Find a Job Online!

If you are independently wealthy or plan to inherit a fortune, then you can skip this information. But if you're like the rest of us working stiffs, take a look at how you can find a better job.

Fill Those Vacant Shoes!

The local newspaper and the employment office are great places to start looking for work, but real careers can be made on the Internet. Since the Internet spans the world, you can make contacts and locate job openings that are not advertised in your local newspaper.

Here's What You Need

All you need is access to the Internet, although a resume wouldn't hurt.

Sites and Features

There are actually lots of places to find work on the Internet. First, try the Web sites of companies that you'd like to work for. Most of the larger companies have links on their home pages for employment information. Clicking one of those links might take you to a listing of jobs, a place to send your resume electronically, or just a description of how to apply for work. It is a great place to start, because you can target your search toward specific companies for which you'd like to work.

Instead of aiming for specific companies, you can also link up with a job-placement service. Two of the most popular on the Internet are www.jobs.com and www.monster.com.

With Jobs.com, you can download a free copy of a program called Resumail Resume 2000. Use this program to write your resume and cover letter, which you can submit to the Jobs.com resume bank for forwarding to prospective employers.

At the Jobs.com Web site, you can search for jobs by city and by category. When you find a job you're interested in, click the Resumail It button to submit your resume.

At monster.com—a rather funky name for a great service listing over 350,000 jobs from more than 30,000 employers—you can find a listing of jobs as easily as entering one or more keywords into a box and clicking Search Jobs. You can also search by location or category. The resulting list of jobs shows the posting date, location, job title, and company.

You can also start your search in one of several communities. The communities change to reflect current employment opportunities, but common ones include Free Agents, Campus, Mid-Career, Dotcom, Technology, HR, Healthcare, Executive, International, and Self Employment. Use one of these communities to track down a job at a certain level or in a specific industry.

The job titles in listings are links—click the title to read details about the offering and how to apply and then click Apply Online to send off your resume.

The site makes it easy to apply, because you can create and store your resume and cover letter on their Web site. You sign up for a free account by just entering your e-mail address. A private username and password will be e-mailed to you, usually within minutes.

Then from the Web site, click My Monster and enter your name and password to access options for storing your resume and cover letter, tracking job offers, and joining online chats.

From the My Monster screen, for example, click the Submit Resume link for an online resume form. The form includes sections for your contact and relocation information, the type of job you're looking for, compensation requirements, and educational background. At the end of the form is a large text box in which you can enter or paste the body of your resume. In fact, you should prepare your resume beforehand and then copy and paste it into the form.

In a similar manner, you can create and store a cover letter from My Monster. The letter and resume will be sent when you click Apply Online from any listed position.

If you prefer going out to get a job, use the Internet to locate job fairs in your area at `dir.yahoo.com/Business_and_Economy/Employment_and_Work/ Jobs/Job_Fairs`. In fact, Yahoo and other search engines offer a wide range of career information. At `careers.yahoo.com`, for example, you can find many career links as shown in Figure 10.1.

FIGURE 10.1   **Career paths at Yahoo!**

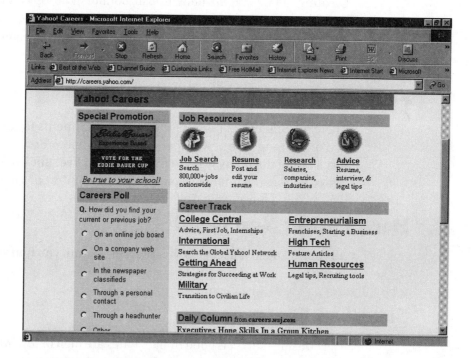

Copyright © 2000 Yahoo! Inc. All rights reserved.

Other sources of employment information can be found at these sites:

- ◆ `www.careerpath.com`
- ◆ `www.hotjobs.com`

◆ www.jobbankusa.com

◆ www.jobsearch.org

◆ www.jobweb.com

11 Need a Roof over Your Head?

Locating the right apartment, house, condo, or co-op can be hard on the legs, wallet, and ego. Start your search for living arrangements on the Internet, where plenty of options abound, whether you're moving around the corner or around the world.

Find a Place to Call Home

There are millions of homes for sale and apartments for rent every day. Looking through the newspaper, banging on doors, and calling realtors are just a few of the many ways to find a place to live. But you can also do a stress-free search for living space from the comfort of a computer.

Here's What You Need

All you will need is access to the Internet . . . until you find your new home, that is!

Sites and Features

The housing market is good or bad. Rates are high or low. Money is tight or loose. There are lots of reasons why finding the right place to live can be difficult, but the Internet can help you find a home and a mortgage to pay for it.

Getting Approved

If you want to make sure you can afford a new home before you look for one, prequalify for a mortgage or, better still, get preapproved.

Prequalification means that you can afford a home up to a certain price and indicates to the seller that you should have no problem getting a mortgage. The prequalification, however, is not a commitment from a lender. Preapproval, on the other hand, means that a lender has actually committed to giving you a mortgage for a certain amount, even though you have not yet picked out a specific property.

Some places to prequalify, get preapproval, and apply for loans are

- ◆ www.eloan.com
- ◆ www.iown.com
- ◆ www.quickenloans.com

You can prequalify at a local bank, of course, but you can also do it online by filling in a form requesting some basic financial information. After filling in the form at www.eloan.com, for example, you'll learn whether you can afford that dream house.

One company, Quickenloans (www.quickenloans.com), even creates a letter stating that you are prequalified for a certain loan amount. You can print it and take it with you to a meeting with the seller.

To get preapproved, you have to enter more detailed information, basically applying for the loan. With a preapproval letter in hand you may be able to strike a better deal.

N O T E Prequalification does not obligate you or the online company to actually establish a loan together. The prequalification is based entirely on your responses to the online form. The lender does not validate your responses until you ask to be preapproved or actually apply for the loan.

Finding Your Home

Once you know what you can afford, you have to find a home in that price range. For that, the multiple listing is a great invention. By listing a house with the Multiple Listing Service (MLS), a realtor can offer a house to every realtor and prospective buyer in the United States. So if you're looking for a home, the first place to start is at www.realtor.com. With almost 1.5 million listings from the MLS, the site offers the widest range of homes available, including condos and co-ops. You can choose homes by geographic area, price, size, and many other criteria in order to narrow down your search.

When you find a good prospect, print a copy of the MLS listing, which usually includes a photograph of the property and a detailed description. Take the printout to a local realtor, or just drive by the house to check it out. If you need to find a local realtor, www.realtor.com can help with that too.

Another excellent source is www.homescout.com. This site includes many MLS as well as non-MLS listings. It also includes a search engine for loans, where you can shop for mortgages.

Finding a Roommate

If you're just looking for a roommate to share expenses, there are some other great sites. Try these to match up with someone compatible:

- ◆ www.roommateexpress.com
- ◆ www.roommatefind.com
- ◆ www.roommatelocator.com

While some companies list roommates throughout the United States, Roommate Express (www.e-roommate.com) specializes in those West Coast areas where housing is at a premium.

12   Hi. What's Your Sign?

Before you dust off those platform shoes or get the wrinkles out of your leisure suit for a happening night on the town, consider making contact over the Internet.

Finding a Date

If you thought finding a job and a place to live could be difficult, how about finding a pleasant, compatible person to spend some time with? Finding a date, friend, or companion is not so easy these days. Sometimes it seems like all the right folks are already taken.

Here's What You Need

All you will need to try out these opportunities is access to the Internet and a free Saturday night.

Sites and Features

There are a whole lot of places to find a date over the Internet. You can try chat rooms, the online equivalent to the local watering hole. The chat rooms in AOL, CompuServe, or some other ISP can be fun and socially rewarding, as long as you use some common sense and caution. Who you are talking to in a chat room may be a mystery.

For a more structured and formal way to meet people, you can try going through online dating services. They work about the same way as other dating services, except you swap information online.

The service at www.one-and-only.com lets you place one free ad before signing on. Check out www.matchamerica.com for a nationwide dating service, or www.1stclassdating.com to start looking.

If you are looking for a how-to on dating, rather than a direct match, try www.fayez.simplenet.com/romanceguide.htm, which calls itself the "ultimate multimedia guide to flirting, dating, love, and romance."

If you want more than a date, you can try matchmaking services such as these:

◆ www.findmymate.com

◆ www.match.com

◆ meetamate.com

Or for something really different, try www.williedaly.com, where a horse whisperer offers matchmaking hints while you go horseback riding in Ireland.

13 Finding Your Roots

Sometimes knowing where you came from is as important as knowing where you are going. Getting a job, a place to live, and a companion on the Internet is about your future. You can also use the Internet to learn about your past.

Genealogy Online

While there's always a chance you'll turn up a skeleton or two, learning about your family history can be an exciting pastime. You never know what famous, infamous, or just interesting people you'll learn about. You'll also get a good sense of who you are and of the trials and tribulations your family went through to get you to where you are today.

Here's What You Need

All you need is access to the Internet. Be prepared, however, with the names of distant relatives, and some understanding of your immediate family tree. Interview relatives to find out whether your family name has been changed or the spelling altered, and to find out the location where relatives might have entered the country and settled. The more you know, the more you'll be able to find.

Sites and Features

The Internet is just packed with information you can use to research your family history.

One of the first places to start, however, is to use the techniques you leaned in Section 9, Tracking Down Lost Souls, to look for relatives that have moved away or with whom you have lost contact. You might just find an aunt, uncle, or cousin you almost forgot about who is also researching the family tree. Don't ignore relatives who are in extended branches—sometimes the most useful bit of information comes serendipitously when you least expect it.

Most of the information you can search online is maintained by organizations of volunteers interested in genealogy, who want to share their information in the hope that they themselves can make contact with relatives. One of the best official government sources, however, is the Social Security Death Index.

The Social Security Death Index contains information about more than 63 million persons. The index can provide information, such as that shown here, that will help you delve further into your family's past:

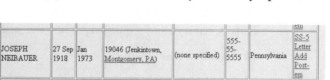

JOSEPH NEIBAUER	27 Sep 1918	Jan 1973	19046 (Jenkintown, Montgomery, PA)	(none specified)	555-55-5555	Pennsylvania	SS-5 Letter Add Post-em

Knowing the birth date, and the state where the person's social security number was issued, may help in getting birth records. Having the date of death, the last known residence, and last payment location may help to locate a death certificate or burial site. You can then use the social security number to access some military, financial, and employment information.

To access the index, go to either of these sites:

◆ ssdi.genealogy.rootsweb.com/

◆ www.ancestry.com/search/rectype/vital/ssdi/main.htm

In the form that appears, enter enough information, such as their first and last names, to identify the person you want to research. Enter just the last name to get a list of persons in the database with the same family name. You can also choose the Soundex option to locate names that sound like the one you enter. This is especially useful if you are not sure of the spelling, or if relatives have changed the surname spelling over the years.

For more information about the person, click the link on the right of the listing—the name of the link will depend on the site you are using for the search. This displays a form letter to the Social Security Administration requesting the person's record. You have to mail the letter away with a check for $7.00 to the address shown on the letter.

Other great sources of genealogy information are at these locations:

◆ www.cyndislist.com

◆ www.gengateway.com

- www.usgenweb.com
- www.familysearch.org
- www.lds.org
- www.ancestry.com/main.htm
- www.rootsweb.com
- www.familytreemaker.com
- www.heritagequest.com

Gengateway.com features a comprehensive series of links to resources of all types, each called a gateway. They include

- Beginners Gateway
- Database Gateway
- Ethnic Gateway
- History Gateway
- Listing Gateway
- Military Gateway
- Obituary Gateway
- Scottish Gateway
- Surname Gateway
- USA Gateway
- Vital Records Gateway
- Worldwide Gateway

The USGenWeb program (www.usgenweb.com) is made up of a massive group of volunteers from around the United States who maintain their own independent sites. Each site contains information and resources at the county level, so you can track down very specific information. The USGen-Web home page also offers links to public domain records, census information, and the Tombstone Project, which contains information from tombstones in surveyed cemeteries.

The records and links at www.familysearch.org and at www.lds.org are maintained by the Church of Jesus Christ of Latter-Day Saints. The Church has one of the world's most extensive collections of genealogy information, including records from many countries around the world.

The sites also explain where you can examine microfilm records of the Church's database of information.

The site at `www.ancestry.com/main.htm` boasts a listing of over 500 million names, including links to the Social Security Death Index, an Ancestry Library of resources, and hundreds of other databases, such as

- ◆ Abstract of Graves of Revolutionary Patriots
- ◆ Irish Records Index, 1500-1920
- ◆ Slave Narratives
- ◆ WWI Civilian Draft Registrations

NOTE While many of the databases at `www.ancestry.com/main.htm` are free to search, most are reserved for registered members of the site. Membership ranges from $19.95 quarterly to $99.95 per year, depending on the length of access and additional features you want.

The RootsWeb.com site (`http:rootsweb.com`) offers links to literally millions of pages of genealogy data, with over 12 million individuals on file. You'll find links to transcripts of marriage certificates, census records, wills, and other public documents.

The site at `www.familytreemaker.com` is maintained by Family Tree Maker Online. In addition to information about purchasing genealogy software, the site offers links to genealogy resources around the world.

You should also check out `www.sierra.com` for a wide range of Generations Family Tree software. You'll find multimedia demonstrations of their products on the CD with this book.

It's About Time

When someone came up with the expression "Time is Money," the Internet wasn't around, but the saying certainly applies to the Internet too. Not only can the Internet charge you for time, it can also take up your time, save you time, and even tell you the time. In this part of the book, we'll look at interesting associations between time and the Internet.

14 Synchronize Your Watches

Does every clock in your home have a different time? Well, spread throughout this planet are timeservers—computers that have the exact time—or as exact as humanly possible.

Use the Internet to Synchronize Your Clocks

The good folks at these timeservers let you synchronize your computer's clock to theirs. You can log on to the Internet and automatically set your computer clock to the exact time.

Here's What You Need

All you need is a shareware or freeware program that you can download from the Internet. You'll find links to several of them on the CD that comes with this book, including EZE Clock, YATS32, Cmdtime, and AtomTime98.

Sites and Features

Using free or inexpensive software, which you can find on the CD or download over the Internet, you can automatically update your computer's clock to the second. If time is that important to you, run one of these programs periodically to keep your clock current. Some programs give you the option of setting your clock each time you connect to the Internet or even when you start your computer.

There are scores of programs that automatically get the current time and update your system clock.

EZE Clock

EZE Clock is one example. This shareware program displays a customizable digital clock on your desktop. The program checks in with the National Institute of Standards Timeserver every time you start your dialup connection to access the Internet and updates your system clock as needed. You can find EZE Clock by downloading it from www.atssoftware.com. You control EZE Clock by right-clicking it to display these options:

Date/Time Properties   Opens Windows's Date/Time Properties window.

Run as Service   Runs EZE Clock every time you start your computer.

Select ISP   Dials your ISP when you manually tell it to sync the time.

Display Clock   Toggles between displaying the clock on the desktop and making the icon invisible.

Keep Clock on Top   Displays the clock above all open windows.

Clock Colors   Sets the foreground and background colors.

Enable Sys Tray Icon   Places an icon for EZE Clock in the system tray.

Set Time Now   Dials into the NIST timeserver and sets your clock.

View Log   Displays a text file showing EZE clock actions.

Help   Opens the EZE Clock help system.

About   Gives you version and registration information.

Close EZE Clock   Closes the program and removes the clock from the screen.

YATS32

YATS32 is another time sync program provided on the accompanying CD. You can also download it from www.dillobits.com.

When you start the program, it may report that there are no timeservers currently defined and ask whether you want to define one or more. Select Yes. You then have the option to choose to evaluate it or to register it. The Evaluate option lets you run it free for a limited time; the Register option allows you to purchase it. If you run YATS32, you will see the following dialog box, which displays several default timeservers, as shown in Figure 14.1.

FIGURE 14.1 Setting your clock with YATS32

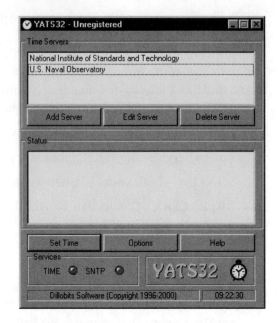

Click the timeserver you want to use and then click Set Time. The program dials into your ISP and sets your clock. The results appear in the dialog box.

You can select additional timeservers by using the Add Server button. The Options button lets you customize YATS32. You have a choice of several options that will run YATS32 each time you connect to the Internet or whenever you start your computer, whichever option you choose.

AtomTime98

AtomTime98 is another shareware synchronization program that is easy to use. You can download it at www.atomtime.com/download.html.

As shown in the following illustration, you just run the program and click the Check button to dial into a default timeserver. If the Local PC Difference box shows any significant difference, click Adjust to make the change to your system's clock.

You can use the Settings button to control how the program works. The button opens a dialog box with five tabs. In the Execution tab, you can set the program to automatically connect to the Internet and check the time at set intervals. The Display tab lets you choose to display the actual time, local time, or Greenwich Mean Time in the AtomTime98 window. The Time Server tab lets you specify a timeserver other than the one maintained by the program. Use the Proxy Server tab if you are connecting to the Internet through a proxy server, and use the License tab to enter your license number if you are using a registered version of the program.

Cmdtime

If you are uncomfortable with programs that take control and appear automatically, you can sync your clock using the command line program **Cmdtime**. This program is on the CD and can also be found at www.softshape.com.

You run Cmdtime from the command line—from the Start ➣ Run option on the taskbar or from the MS-DOS Prompt. Command options give you the choice of a quick adjustment based on three timeservers or a precise adjustment based on ten. They recommend using ten servers if you have a poor connection that might delay the process.

From the Start ➣ Run menu, enter any of the following commands, which assume the program is in the root directory of the C: drive:

C:/cmdtime /?   Shows how to use Cmdtime.

C:/cmdtime /M   Specifies the maximum amount of time your clock can be adjusted. The default is 120 minutes.

`C:/cmdtime /Q`   Performs a quick adjustment using three timeservers.

`C:/cmdtime /P`   Performs a precise adjustment using ten timeservers.

`C:/cmdtime ping`   Shows the servers' response time without adjusting your clock.

`C:/cmdtime /Q +XX`   Adds xx minutes to the time.

`C:/cmdtime /Q –XX`   Subtracts xx minutes from the time.

`C:/cmdtime /T`   Sets the time and shows the servers' response time.

`C:/cmdtime server`   Performs an adjustment using the timeserver listed—you can list up to 10.

`C:/cmdtime /W`   Sets the timeout value—the length of time the program waits until it gives up trying to update the time if the server is not responding. The default is 3000 milliseconds.

`C:/cmdtime +Time`   Adds the specified amount of time to the adjusted clock, as in C:/cmdTime +30

`C:/cmdtime –Time`   Subtracts the specified amount of time.

After you select one of the above commands, the program dials into your ISP, if you are not already connected, gets the time, and sets your date and time based on your time zone.

More Timeservers

Here are a few other URLs and locations of popular timeservers. To use one of these, enter it following the `C:/cmdtime`, as in `C:/cmdtime/ black-ice.cc.vt.edu`.

Web Site	Location
`black-ice.cc.vt.edu`	Virginia Tech Computing Center, Blacksburg, VA
`chime.utoronto.ca`	University of Toronto, Ontario, Canada
`churchy.udel.edu`	University of Delaware, Newark, DE
`clock.psu.edu`	Penn State University, University Park, PA

More Synchronization Programs

Here are a few other programs you can download to synchronize your computer clock:

Program	Download Location
WebTimeSync	www.victechsoftware.com
iTime	www.touchstone.de
Sync-It with Atom	www.tolvanen.com/syncit
WebTime for Windows 95/NT	www.gregorybraun.com

15 Tracking Time Spent Online

As one who knows can tell you, the Internet can become addictive. Before you know it, the sun is shining, you've had no sleep, and you're already late for work.

Preventing Family Trouble

If "Honey, come to bed already" is a familiar mating call in your household, then maybe you need to keep track of your time online. If you want to save your marriage, family, or job, read on.

Here's What You Need

For this essay you won't need much of anything. You may find some useful free or inexpensive software on the CD or available for download from the Internet, however.

Sites and Features

With all of the wonderful features you are learning about in this book, you may be spending more time than you want online. It is not your fault. It is easy to lose track of time. But spending too much time online can break up a relationship, cause family strife, exceed your credit card limits, and make the phone company too happy.

For help in exercising some control over yourself and others in your household, keep track of your time online. The easiest way to do this is to watch the clock in the Windows system tray, on your wrist, or on the wall. This method doesn't cost anything or require any software; it only requires some discipline.

If you need some additional help, check to see if your ISP has a feature for tracking your online time. If they do, you can check your online time regularly to see how close you're getting to—or how far away you are from—your limit of free hours.

If discipline is what you lack, consider some free or inexpensive alternatives. Several programs for tracking your online time are included on the accompanying CD, and there are plenty more that you can download from the Internet.

Online Time

One such program, Online Time, is on the CD and can be downloaded from www.lonewolf.gr/software. Online Time displays an icon (a yellow face) in the system tray—the area of the Windows taskbar where you'll see the time. This icon indicates when you are on and offline. Point to the icon to see the length of time online.

You can also click the icon to open the program window. The window shows the current time, the length of the current session, the length of your longest session, and your total online time. It also displays the number of connections, the number of times you have run the program, the date you installed it, and your system's IP address. You can reset the settings by clicking the Reset icon.

Minimize the window to return it to the icon in the system tray. If you don't like the icon, you can right-click it and choose Icons from the menu to select a new one.

Modem Logger

For a more robust way of tracking your time, try Modem Logger. It can be downloaded from `kiryssoft.cjb.net`.

As you can see from the Modem Logger window shown in Figure 15.1, the program shows the current session time, the length you've been online during the current day, and your total online time.

FIGURE 15.1   **Tracking online time with Modem Logger**

Using the Options menu on the right of the program window, you can associate your browser or e-mail program as the timer "client." You can then run the program and start timing by clicking Options and choosing Run Client.

One nice feature of Modem Logger is its cost log. If you pay for your online time in either ISP or phone-company charges, you can keep track of charges you have accrued. Choose Cost Logging Preferences from the Options menu to open a window, as shown in Figure 15.2. The window in this figure shows what this setup would look like for British Telecom in the United Kingdom. This company charges by the minute. By setting the cost configuration, you can keep track of how much your online time is costing. By using the Autoconfigure option, you can have Modem Logger enter the information for the most popular telephone services for you.

WinAnalyzer

A program that goes a few steps farther to help you control your online time is WinAnalyzer, that you can download from most software collections. This program not only tracks your online time and cost, but can check your e-mail and synchronize your system time. It can also be set to dial in at a specific time or to hang up at a certain time. When WinAnalyzer

FIGURE 15.2 Calculating online costs

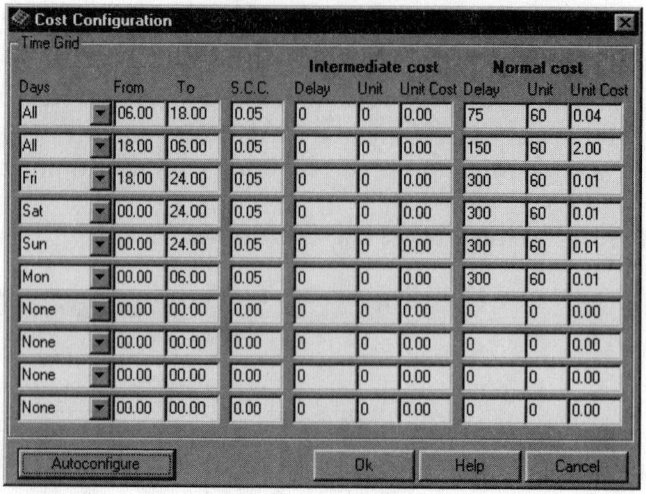
Cost Configuration
Time Grid
Intermediate cost
Normal cost
Days
From
To
S.C.C.
Delay
Unit
Unit Cost
Delay
Unit
Unit Cost
All 06.00 18.00 0.05 0 0 0.00 75 60 0.04
All 18.00 06.00 0.05 0 0 0.00 150 60 2.00
Fri 18.00 24.00 0.05 0 0 0.00 300 60 0.01
Sat 00.00 24.00 0.05 0 0 0.00 300 60 0.01
Sun 00.00 24.00 0.05 0 0 0.00 300 60 0.01
Mon 00.00 06.00 0.05 0 0 0.00 300 60 0.01
None 00.00 00.00 0.00 0 0 0.00 0 0 0.00
None 00.00 00.00 0.00 0 0 0.00 0 0 0.00
None 00.00 00.00 0.00 0 0 0.00 0 0 0.00
None 00.00 00.00 0.00 0 0 0.00 0 0 0.00
Autoconfigure
Ok
Help
Cancel

is installed, an icon is installed in the system tray. When you open WinAnalyzer by clicking this icon, you will see a menu bar and eight command buttons along the left side. Use these to work the program.

You can right-click the icon on the system tray to access configuration options.

By combining settings, you can use WinAnalyzer to dial in, check your mail, and then hang up. Follow the steps below to configure the program and dial your ISP to check your mail.

1. Right-click the WinAnalyzer icon in the system tray and choose Configuration ➢ Connection.
2. In the box that appears, click the dial-up networking connection you want to use, and then click Set as Default.
3. Click the Advanced button in the dialog box.
4. In the box that appears, enter your user name and password, and then click OK.
5. Click Hide.
6. Right-click the icon and choose Configuration ➢ E-mail Watch to open the Preferences dialog box.

7. Enable the check box labeled Check E-mail Immediately Upon Connection.

8. Enter your user name, e-mail password, and the address of your mail server.

9. Click Connection on the left of the box.

10. In the box that appears, pull down the Action menu and choose Auto Hangup.

11. Set the inactivity period to 5 minutes.

12. Select the option Redial Until Connected.

13. Click OK.

14. Right-click the icon and choose Configuration ➤ Timer.

15. Enable the Start Dialing At Time option and set the time you want the program to check your e-mail.

16. Click Start Dialup Sequence.

Now leave your computer just the way it is—go out for the evening or get a good night's sleep. At the time you set, WinAnalyzer will call your ISP (re-dialing if the line is busy), check your e-mail, wait five minutes, and then hang up.

General Timers

If you're interested in the overall time that you're on your computer, not just online, use a more general timing program.

 TimeIt! TimeIt! lets you turn the time on and off, and it allows you to set an alarm. If you only want to go online for 30 minutes, for example, set the alarm for 30 minutes, click the Start button, and then connect to the Internet. Log off when you hear the alarm. TimeIt! is on the CD and can be downloaded from home.skyweb.net/geneg/duquesne_softworks.htm.

 Total Timer Total Timer differs from TimeIt! in the following manner. It just tells you how long your computer has been on and does not use Internet time at all. It is a quick alternative when you want to monitor your computer usage time. Total Timer is on the CD and can be downloaded from the collection of software at www.winfiles.com.

16 Understanding Time Zones

"Hello, sorry to wake you, but I'm selling..."

Doing business internationally, or bicoastally, is great, but don't jeopardize that deal by calling a client in the middle of their night. People get very angry when their pleasant sleep is interrupted by a sales call. Of course, if you do wake the client up, you can always pretend to be a competitor.

Following Time Zone Netiquette

Consider the time zone when using online chats too. Online chats are great for meeting new people, but don't expect a buddy from across the globe to stay up all night to talk to you. Make sure you know what time it is before making that online or long-distance call.

Here's What You Need

The only things you will need are an Internet connection and some handy software that you can find either on the accompanying CD or for download on the Internet.

You should also understand what Greenwich Mean Time (GMT) is. Because Internet services don't really know where you are, they show the time in GMT, the current time in Greenwich, England. (Go figure!) GMT is a standard way to reference time regardless of location, and it is used to coordinate all sorts of worldwide activities.

NOTE GMT is also known as Universal Time Coordinated (UTC), Coordinated Universal Time (CUT), Universal Coordinated Time (UCT), and Zulu time.

Web sites refer to times in other locations as either the actual local time or in relation to GMT. The notation +2, for example, would mean two hours past the GMT displayed. So if the GMT is shown as 16:24, and your time is referenced as +2, then it is 18:24 at your location.

Now what the heck is 18:24? I forgot to mention that GMT uses a 24-hour clock format. Instead of counting from 11 a.m., 12 noon, 1 p.m., 2 p.m., and so on, it counts 11:00, 12:00, 13:00, 14:00, etc. To convert from a 24-hour clock to a 12-hour clock, just subtract 12. This makes 18:24 exactly 6:24 p.m. Times smaller than 12:00 are a.m.; times greater than 12:00 are p.m.

Sites and Features

Before looking for that chat buddy online, or making that long distance call, check out the local time for the person you are trying to reach. You can do so online or by running a program on your computer.

If you're online, or plan to go online, check either of these sites: `www.worldtime.com` or `www.businesswindow.com`.

WORLDTIME

WORLDTIME is a free service that lets you select the location by either clicking the globe or choosing from a list of cities. Once you get to `www.worldtime.com`, click the link Access the service's main page here! to see the site shown in Figure 16.1.

Click the part of the globe that you want to center in the window—you may have to click several times to rotate the globe to the correct location. The centerpoint is the portion of the globe that is used to determine the time in this program; the time will be shown below the globe. The globe will also be shaded to indicate day and night.

You can perform these functions using the links on the left of the site:

◆ Refresh the page to indicate the current time.

◆ Turn the day/night indicator off or on.

◆ Zoom in and out of the graphic.

◆ Display a list of countries that can be used as the map centerpoint.

◆ View the time in selected United States cities, and the dates of public holidays for the current month.

◆ Customize the way the globe appears.

FIGURE 16.1   Global time at WORLDTIME

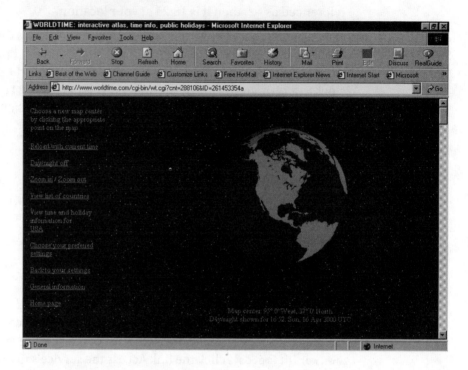

♦ Quickly change to your custom settings.

♦ Get general information on WORLDTIME.

♦ Jump to the WORLDTIME home page.

BusinessWindow

BusinessWindow handles the time differently. This site is a subscription service for members, but it provides a free timetable for many major cities around the world. From the site's home page (www.businesswindow.com), choose World Time from the left-hand pane of the screen. From the next screen, choose an option from the World Time for Non Paying Members section.

You can choose to display a list of countries alphabetically or by zone in relation to GMT. For each location, you'll see the local time as well as the offset from GMT. So, when it is 16:19 GMT, it is already 20:19 (or 8:19 p.m) in Kabul, Afghanistan—well after the end of the office day!

World Time Software

Rather than go online to get the time in various locations, you can download a number of programs from various places on the Internet, and then display the time offline. There are scores of such programs, including World Clocks, GTime, and WorldTime2.

 World Clocks   You'll find World Clocks on the CD with this book. World Clocks lets you display any number of clocks on-screen, each displaying a different time zone, and each showing the location's actual time, not GMT.

So consider using World Clocks to display the time for each chat buddy or for your major overseas clients.

The first time you run World Clocks, you should configure the clock by right-clicking on the clock and choosing Configure. The default setting shows the city, the date, and the offset from GMT. You can modify the caption that appears with the clock and change its foreground and background colors. If you do not want the GMT time to appear in the caption, for example, delete the characters ($GMT), which tell the program to place the GMT time on your screen.

Use the Clock Adjust tab to configure the clock for Daylight Savings Time. Use the General tab to choose a 24-hour format and to show the seconds. Click OK when you're done to display the clock.

To add one or more additional time zones, follow these steps:

1. Right-click the displayed clock and choose New from the shortcut menu. A duplicate clock appears.

2. Right-click one of the duplicates and choose Configure to open the Configure Clock dialog box.

3. Select the city or time zone and then click OK.

You can remove a clock from the screen by right-clicking and choosing Close. Select Exit from the shortcut menu to stop World Clocks, and to remove the icon from the system tray. World Clocks stores the clock configuration in your computer's registry, so the same time zones appear the next time you start the program.

 GTime and WorldTime2   The programs GTime and WorldTime2 take a different approach. They let you display a list of people and where they are located; these programs also display a local time for each location. In order to make these entries, you must already know the difference between your time and the locations you want to add. After these are added, all you will need to do is glance at the list you've created before looking for a chat buddy or making a long distance call.

You'll fine GTime on the CD, or you can download it from www.lonewolf.gr/software.

GTime lets you keep track of time in different locations in relation to your own time, instead of GMT, but you still have to use a 24-hour clock. The program starts with a blank window to which you add the locations you are interested in. From the GTime window, click Add to see a dialog box similar to this one:

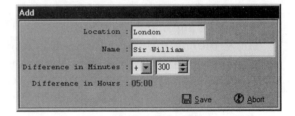

Enter the location and name of the person at that location; also adjust the difference between your time and theirs (the difference is measured in 30-minute intervals—before(-) and after(+) your own time). For example, suppose you're in New York and your client is in London, which is five hours ahead in time. Enter London in the Location box, and the client's name in the Name box. Make sure the Difference in Minutes is set at +, and advance the time to 300.

When you click Save, the locations will appear in the GTime window. You'll see the difference between the two locations, and the current time and date in each location. If you want to add locations, all of the information will be computed for these as well.

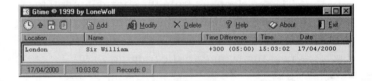

Use the buttons on the program's toolbar to add, modify, or delete a listing. If you find a monthly calendar useful, click the calendar icon. The calendar also shows the number of the week (with weeks numbered 1–52 beginning in January), and you can use the scroll bar to display other months. Click OK in the calendar window to close it.

Use the Notes icon on the toolbar to open a notepad-like window for recording reminders and other text. The text is saved in a file called Notes that opens whenever you click the Note icon. You can also open the file from your desktop using Notepad or any word processing program.

WorldTime2 is also on the CD and can be downloaded from `www.molecular-software.com`.

The WorldTime2 window, along with its List Management dialog box, is shown in Figure 16.2. Click List Management inWorldTime2 to add and remove people from the list.

FIGURE 16.2 **WorldTime2**

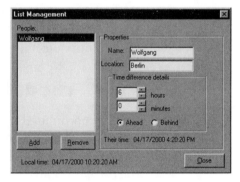

To add a person, follow these steps:

1. Click List Management in WorldTime2.

2. Click Add. The notation <NewPerson> appears in the People list.

3. Enter the person's name in the Name text box. It is echoed in the People list.

4. Enter the location in the Location text box.

5. Set the number of hours and minutes of time difference.

6. Select Ahead or Behind, as appropriate. The time at that location appears at the Their Time prompt.

7. Click Close.

WorldTime2 keeps the clock running in the list even if the window is minimized. To customize how the program works, click Options. In the dialog box that appears, you can set how often the time is updated (up to 60 seconds) when the application is open or minimized. You can also choose to keep the window in the foreground, and you can save its position so it reappears in the foreground each time it is opened.

17 Stay on Time and on Schedule

Never get caught off guard again without your trusty date book or calendar. You can use FREE services to maintain your schedule online and keep track of appointments, meetings, and other events.

Keep Your Schedule Updated Online

Staying coordinated is not always an easy task—that's why calendars, date books, handheld computers, and personal information managers (PIMs) are so popular these days. If you have one of those small handheld devices, you can easily carry it with you to check or arrange appointments and look up addresses. You can also get PIM software, such as Microsoft Outlook, for use on laptops and desktop PCs, or you can do it all online.

Here's What You Need

All you need to maintain a schedule online is a connection to the Internet and free registration with an online calendar service.

Sites and Features

PIMs are great for the busy executive, or anyone who has a busy schedule, a list of contacts, or a to-do list to maintain. If you move around a lot and work at a number of different computers, it is difficult to keep all of the information up-to-date and synchronized. You might schedule a meeting on your laptop, forget to update the data on your desktop, and then miss the meeting because you're reviewing your schedule on the office computer.

A solution to this dilemma is to use a free, Web-based PIM. That's right— your schedule and address book can be maintained on the service's own computer rather than on your laptop or desktop. You can check your schedule, make appointments, and keep an address book from any computer that has access to the Internet. Some of the services even let you synchronize the online data with your own computer; you can then synchronize your schedule with a handheld device, such as a Palm Pilot, Casseopia, or other Windows Consumer Electronics (CE) devices.

While the features vary, some of the online services include the following:

Calendaring   Lets you maintain your appointment schedule online. You can even share it with others to arrange meetings, and you can check the schedules of participants for free time.

Task List   Keeps a list of activities you have to perform and of your progress performing them.

Address Book   Maintains name, address, e-mail, and other information about contacts, customers, and colleagues.

Free E-mail   Gives you an e-mail address for sending and receiving messages.

File Storage   Lets you upload documents and other files for safekeeping to the service's computer. Use this service to keep files handy for access from any Internet computer, to share files with others, or to back up important files.

Personal Web Site   Gives you space for a home page.

Bookmark Management   Lets you maintain a list of favorites or bookmarked sites for easy access from any Internet computer.

Synchronizing   Lets you update your files so your Web-based PIM and your laptop, desktop, or handheld computer have the most current information.

There are dozens of free PIMs on the Internet. All of these services make you register the first time you use them, but the basic services are free. The only problem with these services being free is that the only way they can afford to be so is by advertising.

One other problem of Web-based PIMs is speed. It takes longer to log on to the Internet, sign on to the PIM site, and check your calendar than it does to just open your notebook and check with Microsoft Outlook or some other program. Still, Web-based PIMs can be great resources if you're on the go and hopping from one computer to another.

Because of their popularity, new PIMs are popping up all the time, while some current ones may be folding due to the competition. In this chapter, we'll look at several that offer a wide range of services and which—as of this writing—have been around awhile.

Visto

One of my favorite Web-based PIMs is Visto, a free service you can find at www.visto.com. Signing up is easy: just click Sign Up!, fill in an on-screen form with some basic information, and choose a password. The next time you go to Visto, enter your member name and password and click Log In Now to access your Visto page.

In addition to calendaring and an address book, Visto lets you upload files and graphics for storage and helps you organize them into folders and photo albums. You can maintain a to-do list and organize bookmarks for navigating the Internet. Visto also provides group folders and home pages.

Once you register and log on to Visto, you'll see the choices shown in Figure 17.1. The tabs along the top of the window and the options down the left side provide access to Visto's main functions. Registering for Visto also gives you an e-mail account, as in alan@visto.com. The e-mail page lets you access your Visto e-mail in order to send and receive messages and files, and you can access e-mail you have in other accounts from the Internet or from a wireless device.

The Files area lets you store documents, graphics, and other files on Visto's computer. You can access the files from any Internet connection and share them with other users by specifying a password for them to use. The Files page lets you upload and download files, and create folders in which you can organize them.

Use the address book to store e-mail addresses that you frequently access. Then it will be easy to use the address book to look up people to invite to meetings and to share files with. The address book works just like most computer address books; it lets you add, edit, and delete contacts.

FIGURE 17.1 **The main Visto window**

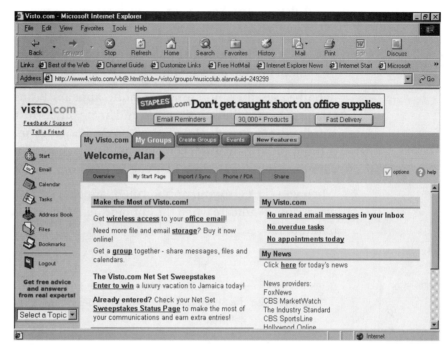

The bookmark page lets you organize your favorite sites, much like Favorites in Microsoft Internet Explorer and Bookmarks in Netscape Navigator. You add the addresses of sites that you want to access, and you can organize them into groups. By storing your bookmarks online, you can access the sites from any Internet connection.

Because calendaring and maintaining task lists are elements in most PIMs, lets look at these in a little more detail.

The Calendar   The heart of all PIMs, Web-based or otherwise, is the calendar. You use the calendar to schedule both appointments and meetings, and to make sure you don't forget them. Web-based PIMs let you share your calendar with others; this way you can plan group meetings, parties, and other events and also check and make sure all of the participants are available.

Once you are in the Calendar screen, use the arrows next to the date to change the date shown, or to click a date in the miniature monthly calendars on the right. You can always click the Today button to return to the current day.

You can add an appointment to the calendar in one of two ways:

♦ Click the Add New Event to Calendar button to create an appointment in which you designate the date and time.

♦ Click the underlined time in the calendar window to create an appointment for that day and time.

In both cases, the appointment window appears. From this screen you enter the details of the appointment and invite others to attend. You can also edit an event you have already created by changing the day, time, or length of the appointment. After you have made any changes to the appointment, click the Attendees button to invite others from your Visto address book.

When you click OK, your appointment appears in the calendar. Use the check box to indicate when the appointment is completed, or click the appointment to edit it.

NOTE Use the Share Calendar button to designate other users who can have access to your calendar.

Task List Chances are you have a "to-do list" somewhere around your home or office. Web-based PIMs let you maintain this list on their Web site so you can track your progress, and let you see which tasks are behind schedule, on schedule, and completed.

Click Tasks in the left of the Visto window to open the task list showing all current tasks.

To insert a new task, follow these steps.

1. Click New in the Task list to open the window, shown in Figure 17.2.

2. Enter the subject of the task as well as its start and due dates (if it has these).

3. Use the Status list to mark the task as Not started, In progress, Completed, Waiting on someone else, or Deferred.

4. Pull down the Priority list and choose High, Normal, or Low.

5. If you've already started the task, enter the percentage complete in the % Done text box.

FIGURE 17.2 **Creating a task**

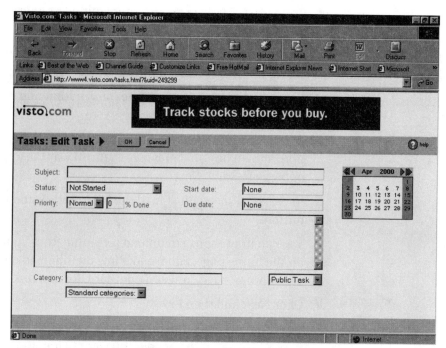

6. In the large text box, enter a description of the task.

7. Type a category for the task, or pull down the Standard Categories list and choose one of the built-in categories.

8. Designate the task as Public or Private.

9. Click OK.

You can review all tasks in the main Task window, and glance at which are complete, which are in progress, and which are overdue.

Visto Groups   A group can be any number of persons with whom you want to share information, messages, and files. In a way, setting up a group is like creating a personal Web site. You can create a group for family members, friends, or business associates. Each group has a message area for posting and replying to messages, file storage, and a common calendar. As the group manager, you create the group and invite others to join. You also establish a password that members must enter to access the group.

To create a group, follow these steps:

1. Connect to www.visto.com, enter your username and password, and click Log In Now.

2. Click Create Groups to start a series of screens in which you enter information and select options.

3. In the first screen, just read the information and click the Next button.

4. In the second screen, enter a name for the group, a one-line description, and an optional message that you want to appear on the group homepage. Click Next.

5. In the third screen, just read the information and click the Next button.

6. You can now choose to upload a graphic from your disk to display on the home page, choose to allow members to change the content of the home page, and add another URL as a link.

7. Click Next and then Finish.

8. You can now invite others to join the group. In the To box, enter the e-mail addresses of the people you want to join the group and separate each e-mail address with a comma. Each invited member receives an e-mail inviting them to join; each message should also contain a link to the group page. You can edit the message if you want.

9. Click Send.

When you log in to Visto, the names of your groups should appear with the other tabs. From these tabs, you and other group members can post and reply to messages, check the calendar for group events, and access shared files.

AnyDay

You can find AnyDay, another powerful Web-based PIM, at www.anyday.com. Registration is quick and easy. Just enter some basic information and then log on with your user name and password to access a calendar, as shown in Figure 17.3.

AnyDay provides your horoscope and the local weather (by using your registration information); it also offers a calendar, a to-do list, and a reminder

FIGURE 17.3   The AnyDay calendar

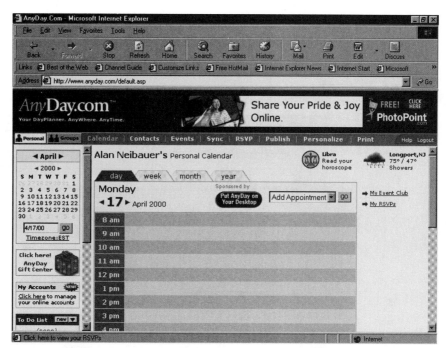

list. To navigate in the calendar view, either use the tabs on the calendar to change between the day, week, month, and yearly views, or use the small monthly calendar on the left to change dates.

To add an appointment to the calendar, click the date of the appointment to display the appointment form. Other options farther down the form let you add e-mail addresses (of others you want to invite to the meetings), designate your preferred type of appointment reminder, and set up recurring appointments on your calendar.

The reminder options let you choose to either display a reminder in a box when you log on to AnyDay, or have an e-mail reminder sent to you at a designated amount of time before the appointment.

The Repeat Appointment options let you designate how often the event occurs and when the appointment stops recurring. For example, you can choose to schedule a series of weekly appointments ending on January 1, 2001.

SuperCalendar

You can also maintain a Web-based calendar at the site www.supercalendar.com. After you register and log in, your calendar appears, as shown in Figure 17.4.

FIGURE 17.4 SuperCalendar

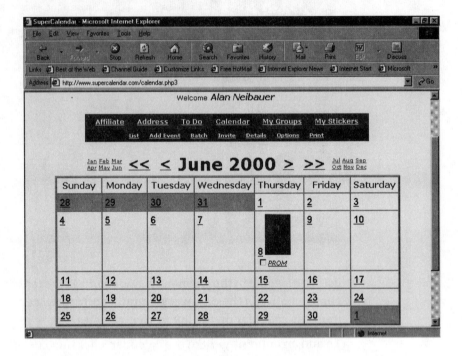

You can join groups that automatically add events to your calendar, including United States holidays, the schedules of selected professional sports teams, and new video releases.

Use the links and options above the calendar to change the month and year, show a list of meetings, and add new ones. You can also invite others to a meeting or to join a group.

As shown in Figure 17.4, you can add graphics called stickers to a calendar when you create an event. Use the My Stickers command to use graphics that you have on your disk.

Some Other PIMs

In addition to the services described in detail above, here are some other Web-based PIMs worth exploring:

Name	Site
Day-Timer Digital	`digital.daytimer.com`
GTFreemail	`www.gtfreemail.com`
Onebox	`www.onebox.com`
Jump!	`www.jump.com`
PlanetAll	`www.planetall.com`
MagicalDesk	`www.magicaldesk.com`
When.com	`www.when.com`
Yahoo	`calendar.yahoo.com`

News and Mail

The Internet can keep you informed about current news, weather, and sports. It will also keep you up-to-date on the latest gossip via e-mail from friend and foe alike. Tame the news/mail Internet beast with the features you'll learn here.

18 Where's the Sports Section?

If you're too busy to enjoy reading your local newspaper, or to watch the local news over a cup of java in the morning, take a look at the news on-screen.

Read Local News, Weather, and Sports

A growing number of newspapers and television stations are going online with electronic versions of their daily papers and news reports. You can do anything from reading the current news to checking out the lottery results, and you can generally find out what's happening in your city and around the world—all online.

Here's What You Need

You'll need access to the Internet and a local newspaper or television station that provides online news.

Sites and Features

One place to start looking for local news, sports, and weather is at `dir.yahoo.com/News_and_Media`.

From there, you can choose to view newspapers, magazines, radio stations, television stations, and other types of media. If you select newspapers, for example, you can choose a category of newspaper or select from a list of papers that have online sites.

Once you select a specific newspaper, the features available vary. All of the newspapers let you read the day's top stories and access other sections. The *Houston Chronicle* (www.chron.com) has links to various sections of its paper along the left of the screen. A page with news about the Philadelphia region (philly.com) that features the *Philadelphia Inquirer,* the *Philadelphia Daily News,* and the television station *6ABC,* is similar, with tabs along the top of the page to go to major sections of the paper, and links along the left to search by category.

If you select magazines from the Yahoo! site, you can first select a category, as shown in Figure 18.1, and then a specific magazine. Radio and television stations work about the same way.

FIGURE 18.1 **Magazine categories**

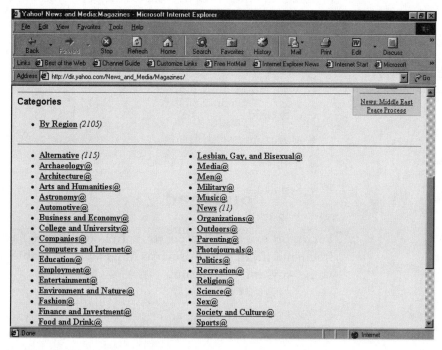

Copyright © 2000 Yahoo! Inc. All rights reserved.

If you're interested in news, local or not, then try www.totalnews.com. You can search for news stories based on a keyword, or you can click a category from a collection of links. Clicking a link displays a list of sources for news—print and broadcast.

Perhaps the best place to get news from around the world, however, is at www.mediainfo.com/emedia.

This site lets you find online newspapers, magazines, and other news sources by region, by category, or by a number of other criteria. It is a perfect place to locate news sources in almost any language.

The regional choices are USA/Canada, Africa, Asia, Oceania, Europe, Latin America, and the Middle East. If you're looking for a newspaper from Brazil, for example, click the map of Latin America to see a list of online papers in Brazil, and then click the link for the paper you want to read.

You can also search for news by first selecting from the categories shown here, and then entering a region, state, or city:

- Newspaper
- Association
- City Guide
- Magazine
- Radio
- Syndicate
- Television

For a more extensive search, you can choose the media category, location, frequency (from options such as AM, FM, Daily, Cable, and Satellite), name, city, and type of site.

19 Appearing at a Location Near You

If you're looking for a good movie to see, a concert to attend, or just what special events are going on in your city, then log on to the Internet.

Locate Local Entertainment

It seems just about everyone is on the Internet. Chances are your city is too. Through local government, neighborhood organizations, and companies' home pages, you can learn what's happening in your city or town.

Here's What You Need

The only things you need are access to the Internet and the name of the city you want information about.

Sites and Features

Some city listings in the Internet are detailed—with movie locations and times, happenings in local clubs, charity events, and the like. Others are more commercially oriented, with restaurant information, tourist sites, and other standard information. And remember, you can use city information not just for your own town but for places you plan to visit. Be prepared for a rainy night when you're at the beach, or to take advantage of those special events in far away places.

Citysearch

The best place to start is at www.citysearch.com. Try entering this in the address line: yourcity.citysearch.com/.

Of course, substitute yourcity with the name of your town, as in atlanta.citysearch.com/. If your city is covered by the Citysearch service, you'll see information as shown in Figure 19.1.

FIGURE 19.1 City information on Citysearch

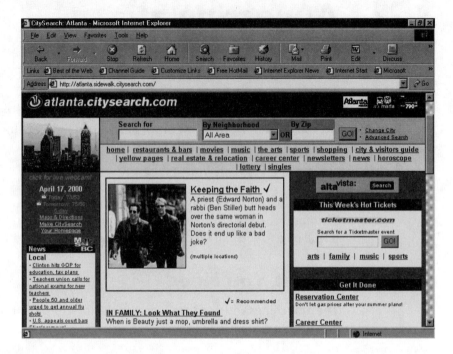

Copyright © 2000 Microsoft and/or its suppliers, One Microsoft Way, Redmond, Washington 98052-6399 U.S.A. All rights reserved.

Get movie listings by clicking the Movies link at the top of the page. In the screen that appears, use the lists in the Movie Search section to locate a movie you are interested in seeing and then click Go!

◆ Use the Movies list to select a film by its title.

◆ Use the Genre list to select a film by its type.

◆ Use the Choose a Theater list, or enter a zip code, to display theaters by neighborhood.

If you get an error message, then your city is not among those maintained in this site's database. In that case, go to www.citysearch.com/, which accesses the service's main home page and displays this dialog box:

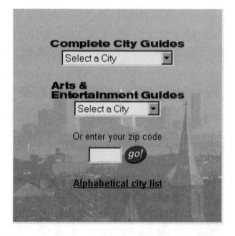

Copyright © 2000 Microsoft and/or its suppliers, One Microsoft Way, Redmond, Washington 98052-6399 U.S.A. All rights reserved.

Choose a city in the first list to get a complete guide or select a city in the second list for an arts and entertainment guide. If the city isn't listed, enter your ZIP code and click Go!. You can then select the type of entertainment information you want in the screen that appears to access listings for movies, concerts, and other activities.

infospace.com

Another way to find information on your town is to navigate to infospace.com and click the City Guide link. In the screen that appears, enter your city and state, or your zip code, and click the Find button. In addition to other information on your city, you'll see links to access categories of information.

One special feature of InfoSpace is their community message boards. You can leave and reply to messages, sharing information with friends and strangers about almost anything. Click Area Message Boards in the Community and Government section of your city's page to see the beginning of a list of message boards. To view more links, click Message Boards Index.

You can read messages very easily—just click a topic to see the individual messages and then click a message that you want to read. If you want to leave a message or reply to one, however, you have to sign up for a free InfoSpace account. The first time you click either Post a Message or Reply, you'll be asked for your InfoIpace username and password. If you haven't yet signed up, click the Register Now link, and complete the requested information.

Other Options

When neither Citysearch nor InfoSpace contains the local information you're looking for, try working through your state. To access your state's home page, go to www.state.yourstate.us, as in www.state.ca.us for California, or www.state.pa.us for Pennsylvania. Once you get to your state's home page, look for links to local communities.

20 Breaking News, as It Happens

Watch late-breaking news, sports, and weather scroll across your screen, and customize news reports to get just what you are interested in knowing.

View Headline News

You'll get the latest headlines delivered right to your screen, and if you see a story you're interested in, just click to get all of the details.

Here's What You Need

You need an Internet provider that offers a dial-up networking connection and a news broadcasting program that you can find on the CD or download from the Internet.

Sites and Features

Getting news delivered right to your desktop is called *push* technology because information from the Internet is pushed your way—it goes to you rather than you requesting a site to be downloaded. To get information pushed to your screen, you'll need a news service program. The program accesses the service's Web site and downloads the current headlines and news, which it displays on your screen. The programs and the service are free. You "pay" for it by seeing ads from sponsors along with the headlines. It is a small price to pay, however, for being kept informed in real time. If the ads bother you, there are programs that can keep some of them away, as you'll learn in Section 49, "Busting Those Ads".

You can specify the type of news you'd like to receive and, in some cases, even customize it for your location. Of course you'll need to be online to receive the news, but as you're working or browsing you'll see headlines scroll across your screen. One program even replaces your screen saver, so the news continues even during periods of inactivity.

There are a number of push programs available for free on the Internet. We'll take a look at several of them now in two categories—news tickers and news windows. News tickers display headlines and other information in a scrolling bar. News windows list headlines in a window.

We've included several of them—NewsDart, HeadlineViewer, and EntryPoint—on the CD with this book. Let's take a look at several of them now.

NOTE Remember, the latest version of America Online Instant Messenger includes a news ticker.

Desktop News

One handy news ticker program available for downloading is Desktop News. You can download it from `www.desktopnews.com`.

When you start Desktop News, it dials into your ISP (if you are not already connected) and starts displaying the current headlines and stock prices, along with their source, in its own on-screen window, shown here. To read details of a story, click the headline.

NOTE Be patient. It may take a few seconds for the news to be retrieved and displayed.

You can customize Desktop News in several ways. Right-click the button on the far right of the Desktop News window or the Desktop News icon in the system tray and choose from these options:

Upgrade

Auto Hide
Always On Top
Pause Ticker
Work Offline
Stealth Mode
Auto Click

Preferences
Tips
Mark All Read
Re-Dock

About Desktop News
Homepage
Help

✔ Dock on Top
Dock on Bottom

Exit

To customize the type of news that appears, choose Preferences. In the dialog box that appears, you can unsubscribe from categories so they no longer appear, change the buttons and other components of the ticker window, determine which stock quotes appear, and adjust how fast headlines scroll and other ways that the ticker operates.

Web Ticker

Web Ticker, which you can download from `www.spaeder.com/index.htm`, displays headlines as well as summaries of major stories, as shown here:

tained scores of anti-globalization demonstrators Monday and hurled tear gas and sprayed pepper to crush protests aimed at disrupting the

Double-click a story to open it in a browser window. Many of the stories are taken from the Yahoo! daily news summary, but another source is `www.nandotimes.com`.

Right-click the program's icon in the system tray and select Configuration to set the ticker speed, frequency of updating, and other aspects of its operation and appearance.

Headline Viewer

Headline Viewer, you can download from `www.vertexdev.com`, displays a window as shown in Figure 20.1.

FIGURE 20.1 Getting news from Headline Viewer

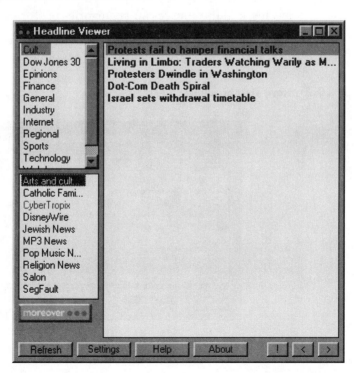

On the left side of the window are two lists—the Category List and the Active Providers List. The Category List contains categories of news that you can select. Choosing a category shows the sources of the news in the Active Providers List. Select an active provider to see its headlines in the Article List on the right. Double-click an article to open it in your browser or double-click an active provider to go to its Web site.

You can also click the ! button to open the provider's site, and the ← and → buttons to move forward and backward through the list of providers.

Use the Refresh button to update the list of headlines from the selected active provider.

Use the Settings button to open the Settings dialog box. Here you can customize the way Headline Viewer works, select other providers, display statistics on your use of providers, and change the appearance of the window.

News Dart

News Dart is another program that lists headlines in a window. You can download it from www.3dig.com. When you run News Dart for the first time, you have to configure it by specifying keywords that you want to appear in stories, and the sources and categories of stories.

News Dart then scans its sources, displaying them in a window as shown in Figure 20.2. Double-click a story to read its details.

FIGURE 20.2 **News Dart headlines**

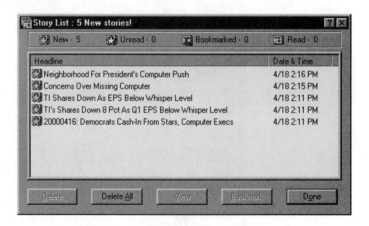

Right-click the News Dart icon in the system tray to stop and pause the scan for news stories and to open its Properties dialog box for changing keywords, news sources, and other settings.

EntryPoint

A program called PointCast was one of the most popular news programs because of the range of services that it offered. PointCast has been replaced by a new program, EntryPoint, that offers news, weather—even a music player and a lot more in both a scrolling ticker and lists. You can download the program from www.entrypoint.com, but you'll also find two versions of EntryPoint on the CD. In the EntryPoint folder of the CD, you'll find the basic program that gives you all of the news and weather features that you'll learn about in this section. In the EntryPoint2 folder, you'll find a more comprehensive version of the program that also provides a multimedia file player that you can set as your computer's default player, as well as an e-wallet feature for making secure on-line purchases using your credit card.

The EntryPoint window, shown here, includes the scrolling ticker—click a headline to open it in its own window.

To the right of the ticker are stock and weather sections. Point to a section to see a box with details about stock prices or weather. You may have to first click elsewhere in the EntryPoint window and then point to the section to display the information. Click the section to open detailed information about stocks or weather in the browser.

NOTE Click the button on the left of the ticker to stop and restart the scrolling.

Above the ticker is a series of buttons that display windows of information or open Web sites in your browser window:

◆ News displays a separate window with links to news sources and headlines.

◆ Sports displays a separate window with links to sports sources and headlines.

- Fun displays a separate window with links to entertainment sources such as comics, games, horoscopes, show times, and TV listings.

- Shop opens the EntryPoint shopping service in your browser.

- EWALLET lets you store credit card information on a secure site for on-line purchases.

- Finance displays a menu of financial features such as online brokers and banking.

- Travel displays a menu of travel services such as airline tickets and travel books.

- Info displays a menu of information sources including city guides, en-cyclopedias, maps, and directions.

To the right of the buttons are two search boxes that you use to search the Internet. Pull down the list associated with the first box and choose the search engine to use. In the next box, enter keywords for the search or pull down its list to choose a previously used search. Click Go to perform the search, displaying the results in your browser window.

Below the Go button is the EntryPoint Player control panel. Click on the Song List button on the right to begin downloading the EntryPoint Player application, a program for playing music files. After the program is down-loaded, it appears as shown in Figure 20.3. Use it to create and play a list of music tracks. You can control the playing, using the buttons in the Player or the panel in the EntryPoint ticker.

Click the EntryPoint button on the far left for a menu of these functions:

- Go To EntryPoint
- Personalize
- Options
- Minimize
- Refresh
- Change User
- Suggestions & Feedback
- Customer Support
- Frequently Asked Questions

FIGURE 20.3   **EntryPoint Player**

- ◆ Invite a Friend to Try EntryPoint
- ◆ About

Personalizing EntryPoint   You can customize EntryPoint to get the type of news that you're interested in. You can set personalization options only when online.

Click the EntryPoint button on the left of the EntryPoint window and then choose Personalize to access the Personalize pages of the EntryPoint Web site. The page presents six options:

- ◆ Personalize News
- ◆ Personalize Stocks
- ◆ Personalize Weather
- ◆ Personalize Sports
- ◆ Personalize Entertainment
- ◆ Personalize Alerts

Select the item you want to personalize to see a list of options that you may select. Choosing Personalize News, for example, lets you select the sources and types of news that appear on your ticker. Selecting Personalize Weather lets you choose the city or region for which weather is reported.

After making your selections from a page, move to another or click the button labeled I'm Done, Submit.

Choosing Options from the EntryPoint list opens the dialog box shown in Figure 20.4. Use these options to determine whether the EntryPoint window always appears over other windows, signs in automatically, or starts automatically. Use the Proxy Settings option if you are running EntryPoint behind a proxy server.

FIGURE 20.4   **EntryPoint options**

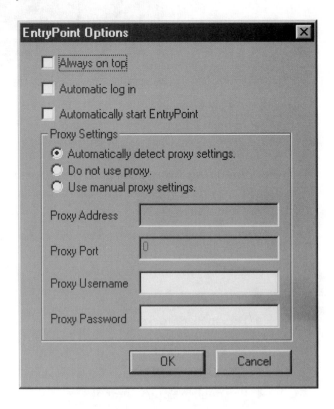

21 Free E-Mail

Think that one e-mail account is enough? No way! There are plenty of reasons to sign up for more free e-mail accounts.

Sign Up for Free E-Mail Accounts

Free e-mail offers are all over the Internet, and millions of folks are taking advantage of them. Why do companies offer e-mail for free? Repeat after me—ADVERTISING. The more hits, the more revenue, and the more likely you are to partake in some of the fee-based services that are available.

Here's What You Need

You'll need access to the Internet. You don't even need to have an ISP; you just need to be able to get into the Internet from any location.

Sites and Features

Your first question may be, "Why do I need more than one e-mail address?" Oh, let me count the ways!

◆ Do you have an e-mail account at work and think (or know) your boss is reading your mail? Sign up for free e-mail to keep your personal mail just that—personal.

◆ Do you share an e-mail account with other members of your family and know that your spouse/children/significant other is reading your mail? Use free e-mail so every member of your family has their own address. (Some ISPs let you sign up for more than one e-mail address on one account anyway.)

◆ Do you have an ISP that you can access only from your home computer, or from a computer where their special software is installed? Get free e-mail so you can get your mail from any computer connected to the Internet.

◆ Are you getting too much junk e-mail? Get a free e-mail account to use when filling out forms so junk mail is channeled there.

◆ Would you like an e-mail address with a snappy name, like `the_boss@hotmail.com` or `clint@do.you.feel.lucky.punk.com`? Yep, you can do that with free e-mail.

◆ Want to send an electronic complaint but not under your "real" address? Sign up for a free e-mail address and complain from there.

◆ Would you like to double-up on some free offers? You don't know whether the folks who give the offers would appreciate this, but many of them use your e-mail address to check whether you've already signed up. With a free e-mail account, you get another address to use.

If you answered YES! to any of those questions, then you are a perfect candidate for free e-mail. Here are some facts about free e-mail accounts.

All of the free e-mail programs are Web-based.   This means that you don't need any special software to get your e-mail, and you can get it from ANY location that has access to the Internet. You won't need any special e-mail program or special program provided by the ISP. You can get your mail from the library, the school, the local Internet café—from anywhere there is an Internet connection you can use.

The free e-mail programs are server-based.   This means that the e-mail is stored on their computer even after you read it. So if you check your mail at work, it will still be there for you to read again when you get home. You have to tell the system to delete it.

Some of the services also provide e-mail forwarding.   This means that you can have mail from other accounts sent to their server. So all of your mail will be waiting for you in one location. The one drawback is that many of the services add a small ad to each message you send.

Who offers free e-mail? Just about everyone:

◆ www.v3mail.com

◆ www.excite.com

◆ www.homepageware.com

◆ www.lycos.com

◆ www.netscape.com

◆ www.visto.com

◆ www.yahoo.com

◆ www.iname.com

◆ www.mail.com

Hotmail

You can hardly browse anywhere on the Internet without tripping over a free e-mail program.

As an example, let's look at signing up for free mail on www.hotmail.com, a very popular free e-mail service. The process is about the same with the others; only the links are different.

1. Log on to www.hotmail.com.

2. Click Sign up now!

3. Enter the information requested. This includes entering a login name that will be your e-mail name, a password, your first and last name, your country, gender, and the year of your birth. You can also choose to have your name and location listed in the Hotmail directory and to have Hotmail add your name and e-mail address to general Internet directories.

4. When you're done, click Sign Up. A confirmation message appears showing your Hotmail login name.

5. Click Continue to Hotmail. You can now sign up for a free service to have news and other information automatically delivered to your Hotmail address.

6. Select the checkboxes for the types of information you want delivered and click Continue.

You can enter your login name and password to access your Hotmail e-mail and to send e-mail from the initial Hotmail screen.

A typical Hotmail inbox is shown in Figure 21.1. You can read or delete messages, move a message to another folder, and compose a new message.

The options on the left of the screen let you access other Hotmail features, such as a calendar and a notepad for storing reminders. If you click POP Mail, you can designate up to four mail servers that this e-mail will be linked to, such as your ISP or other free mail systems. Among other features, Hotmail and similar services let you create an online address book. Click Addresses from the list of options across the top to open your address book. Here you can add recipients and give them nicknames.

FIGURE 21.1 Hotmail inbox

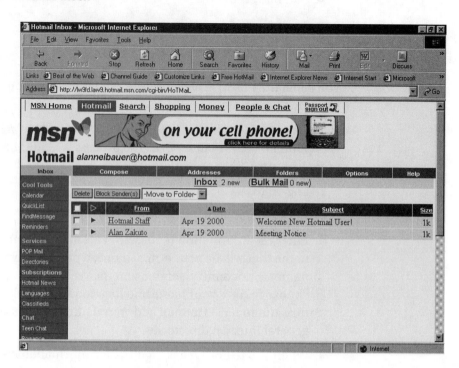

Copyright © 2000 Microsoft and/or its suppliers, One Microsoft Way, Redmond, Washington 98052-6399 U.S.A. All rights reserved.

To read a message, click its link in the From column. To delete mail, enable the check box next to it and click Delete. You can also move an e-mail to one of the other folders that Hotmail provides—Sent Messages, Drafts, the Trash Can, or a custom folder that you create.

To send a message, click Compose along the top of the screen. The mail composition window is shown in Figure 21.2. You can either type the recipient's e-mail address in the To line, or click To to access your address book. The same goes for the cc and bcc lines. You can also click Directories to look up e-mail addresses.

Enter the subject of the message and then its text. Using the buttons, you can save the message in your Drafts folder, add an attachment, check your spelling, use the thesaurus, or look up a word in the dictionary. Click Egreetings to select and send an electronic greeting card, as you'll learn how to do in Section 28.

When you're done with the message, click Send.

FIGURE 21.2 Composing mail with Hotmail

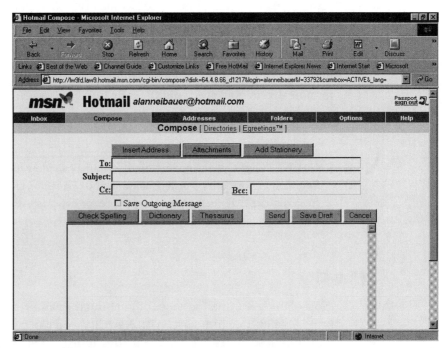

Copyright © 2000 Microsoft and/or its suppliers, One Microsoft Way, Redmond, Washington 98052-6399 U.S.A. All rights reserved.

Also, the Add Stationery button lets you decorate your e-mail with a fancy graphic design. Click Add Stationery and, in the screen that appears, pull down the Background list to select from over 20 stationery designs. A preview of the design appears onscreen. Click Ok to add the design to your e-mail and return to the Compose form. Your design will be sent with the message, but it will not appear in the Compose form.

With all e-mail services, junk mail can be a problem. If you are getting mail from an annoying source, select the checkbox next to their message in the Inbox and click Block Sender(s). In the screen that appears, click OK to confirm blocking their mail so it will not appear in your inbox.

You can also turn on the Inbox Protector feature to channel mass marketing and other unwanted mail to a special Bulk Mail folder. Click Bulk Mail in the Inbox to open the Inbox Protector window, and then click the On option button to activate the feature.

Inbox Protector applies a set of rules to determine junk mail that will be sent to the Bulk Mail folder. In the Inbox Protector window you can choose to have these rules applied to mail from all Hotmail and Passport users, content from Microsoft and MSN, Passport partners, and specific addresses or domains that you enter. You can also choose to send the filtered mail to the Bulk Mail or Trash Can folder. Messages in the Trash Can are automatically deleted every night, while bulk mail is retained for 30 days.

NOTE Click Options on the top of a Hotmail window to change your profile information, customize blocked mail and Inbox Protector, create filters to channel mail, retrieve POP mail, create a signature for new mail, and set other Hotmail preferences.

NewCity

Most of the free e-mail services offer about the same features, but NewCity provides a unique fun twist. With NewCity, you can create any number of personalities. A personality is a custom address that will appear in the From line of your e-mail, such as alan@who.loves.you.baby.com, or bigboss@you.are.fired.com.

In addition to the custom address, you can also create any number of personal handles. A handle is a name that appears in the From line in place of an e-mail address. For example, here's the header of an e-mail that uses a NewCity handle:

> From: Love God

If the recipient looks at the e-mail address for the sender, they will see the custom address of the personality, like this:

> E-Mail Address: alan@who.loves.you.baby.com

NewCity also lets you create a signature—text that is automatically inserted at the end of your e-mail.

WARNING If you use a custom e-mail address instead of your regular NewCity address, the recipient will not be able to reply to your message.

Go to www.newcity.com and register for the free service. Then click Mail in the NewCity home page and enter your username and password to access your Inbox. From the Inbox, you can read and compose new mail. Your NewCity e-mail address is your username, as in alan@newcity.com.

To create a personality, however, click Preferences on the left of the inbox, and then click Personalities & Signatures. You will see the built-in personality called Me that uses your NewCity e-mail address, and a list of any personalities you have already created. Now follow these steps:

1. Click Create New.

2. Enter a name that will represent this personality in the list.

3. Enter the custom address.

4. Enter an optional handle. Do not enter a handle if you want the custom address to appear in the From portion of your e-mail.

5. Enter text up to 2000 characters to be used as a signature.

6. Click OK.

7. Click the Make Default button next to the personality you want NewCity to use for your e-mails by default.

To send an e-mail, click Write Mail to open the composition window. To choose a personality other than the default, pull down the From list and choose the personality to use for the message. Complete the e-mail and click Send.

MailStart

For a quick way to send e-mail using a custom, nonreturnable address, check out MailStart. MailStart offers a number of features that you'll learn about in later chapters, but its e-mail feature can be fun and can ensure your privacy. You don't need to register with MailStart to send mail, and no special software is required.

To send mail, go to www.mailstart.com and click on the link Send E-Mail to Someone you Know to open the form shown in Figure 21.3.

FIGURE 21.3 **Sending e-mail from MailStart**

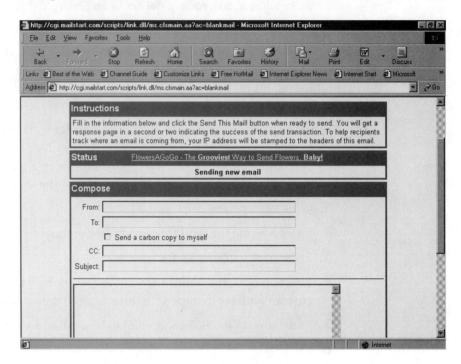

Enter your own e-mail address in the From line, or make something up for fun that looks like an e-mail address. Complete the form by entering the recipient's e-mail address, subject, and text of the message, and then click Send This Mail at the bottom of the form. The recipient will get the e-mail showing whatever address you entered in the From line as the sender.

N O T E   Your computer's IP address, however, will be sent along with the message in the header. The IP address can be used to track you down, so use **MailStart** only for legitimate purposes.

22 Pick Up E-Mail From Anywhere

Getting mail is the other side of the coin of sending it. While you may have an e-mail program on your home or office computer, you may be away from home or the office and need to check for important mail. All is not lost!

Get Your E-Mail Using Any Web Browser

It seems that Internet access is just about everywhere—the local library, cyber cafés, even in many companies that cater to the technologically aware. When you're away from your desktop or laptop computer, you can still check for e-mail from any computer that has Web access. Of course, you can check and read your mail without placing your private messages on a public computer, or storing a cookie or other file with your e-mail address and password.

Here's What You Need

You just need access to the Internet, your e-mail address, and your password. With Yahoo, Excite, and other free e-mail services, your e-mail password is the same as your service login password. Some ISPs, however, such as AT&T WorldNet, use separate logon and e-mail passwords. To access these types of mail through Web-based services, you need only your e-mail password.

NOTE Some ISP e-mail systems use special software that blocks access by other servers.

Sites and Features

If you need to check your mail from someone else's computer, just get onto the net and go to /www.mailstart.com to see this form:

Enter your e-mail address and e-mail password and click Check My Mail. MailStart will access your mail server and get a copy of any mail stored there. It will not delete the mail from the server, just copy it, so you can later access the mail from your computer. Your mail appears on-screen as shown in Figure 22.1.

Click the mail's subject to open the message and respond to it. You can also click Send New to compose a new e-mail using the address you entered to check your mail. To delete a message from your server's mailbox, select the checkbox next to it and click the Delete button. Click Delete All to remove all of your messages from your server's mailbox.

As an alternative to MailStart, check out www.readmail.com. At that site, enter your e-mail address and password in the form and click Check Mail to get your e-mail.

FIGURE 22.1   Checking mail online at MailStart

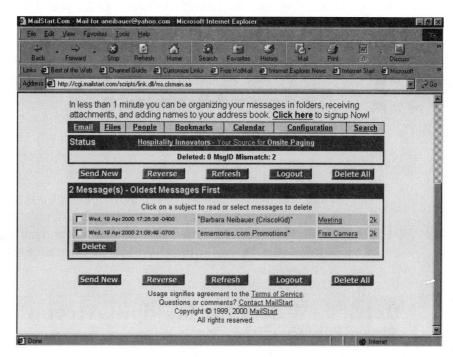

MailMirror

You can also sign up for a free account at MailMirror. This unique service maintains a copy of your mail on its own server. If you are away from your computer and need to reference mail that you sent or received at home, for example, you can log on to MailMirror to read the messages.

The MailMirror system works in conjunction with your default e-mail program. When you install and configure the MailMirror software, it monitors the mail folders that you designate, such as your Inbox and Sent Items folders, and maintains an exact duplicate of the messages on the MailMirror computer. You then log on to your MailMirror account from any Internet connection to access your own mail folders.

You can download MailMirror from www.cdrsoft.com, where you also signup for the service.

There are three types of accounts that you can establish. The Basic account is free but is limited to mirroring a maximum of 50 messages from two mailboxes. The Professional account will mirror up to 200 messages in 8 mailboxes, and costs only $19.99 for an entire year. The Unlimited account cost $24.95 per year for no limits on messages or mailboxes.

23 Access Multiple E-Mail Accounts

Some Internet providers give you more than one e-mail account. You might use the accounts for each member of the family, or just use different names for various purposes, such as business and personal. But having multiple accounts means you have to remember to check for mail on each. No problem.

Retrieve E-Mail for Multiple Accounts Simultaneously

Once you have more than one e-mail account, you have to remember to check each for new mail. With all of the free e-mail offers available, and with multiple accounts at one ISP, you could end up checking two, three, four, or more mail accounts each time. It would be too easy to skip an account and miss some important piece of mail.

Here's What You Need

You'll need a program that lets you access multiple accounts at one time. There is one free with Microsoft Internet Explorer—Outlook Express—and you'll find another on the CD that comes with this book.

Sites and Features

Checking more than one mail account at a time is easy. In fact, you can take advantage of free or inexpensive software to automatically check all of your accounts at the same time.

Before looking at these programs, however, you should understand about the two general types of e-mail systems–POP and Web-based.

Mail systems that use POP (Post Office Protocol) hold your mail on their computer until you access it. When you use a program to get your mail, your messages are downloaded to your computer and deleted from the service's computers.

Web-based mail is stored on the service's computer until you tell the service to delete a message. You access your mail by getting on the Internet and logging on to the service with your username and password.

With that said, you should be aware that many systems use both POP and Web-based protocols. If you have an account with AT&T Worldnet, for example, you can use a program to download the mail using POP, or you can log on to the Internet and access your mail on the Web. While many Web-based mail services allow access to your mail only through your Web browser, some like Hotmail, Yahoo, and others also offer the option of POP access, so you get the both of best worlds. If you have a free Web-based mail account, ask the provider if they also offer POP access.

Using Outlook Express

Outlook Express is an e-mail program that comes free with Microsoft Internet Explorer, which comes free with Microsoft Office and with plenty of other programs. With Outlook Express, you set up one or more accounts that you want to use to send and receive POP-based mail. You can choose to send and receive from any or all accounts at the same time.

To set up an account in Outlook Express, start the program and then follow these steps.

1. Select Tools ➤ Accounts to open the Internet Accounts dialog box.

2. Click the Mail tab, click Add, and choose Mail. This starts the Internet Connection Wizard.

3. Enter the details of your account in the dialog boxes that follow. You will be asked for the name that you want displayed in messages, your e-mail address, the type of server, and the name of the incoming and outgoing servers, and your account name and password.

4. Click Finish in the last Wizard dialog box.

N O T E   Outlook Express 5 also lets you sign up for a Hotmail account and send and receive Hotmail mail through POP. To sign up for a Hotmail account, choose Tools ➤ New Account Signup ➤ Hotmail. Follow the steps shown previously for adding a new account, but specify your Hotmail address in the second Wizard dialog box. You can also access your Hotmail account over the Internet using your Web browser.

When you click Finish in the last Wizard dialog box, your accounts will be listed in the Accounts dialog box. The default account will be used automatically for all mail that you send. You can tell which account is the default by looking for the word (default) in the list of accounts. Use the Set as Default button to select another account as your default.

Before using the account, follow these steps:

1. Click the account in the Accounts dialog box.

2. Click Properties to see the dialog box in Figure 23.1.

FIGURE 23.1   **Account properties**

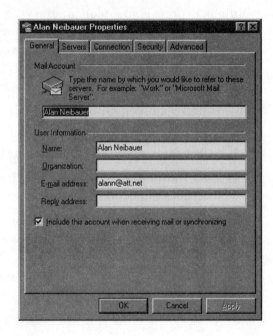

3. In the text box at the top, enter the name that you want to appear for the mail account in Outlook Express boxes.

4. Notice the check box at the bottom labeled Include This Account When Receiving Mail or Synchronizing. Enable the check box if you want Outlook Express to automatically include this account when you send and receive mail.

5. Click the Connection tab.

6. Click Always Connect Using, and then select the dial-up networking account.

7. Click OK.

Now when you are ready to send mail, you have to select the account to use. Click New Mail in the Outlook Express toolbar to open a mail window. Pull down the list at the end of the From box and select the mail account that you want to use. Complete the message and then click Send.

NOTE The instructions for sending mail are for Outlook Express version 5. If you have an earlier version of the program, complete the mail messages, choose File ➢ Send Later Using, and then click the account to use.

When you click Send, Outlook Express adds the message to your Outbox. If Outlook Express isn't set up to send your mail immediately, click the Send/Rec button on the toolbar. Outlook Express dials your Internet provider, sends your mail from your Outbox, and checks for new mail. If you want to send mail without checking for new messages, pull down the list next to the Send/Rec button and choose Send All. You can also choose a specific account to use.

Changing Identities When you check for mail with multiple accounts set up, all new mail appears in the same inbox. So, you'll be able to read everyone's mail, and they'll be able to read yours. If you want to keep your mail separate and private, create an identity for each member of the family who has an e-mail account. The identity records the person's name and e-mail address, and creates an entirely new set of folders for each.

To create an identity, choose File ➤ Identities ➤ Add New Identity to open the dialog box shown here:

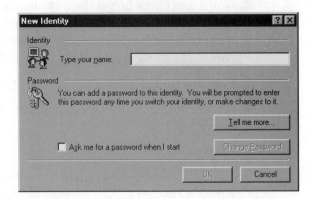

Type a name for the identity. If you want to password protect the folders so others cannot read the identity's e-mail, click Ask Me For a Password When I Start. Enter the password in both text boxes and click OK.

Now click OK in the New Identity dialog box. You'll be asked if you want to switch to that identity. If you select Yes, a whole new set of Outlook Express folders appears. If you select No, you can later change identities by selecting File ➤ Switch Identity. This will open the box shown in Figure 23.2. Click the identity in the box that appears, and then click OK.

FIGURE 23.2 **Switching identities**

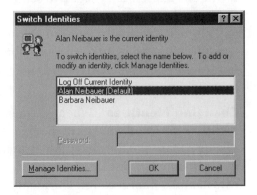

For each identity, you have to create an e-mail account. When you first create the identity, the Internet Connection Wizard starts. You'll first be asked if you want to use an existing account or create a new one. Click Create a

New Internet Mail Account and then click Next. Complete the Wizard and then click Finish.

To choose which identity to use as the default when you start Outlook Express, select File ➤ Identities ➤ Manage Identities to see a list of defined identities. Choose the identity to use as the default and then click the Make Default button. Select Ask Me in this list if you want to choose the identity when you start Outlook Express.

Before creating or sending mail, make sure you are using your own identity. Choose File ➤ Switch Identity; click the identity in the box that appears, and then click OK.

NOTE The Netscape Navigator Web browser supports "profiles" that are totally separate environments for each user. Each user specifies their own e-mail configurations, and they get their own browser bookmarks and other settings. You get to choose a profile when you start up Netscape, if you have more than one.

MailAlert

As an alternative to setting up multiple accounts in Outlook Express, you can use the program MailAlert to check for e-mail and alert you when it has arrived. MailAlert is a highly customizable program that can not only tell when you have received mail, but can beep your pager as well. You can download it from www.diamondridge.com.

The program works with most POP and IMAP mail systems, as well as with mail systems such as Microsoft Exchange and Windows Messaging. You can have MailAlert check for mail and, if any is received, automatically open your e-mail program and display the new messages. You can also use MailAlert as a mail program itself with which you can compose, reply to, forward, and delete mail.

MailAlert gets its initial settings from your current e-mail program. When you first install MailAlert, it will ask you to select from the e-mail programs on your computer, and then it will use the information from the first account it finds in that program, such as its names, mail servers, connection type, and your member name and password.

You can then add additional accounts, determine when MailAlert checks for and alerts you about mail, and set other program options in the window shown in Figure 23.3.

FIGURE 23.3 Setting up MailAlert

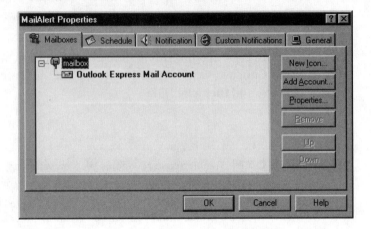

MailAlert will automatically check for mail at the times you specify in the Schedule tab of the window, and you can have it check at any other time using the MailAlert icon in the system tray of the Windows taskbar.

When mail is received, the program opens its own mail window, shown in Figure 23.4. Double-click a message to open it in its own window or click Run Mail to open your default e-mail program. Use the Run Mail list to select one of the e-mail programs on your system, or use these other MailAlert buttons to perform e-mail tasks:

◆ Close MailAlert

◆ Preview selected mail

◆ Reply to sender

◆ Reply to all

◆ Forward message

◆ Print message

◆ Delete message

◆ Compose new message

◆ Perform MailAlert commands

FIGURE 23.4   MailAlert mail window

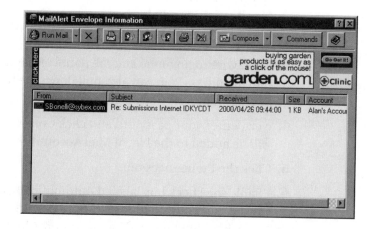

Using Ristra Mail Monitor

While you can access multiple POP accounts using Outlook Express, the program cannot download mail from services that only offer Web access.

If you have several of these free e-mail accounts, you can check them all for new mail using a program called Ristra Mail Monitor. You can download it from `welcome.to/ristra`.

Running the program places an icon for it in the system tray on the Windows taskbar. It also adds it to the Start group so the program runs automatically each time you start Windows. Right-click the icon to display these options:

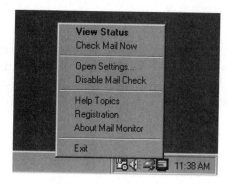

You first have to set up the program to access each of your Web-based e-mail accounts. To do this, follow these steps:

1. Select Open Settings from the shortcut menu to open the Ristra Mail Monitor Settings dialog box.

2. Click Add to see a list of accounts.

3. Enter your login name and the name of the service to complete your e-mail address. You can also pull down the list at the end of the Login Name box to select from supported services.

4. Next, enter your password and click Confirm. The e-mail address will be added to the List of Mail Accounts box.

5. Click the Preferences tab.

6. Enable the check box labeled Automatically Enter Login and Password When Logging In to the Mail Account. This setting will check for mail without you having to enter the login information to have Ristra check the mail.

When you want to check your mail at all of the accounts, just click Check Mail in the Settings dialog box, or choose Check Mail Now from the Ristra shortcut menu on the system tray. Ristra dials into your ISP and checks for new mail at each of the listed services, displaying the results in the Status dialog box.

To read mail, click the account and then click Log In to read your mail.

The Best of Both!

If you have both POP and Web-based mail systems, you might consider a program that accesses both types at one time.

Appload Notify, which you can download from www.appload.com, is an advertising-supported program that lets you check both types of mail. You can configure it for any number of POP and Web-based mail systems, and have it check them for mail all at one time. When Appload Notify finds mail, it displays an animated graphic, shown here, and then opens a window listing all of your mail accounts, as well as advertisements from the program's sponsors. Select an account to see a list of messages that have been received, as in Figure 23.5.

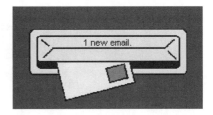

FIGURE 23.5 Getting mail with Appload Notify

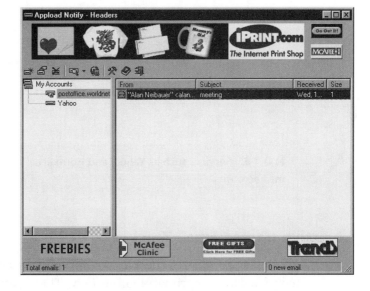

Jo Mail, available at www.download.com, offers the same features. When you first install Jo Mail, you designate either one POP or one Web-based system that you want to check for mail. When you run the program, however, you can add other mail accounts of either type, and then access your mail using the window shown in Figure 23.6.

Other programs for checking multiple mail accounts include Cyber-Info Webmail Notify for checking Web-based mail, Cyber-Info Email Notify for checking POP mail (from www.cyber-info.com), and @nymail (from www.tntsb.com/anymail).

FIGURE 23.6 Getting mail with JoMail

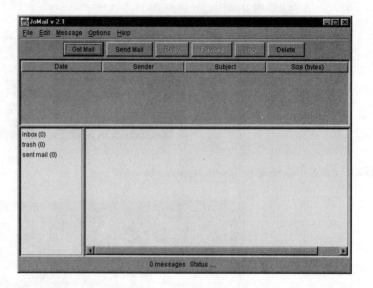

NOTE Services such as Yahoo! and Hotmail also let you access multiple POP mail accounts.

Active Names Email Tracker

Another alternative to checking mail at multiple accounts is to have mail redirected to your primary mail account. The program Active Names Email Tracker, for example, will automatically check your mail at various locations and send it to the e-mail address of your choice. You'll find a hot link button for Active Names Email Tracker on the CD so you can download it from www.activenames.com.

Active Names Email Tracker— it can confirm that e-mail addresses to which you send mail are still active. Before sending mail, add the recipient's e-mail address to your Active Names address book. The program will connect to the mail server at that address and confirm that the recipient's account is still active. You can also invite your recipients to register with Active Names so it can keep track of changes to their e-mail addresses.

24 Be Heard and Seen

While we're on the subject of e-mail, are you tired of sending the same old boring written e-mails? Send a personal spoken message, or even a video instead!

Voice and Video E-Mail

Anyone with a computer and Internet connection can send e-mail these days. But to really capture attention, you can send your own recorded voice message so the recipient can hear your voice. Voice messages are great for birthday greetings, special announcements, and other messages that you really want to make personal. If you have the proper equipment on your computer, you can also send a snapshot or video of yourself.

Here's What You Need

To send voice e-mail messages, you'll need a microphone, speakers, and a sound card in your computer. If you want to send video mail, you'll need a video-conferencing camera. Most computers come with speakers these days, and many with microphones. If yours does not, you can purchase speakers and a microphone inexpensively at most stores that carry computers. Video-conferencing cameras, once only for business users, are now less than $100 and are easy to connect to a computer's USB port.

Sites and Features

If you want to quickly send a voice message, surf over to `messagebay.snap.com/vg/compose.php3`. This feature of Snap, a popular search and shopping site, lets you record and e-mail a voice message to anyone. You'll see an e-mail form with a recording control panel.

NOTE The first time you record a message, you may have to download a small browser plug-in.

Follow these steps to create and send a voice e-mail.

1. Click the Play button to hear a short message that tests the level of your speakers.

2. Click the Record button and record a short message by speaking into your microphone.

3. Click Stop.

4. Click Play to hear your message.

5. In the To box of the e-mail form, enter the recipient's e-mail address.

6. In the From box of the form, enter your e-mail address.

7. Enter any text that you want to appear with the recording message.

8. Click Send

The recipient will get an e-mail from Snap reporting that a voice message is waiting. They just click the link in the message to go to the Snap site that shows your e-mail form, where they click the Play button to listen to your message and to record their own reply.

As an alternative, you can record a voice message over the telephone and have it e-mailed to recipients through vsnetcall.vstream.com/beep/beep_nonmemb.asp. If you don't want to enter that long URL, go to www.evoke.com and click Send a Talking Email. In the form that appears, enter your e-mail address and the e-mail address of the people to get the message, separating each by a space; enter a subject and then click Go.

You'll now see instructions on how to record your message. These include a toll-free phone number and a message code number. Dial the phone number, enter the code followed by the pound sign (#), leave your message and hang up. The recipients will get an e-mail with a link to click to hear the message.

V3Mail

If you want to include your voice or even a video message with an actual e-mail, rather than a link to the Internet, install the program V3Mail. You can download it from www.v3mail.com.

V3Mail is an e-mail program that lets you compose and send mail, but not receive it. Your message can include text and attachments, as well as sound recordings, snapshots, and video.

When you first install V3Mail, it accesses your default e-mail program, such as Outlook Express, and asks you to select the e-mail you want to use for your V3Mail messages. The program configures itself to send its mail over the Internet through the mail server used for the selected address, and also uses that as a return address so recipients can easily click to reply.

Running the program connects you to the Internet, so it can access your mail server, and displays the window shown in Figure 24.1, which serves as the message composition form.

FIGURE 24.1 Preparing voice or video mail

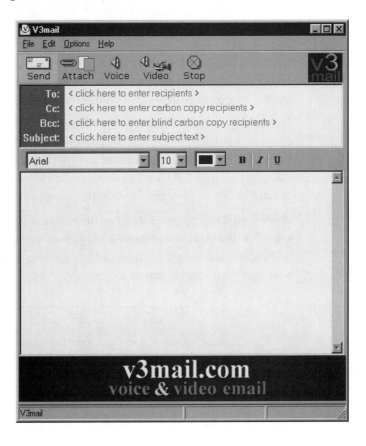

Enter the e-mail address of the recipient, and any cc or bcc recipients. Enter the subject of the message and any text you want to appear in the body of the e-mail. Use the Attach button on the toolbar if you want to send attached files.

To record an audio message, click the Voice button to open this dialog box:

Click the REC button, and record your message by speaking into your microphone. Click the stop button when you're done and then click Attach to insert the message into the e-mail as an attachment.

If you have a video-conferencing camera, you can also send a snapshot or video clip. Click the Video button to open the window shown in Figure 24.2. Click the button with the icon of a camera to record a single-frame snapshot, or click the REC button to record a video, clicking Stop when you're done. Finally, click Attach to add the snapshot or video to the e-mail.

When you click Send, V3Mail connects to the mail server specified by your e-mail address, and sends the e-mail message along with any file, audio, and video attachments. The recipient gets an e-mail with the audio, snapshot, or video clip shown as icons:

The recipient double-clicks on the icon to listen to the audio file or display the snapshot or video.

FIGURE 24.2 Sending a video clip

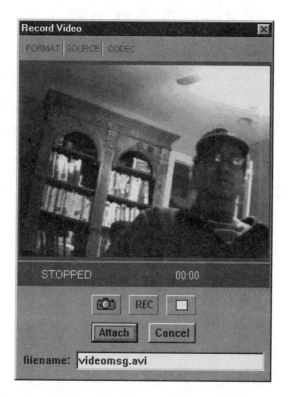

NOTE The icons depend on the default program installed in the recipient's computer to display graphics and play multimedia files.

For other programs for sending audio and video e-mail, check these out:

- ◆ Objective Voice EMail for Windows at www.objectivevoice.com
- ◆ Voice E-Mail 4.0 at www.bonzi.com
- ◆ PureVoice at www.eudora.com/purevoice/pluginDL.html
- ◆ Cubic VideoComm at www.cvideonow.com
- ◆ Voice Express and Video Express at www.imagemind.com

25 Eating Spam

Spam is a meat-based product manufactured by Hormel Foods Corporation. But the Internet community has further immortalized Spam so that it has come to mean unsolicited e-mails that are sent to a large number of users on the Internet. No matter how you feel about the meat-based product (try it grilled like a hamburger), the Internet type of spam is bad.

Stop Junk Mail

If you're getting tired of the junk mail that fills up your inbox, strike back. You can prevent junk mail from ever reaching your computer.

Here's What You Need

You'll need an e-mail program with a junk mail filter, or download a program from the Web, or use PureMail that you'll find on the CD.

Sites and Features

An occasional piece of spam wouldn't be too bad, but have you been hit by five, ten, or more chunks of spam at the same time? If not, you probably will be. Here's the typical scenario—you see that 20 e-mails are coming in, get excited because you think you're so popular, and then you find out it's the same spammer flooding your inbox.

Fighting Back

Fighting back is not always easy, but there are steps you can take. First, you can try contacting your ISP to see if they can take some action by blocking known spammers. Many ISPs offer customer support advice for dealing with junk mail.

You can also try responding to the spam by asking to be removed from the list. Some spammers even tell you how to be removed from their list by returning the message with Remove as the subject, or by e-mailing another address. This doesn't work all of the time though. Some spammers send out their junk and close down the address so your reply is returned; some spammers welcome your reply because it confirms that your e-mail address is legitimate, and therefore they will continue to send you junk mail.

You could also try flooding the spammer's mailbox with your own junk mail and long file attachments, a technique called bombing. But this may not work, because most of the time all of your junk mail to them will bounce right back.

You can also send an e-mail to the spammer's domain. If you get junk mail from someone at America Online, for example, send a complaint to `abuse@aol.com`. With other ISPs try `postmaster@their_domain_name`.

The fight against junk mail is far from hopeless, especially with a little help from the Internet and software developers.

Some e-mail programs, for example, maintain junk mailer lists. E-mail addresses that you add to the list can be deleted as soon as they come in. You don't actually avoid downloading their messages, you just don't see them.

In Microsoft's Outlook Express, for example, select a junk mail message in the Inbox, and then choose Block Sender from the Message menu. You'll see a message asking if you want to also delete all of the messages from that sender. Click Yes if you do. When any new mail arrives from the sender, it will automatically be moved to the Deleted Items folder.

If you change your mind about blocking mail from the sender, select Message Rules from the Tools menu and click Blocked Senders List. In the dialog box that appears, select the e-mail address of the person you no longer want to block and click Remove. Select Yes to confirm the deletion, and then close the Message Rules dialog box.

Spam-Eating Software

An even better solution to junk messages, however, is to delete them even before they download onto your computer. If you get your mail over the Internet through a POP3 mail server, you can do just that. There are programs that dial into your ISP's post office and check the mail waiting for you. If the program finds an address or domain that you've identified as junk, it deletes the message without having to download it.

The program SpamEater, which you can download from `www.hms.com/default.asp`, comes with a long list of known spammers, but you can add your own as well. There is a standard version that is distributed for free and a professional version with additional features available for a 30-day trial period.

The program can automatically check for spam and delete it, or it will let you view your messages' headers (the To, From, and Subject part of the message) to determine which you want to delete.

To see how SpamEater operates, choose Preferences from the File menu to create a profile in the dialog box shown in Figure 25.1. You will see that the profile includes the address of your ISP's e-mail server and your logon name and password. You use the Spammers tab of the dialog box to view the list of known spammers, and to add your own.

FIGURE 25.1   **SpamEater**

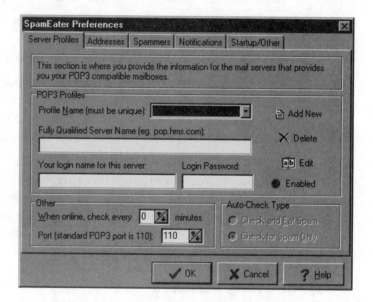

You then use the Action menu in the SpamEater window to perform these actions:

Check and Eat Spam   Checks your waiting mail and deletes messages from people on the spammers list.

Check Only for Spam   Scans your mailbox for spam.

Check and View Headers   Displays the headers of messages so you can delete interactively.

Spam Off, which you can download from `lelsoft.hypermart.net/spamoff`, is another anti-spam program. It works about the same way SpamEater does, deleting messages from identified spammers. After installing the program, right-click its icon in the system tray, as shown here:

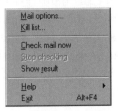

Use the Mail Options menu choice to specify your e-mail server, login name, and password.

Use the Kill List command to designate the e-mail addresses of spammers or just their domains. The capability of adding domains to the list, rather than specific addresses on the domain, lets you capture spam from anyone using a spam-friendly mail server.

Select Check Mail Now to dial into your e-mail server and delete messages from listed spammers.

Spam Buster is an advertiser-supported freeware program for filtering unwanted messages. You can download it from `www.contactplus.com`. When you install the Spam Buster, you can choose from areas of interest that will determine which sponsors' advertisements will be sent to you. The program includes a list of identified spammers but also uses keywords and other indicators to identify spam by subject, header, and the sender's domain name.

A Spam-Fighting Server

A company called Brightmail (`www.brightmail.com`) offers a different approach to fighting spam. Rather than have the spam-fighting software and rules for filtering on your computer, Brightmail acts as an intermediary between you and your POP mail server.

To use the Brightmail service, you need to register for a free Brightmail account and download its setup program. You run the Brightmail program to reconfigure your e-mail program, such as Outlook Express, to connect to the mail servers at Brightmail instead of to your POP account. No

Brightmail software is actually installed on your computer, except for an uninstaller that will reconfigure your e-mail program to connect directly to your POP account if you choose to stop using the Brightmail service.

Brightmail connects to your mail server, downloads your waiting mail, and examines it for spam. It stores the spam messages on its own computers and forwards the other mail to your computer so you can read it with your e-mail software. Spam is maintained on the Brightmail server for 30 days, so you can periodically scan the messages before they are deleted to insure that legitimate mail was not held by mistake.

PureMail

The program PureMail takes another unique approach to fighting spam. You'll find a copy of PureMail on the CD with this book, and you can download it from `http://travel.to/louieorbeta`.

Using PureMail, you give every person from whom you want to accept mail a special code called the PureMail Stamp. PureMail then works in the background, checking your mail server and only accepting email with the PureMail Stamp attached.

For more information and programs about fighting spam, check out these sites:

◆ `www.junkbusters.com/ht/en/index.html`

◆ `www.mindworkshop.com/alchemy/nospam.html`

◆ `www.cyber-info.com`

◆ `www.spamkiller.com`

More Free Stuff

So far, you've learned how to get free music, videos, and e-mail over the Internet, but that just touches on the free stuff that's available. There are all sorts of free things that you can get, so put your charge card away!

26 Test Free Service Offers

Whoever said "there's no such thing as a free lunch" was never the lucky recipient of those free America Online (AOL) CDs clogging up the mailbox. Don't throw them away! Even if you already have an ISP, you should take advantage of the free trial offers provided by AOL and other companies.

Enjoy a Free Month of Internet Access

The free monthly offers from ISPs (such as AOL, CompuServe, and others) let you browse the Internet, send and receive e-mail, and download files without spending a dime. The offers are especially attractive if your current ISP charges for extra hours or does not have a local toll-free number. After all, the trial period is free, and you just might find an ISP you like better!

Here's What You Need

You need a credit card and a calendar—and sometimes the patience to wait on hold for a long time!

Sites and Features

Suppose you want to download some humongous file, or you need to spend an extended period online browsing. If you have limited free time on your ISP, you'll find it gets used up quickly.

Rather than waste your precious money, take advantage of free monthly offers. Sign up, download those large files, or do that extended browsing, and then cancel the service. The trick is to cancel the service BEFORE the free time period or free hours are exceeded.

First, find out exactly what the free offer entails by asking the following questions:

- ◆ Is it a free month?
  - ◆ Calendar month or 30 days from signing up?
  - ◆ Exactly what is the last free day to use it?
- ◆ Is it free hours?
  - ◆ How many?
  - ◆ When do they start?
  - ◆ When do they end?
  - ◆ What's the charge for additional hours?

Next, be prepared by getting any required software first. If you didn't get any free CDs in the mail, look for free signup CDs in local computer stores or packed in computer magazines. When you install the software, choose to retain your current browser if that is an option. This will create less possible havoc if you decide to cancel the ISP after the trial period and remove its software.

Dial-Up Networking

Depending on the service, you may not need any new software. Some ISPs let you connect using the Dial-Up Networking that is built into Windows. You can use whatever browser and e-mail program you already have. So, if you are connected to one ISP through Dial-Up Networking, you might only need to create another connection in the Dial-Up Networking window. This saves you the trouble of installing special software only to uninstall it after the free trial. Some uninstall programs leave too many traces of their programs around anyway.

To find out whether you can use Dial-Up Networking rather than the ISP's software, make sure to call the ISP whose trial period you want to use, rather than signing up automatically using their free software. If they will let you sign up without using their software, ask them to provide you with the local telephone number to dial, your username, and your password.

Also ask them to give you the Dial-Up Networking type (usually PPP: Internet, Windows NT Server, Windows 98), the primary DNS, the secondary DNS, and any other Dial-Up Networking (DUN) settings.

Once you've given them your charge card information, follow these steps:

1. Open My Computer and then Dial-Up Networking.

2. Open Make New Connection to see the first Make New Connection dialog box, shown in Figure 26.1.

FIGURE 26.1 **Making a new connection**

3. Type a name for the connection.

4. If the modem listed is incorrect, pull down the list under the Select a Device heading and choose the modem you want to use. Click the Configure button only if you need to change any of the modem settings, AND YOU REALLY KNOW WHAT YOU ARE DOING.

5. Click Next to see the second Make New Connection dialog box.

6. Enter the area code and phone number of the free-trial ISP.

7. Click Next to see the last Make New Connection dialog box.

8. Click Finish.

9. Now right-click the connection you just made (it will have the name you entered in step 3 above) and choose Properties. The first tab of the box that appears should show the same phone number and modem you set up in the Make New Connection boxes. If not, enter the correct number and choose the correct modem.

10. Now click the Server Types tab to see the options shown in Figure 26.2.

FIGURE 26.2 Setting dialup properties

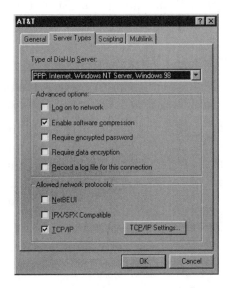

11. Check the setting in the Type of Dial-Up Server box. It should normally be PPP: Internet, Windows NT Server, Windows 98.

12. Make sure the Advanced Options are set correctly. If you are unsure, leave them alone.

13. Click the TCP/IP Settings button.

14. If your ISP gave you a DNS number, enable the option Specify Name Server Address.

15. Enter the Primary DNS.

16. Enter the Secondary DNS, if you were given one by the ISP.

17. Click OK until all of the dialog boxes are closed.

You now have more than one Dial-Up Networking connection created. To dial into the trial ISP, double-click the connection you created for it. The first time you connect, you'll have to enter your user name and password.

Enter the information and enable the option labeled Save Password. Once the connection is made, start your browser—you're ready to go!

Some ISPs let you bring your own Internet connection. This means that you can save money if you sign up for two Internet services by using one to connect to the other. You'll learn more about this later. Do not select this option for your trial period. Why not? With BYOA, you dial into the new ISP through your current one, so you are still using its dial-up network and accumulating usage time.

Additional Information

Try these Web sites to check out information about free trial periods: `www.att.net`, `www.aol.com`, `www.compuserve.com`, and `www.prodigy.com`.

Now, about canceling. Make sure you can cancel using a toll-free phone number. Being able to cancel online is fine, but the time spent canceling could bring you over the allowed limit. If you can cancel by phone, this is where the patience referred to earlier comes in. Sometimes, and depending on when you call, the wait to speak with a service representative can be interminable.

N O T E   Many computer stores offer rebates of up to $400 if you sign up with a specific ISP for a number of years. You actually do get the money off your purchase, but you have to lock yourself in to one ISP. If you experience busy signals or poor service, you'll find that the rebate was not worth it.

27   Totally Free Internet

While the ISP test drives are great, getting an ISP totally for free is even better. That's right. You can sign up to get the Internet for absolutely nothing—no sign up fees and no monthly charges.

Enjoy Free Internet Access

Isn't advertising wonderful! For the trouble of seeing a few ads onscreen or letting a marketer track your Internet usage, you get connected to the

Internet for nothing. Most of the free ISPs display a small window on the screen that contains links to popular sites as well as advertising messages. As long as you leave the window on the screen, you can browse to your heart's content. There's even one free ISP that lets you surf without seeing any ads at all, as long as you start your surfing from its home page.

Here's What You Need

You don't need a credit card, because its all free! You'll need to register with the free ISP service and, in most cases, download and install a program that lets you connect to the ISP and start surfing the net.

Some of the companies offer free access throughout the United States, but you'll need to check the access numbers to make sure they are local and toll free.

NOTE When you use a free ISP that has its own dialing software, you should set Internet Explorer so it does not dial into the Net itself. Right-click on the Internet Explorer icon on your desktop, select Properties, and choose Never Dial a Connection on the Connections tab.

Sites and Features

There are a number of companies that offer free Internet service to specific communities. In this chapter, however, we'll look at services that have access numbers across the United States.

These companies are:

www.freewwweb.com

www.ifreedom.com

www.freensafe.com

www.dotnow.com

www.juno.com

www.altavista.com

```
www.freei.net
www.netzero.com
www.address.com
www.xoom.com
www.bluelight.com
www.nettaxi.com
```

None of the sites except Freensafe places restrictions on the sites you visit. Freensafe is a family-oriented provider that filters out adult-oriented material.

Freewwweb

My favorite free ISP is Freewwweb, at `www.freewwweb.com`, which calls itself the "Creator and Leader of the FREE WORLD." Freewwweb shows no ads at all, doesn't require you to download any software if you already have a Web browser and dial-up networking, and gives you a POP e-mail account that you can access from programs such as Outlook Express. All it asks is that you use `home.freewwweb.com` as your home page.

NOTE Freewwweb also has local access numbers throughout Canada.

Go to the site at `www.freewwweb.com/pricing/pricmain.html` to learn how to register for the service and to set up dial-up networking, as explained in Section 26. You'll find a link to `autoreg.freewwweb.com` where you complete the multiple page registration form, which asks for your name, address, and phone number. In the box that asks for the Registration Code, enter FWDL-2.1. You'll also have to select a username and password, and select and write down an access phone number for your area.

WARNING It is your responsibility to check that the local access number you select is toll-free.

Freewwweb will verify that your user name and password are acceptable, and then download a small Internet setup file. Rather than run the downloaded setup file, which will change your computer's Internet settings, set up dial-up networking, using the techniques discussed in Section 26. This way you can leave your current ISP settings intact and choose to use the free account when you want.

1. Create a new connection called Freewwweb using the access number that you selected during registration. Right-click on the connection and choose Properties.

2. Choose your modem in the Connect Using box in the General tab.

3. Click the Server Types tab. Choose the PPP option in the Type of Dial-Up Server list and make sure only two check boxes are selected—Check Enable Software Compression and TCP/IP.

4. Click the TCP/IP Settings button.

5. Select the option Server Assigned IP Address.

6. Select the option Specify Name Server Address.

7. Enter 216.70.64.1 as the Primary DNS number

8. Enter 216.70.64.2 as the Secondary DNS number.

9. Check the boxes Use IP Header Compression and Use Default Gateway on Remote Computer.

10. Click OK twice.

11. Right-click again on the Freewwweb connection.

12. Click Create a Shortcut and then click Yes.

You now have a shortcut to the Freewwweb connection on your desktop. When you want to connect to the Internet, double-click the shortcut icon. The first time you use the connection, enter your username and password and click Save Password. Your username for logging on is your complete Freewwweb e-mail address, as in alan@freewwweb.com.

Click Connect to dial in to Freewwweb. When a message appears reporting that you are connected, launch your Web browser to surf the Net!

To set up your e-mail account in a program such as Outlook Express, enter your complete e-mail address as your username, and specify the outgoing mail server as `smtp.freewwweb.com` and the incoming mail server as `pop3.freewwweb.com`.

Other Free ISPs

All of the other free ISPs listed previously display some sort of advertising on-screen as you browse. In most cases, the advertising appears in a separate window that appears in the foreground of your browser, but you can move the window around the screen. Other sites display their advertising banner in a frame at the top of your screen. The frame does not cover up or interfere with your browser window; it just makes the browser window smaller than full-screen.

While AltaVista (`www.altavista.com`) will disconnect you if you don't click on an ad in their window every 30 minutes or so, the other companies are more liberal. Ifreedom (`www.ifreedom.com`) will even remove their banner advertisement for 20 minutes after each visit you make to an advertised site.

Four of the sites listed (`address.com`, `xoom.com`, `bluelight.com`, and `nettaxi.com`) use the same Internet dialer and list of access codes. The actual connectivity is provided by a company called Spinway (`www.spinway.com`). When you use these programs to connect to the Net, you'll see and hear a commercial as you are connecting, as shown in Figure 27.1. You may experience some delays in surfing as new commercials are downloaded to your computer.

You can download the dialer programs for these services at their Web sites.

FIGURE 27.1 Signing on to BlueLight

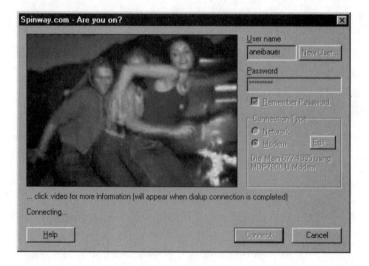

28 Don't Lick Stamps!

While not everyone is online, a heck of a lot of people are. So for birthdays, anniversaries, and other occasions, consider sending your greeting card electronically. Your friends and relatives will love getting animated and musical greetings, with personalized messages, delivered directly to their computer screen.

Send E-Cards for Every Occasion

Most online cards are FREE, and most include snappy animations and music. You select the type of card and what you want it to look like, and you add your own custom text. There are cards for birthdays, anniversaries, and almost every other imaginable holiday. There are even cards for breaking up a relationship.

Here's What You Need

All you need to send electronic greeting cards is access to the Internet!

Sites and Features

Electronic greeting cards are quick and easy to send. The cards work in two ways:

1. With most systems, the recipient gets an e-mail informing them that an online greeting is waiting for them. All they do is click a link in the e-mail to launch their Web browser and get the card on their screen. Cards are saved from one to three weeks, depending on the company.

2. Other companies let you download the card to your computer, or purchase it on a CD, where you customize it and send it as an e-mail attachment. The recipient just opens the attachment to view the card, without having to stay online.

NOTE If you want to send real greeting cards through the mail for a fee, check out www.sparks.com.

Free and Low-Cost Electronic Greeting Cards

There are hundreds of sites that provide free or low-cost cards, but the ones I like best are www.egreetings.com, www.bluemountain.com, and www.barkingcard.com. These sites have plenty of choices, and they provide special holiday cards for almost every occasion.

Egreetings   The first time you send a card, you have to register by giving your e-mail address and picking a password. Registration is free. Then, whenever you want to send another card, just sign in with your e-mail address and password. For example, here's how to use Egreetings.

1. Navigate to www.egreetings.com.

2. Click one of the featured categories in the section Totally Free Greetings. You see several choices of cards.

3. Click the card that you want to send.

4. Now fill out the card: enter your e-mail address and the recipient's e-mail address, and then fill in a subject line and any personal text you want to enter. You can also specify a date that the card should be sent if you don't want to send it immediately, and you can attach a gift certificate to one of a number of online stores. You select the amount of the certificate and the online store, and then pay for it with your charge card, so the recipient can redeem the certificate for merchandise.

5. Click Preview to see how your card looks or click Send to send it immediately.

6. If you selected to preview the card, click Send to send the card, or Change if you want to modify it.

The recipient gets an e-mail message that includes a link that the recipient can click to go directly to the Egreetings site to see the card.

Blue Mountain Arts   The Blue Mountain Arts site works about the same way, and also has a wide variety of cards to select.

1. Navigate to www.bluemountain.com, and select the category and the card.

2. When the sample card appears, click the link that says Personalize and Send. You see a screen that lets you customize the card by entering the name and e-mail address of the recipient, your own e-mail address and name, and one or more lines of a custom message.

3. Complete all of the information and then click Preview Here Before Sending.

4. If the card looks OK, click Send. Otherwise, you can click Edit Before Sending to make any necessary changes. For some cards, you may even be able to select the date you wish to send it.

The recipient gets an e-mail message telling them that you've sent them an electronic card, and if you chose that option, you will get an e-mail confirming that the card has been picked up. The recipient should click the link to go directly to the Blue Mountain Arts site to see the card.

 Barking Cards   Barking Cards, at www.barkingcard.com, is a FEE-BASED greeting card company. Barking Cards offers a free sample collection of cards, which are included on the accompanying CD or are available for download from www.barkingcard.com. Run the Setup program to install the sample value pack on your computer. If you order an e-mail card online (usually less than $2 a card), you fill out some charge card information and enter the name and e-mail address of the recipient.

For a special value, you can purchase value packs of greeting cards on CD-ROM. Each pack includes a number of cards that you can customize with text, graphics, and sounds. You can send these cards to as many people as you want, for as long as you want. You create the card on your computer by first selecting a category and then a specific card. You then modify the card by adding your own text, graphics, and sounds.

When you're done customizing the card, you are asked if you want to save it with the Barking Card Player. The player allows the recipient to install the card on their computer, where they can play it. Saving the card without the player lets you later open and edit the card. You must choose to save it with the player before sending it to the recipient.

You send the card as an attachment to an e-mail message. The attachment appears as an executable program that the recipient saves and then runs. Running the program displays the card and adds it as a program item in the recipient's Start ➤ Programs menu so they can view it again and again.

WARNING   Because of the chance of a computer virus, be careful when running any executable file that you get over the Internet. Make sure the card is from a reputable and recognized sender. If you do not recognize the name or e-mail address of the sender, or if none is given, do not run the executable program.

More Electronic Card Options

Here's a list of other sites for free or inexpensive electronic cards:

- ◆ findmyhome.com/card2.htm

- ◆ www.arkworld.com/pete/greetings

- ◆ www.123greetings.com

- ◆ www.greeting-cards.com/pg/p

- ◆ www.hallmarkconnections.com

- ◆ www.virtualpresents.com/cards.html

- ◆ www.snap.com (click E-cards.)

And for that very special occasion, try visiting www.c-ya.com. This site specializes in relationship closure cards—when flowers and candy definitely send the wrong message. How about saying:

Although our lives have only crossed

Each others' paths for a short time,

I can already tell you this:

It's been long enough. C-ya.

Just don't mess up and send one of these cards to your current gal or guy.

29 Print! Don't Lick!

When you really do have to mail a greeting card, letter, priority package, or some other mail, save yourself the trouble of going to the post office. Get and print mail from the comfort of your own computer.

Buying Stamps online

The United States Postal Service now lets you purchase postage on line, and print it directly on envelopes or labels right from your computer. It is just like having a postage meter at home. You select the amount of postage you want, enter the recipient's address, and print away.

Here's What You Need

You don't actually buy online stamps directly from the Post Office at these sites. You create an account with one of the online postage companies, download or order their software, and then purchase postage through them. There are two major online retailers of postage. They can be found at www.stamps.com and www.estamp.com.

The online company will take your information and submit it to the Postal Service for a free Postage Meter License. The license gives you permission to use a postage meter to print stamps. In this case, the postage meter is your own computer and printer, but you still need the license.

Of course, there is a price to pay for this convenience. You'll have to pay the online postage company either a monthly fee or a percentage of the cost of the postage you buy.

Sites and Features

Both the Stamps.com and Estamp.com sites offer the convenience of buying and printing stamps online, but both have certain restrictions imposed on them by the United States Postal Service.

You won't be able to print the postage on a blank envelope for use at any time, for example. The printed postage must be used within 24 hours and it is linked to a specific address. While you can select from a range of envelopes and labels, you may not be able to print on a custom-size envelope, and you may need to purchase special labels for some large items such as priority packages and parcels.

Even with these restrictions, getting stamps online can beat waiting in a post office line.

NOTE You can also buy stamps, stamp-collecting supplies, phone cards, and other stuff directly from the United States Postal Service at www.stampsonline.com.

Stamps.com

Stamps.com offers two basic service plans.

The Simple Plan charges 10 percent of the postage you use each month, with a $1.99 minimum and a $19.99 maximum. The company usually offers a one-month trial period free of their charges, and sometimes even some free postage as well.

The Power Plan costs $15.99 per month no matter how much, or how little, postage you use. However, you'll get a free digital postage scale and sometimes up to $50 in free postage. You can connect the scale to your computer to have it weigh a piece of mail and print the proper amount of postage.

Once you register for the service and your postage meter license, you download or order the Stamps.com free software, shown in Figure 29.1. You can then create and manage an address book, buy and print postage, manage your account, and set program options. You can also order envelopes, labels, and other mailing supplies from the company.

Choosing Print Postage opens the window shown in Figure 29.2. You can enter your return address and the recipient's address, and you can select the type of mail, envelope, or label size. You can also specify its weight and select the amount of postage you want to add. The Options button lets you add additional postage or postdate the stamp so you can mail it at a later date.

FIGURE 29.1   Postage with Stamps.com

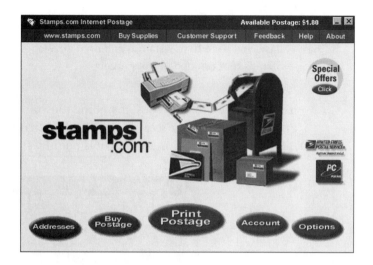

FIGURE 29.2   Printing Postage with Stamps.com

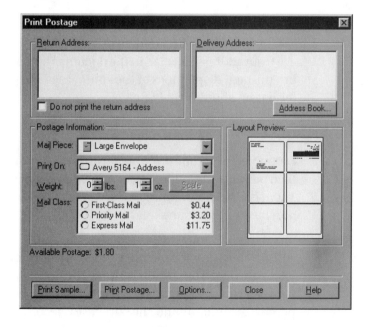

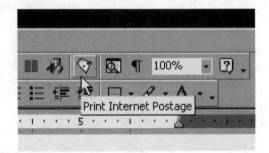

NOTE Stamps.com keeps track of your available postage in their own database; you have to buy stamps and print envelopes when you are online so Stamps.com can update your account.

If you have Microsoft Word, installing the Stamps.com software places a Print Internet Postage icon on the Word toolbar and adds the Stamps.com Internet Postage option to the Tools menu, as shown here.

Use the toolbar button and menu options to print an envelope with postage to an address selected in the document. The menu options also let you buy postage, display logs of your purchases and printed stamps, and get information about postal rates.

Estamp.com

Estamp.com has one price plan. You must purchase a $49.95 starter kit and then pay an additional 10 percent of the cost of the postage you purchase. There is a $4.99 minimum and a $24.99 maximum charge each time you purchase online stamps.

The starter kit contains Estamp's software, a CD that checks your addresses and zip codes for accuracy, a sample pack of labels, and the Electronic Vault. The Electronic Vault is a small device, called a *dongle,* that connects between your computer's parallel printer port and your printer. When you purchase stamps online, the purchase is recorded in the Electronic Vault so you can later print postage without connecting to the Internet. The vault also stores your address book and account information.

30 Enjoy Free Faxing

Even though many modems today can send and receive faxes, you're still responsible for the long distance call charges. Rather than make those long distance calls, send faxes free over the Internet!

Fax Documents Anywhere

My wife just hates making long distance fax calls. It's not the money, it's struggling with all of the numbers. She just hopes that she gets the number correct and actually reaches a fax machine. (OK, so maybe the money does enter into it somewhere.)

Faxing is a great way to communicate, but those long distance telephone charges can be a killer. That's assuming you have a fax machine or a fax modem. Have you ever checked out the prices that some places charge you to fax? It can be up to four or five dollars per page. Pretty expensive for the cost of a phone call!

Well, thanks to the kindness of strangers, you can send free faxes from your computer (even without a fax modem) to telephones around the world.

First, there are some caveats:

◆ The totally free fax services are limited to certain geographic areas. They often rely on volunteers to actually make the local connection, and the service is limited to their areas.

◆ The not-so-totally free services let you send a few faxes for free as a way to test their system. Even if you do have to pay, however, it is still sometimes cheaper than the long distance calls.

NOTE See Section 31, "Free Faxing Revisited," to find out how you can get a free phone number for receiving faxes!

Here's What You Need

Basically, to take advantage of these services you won't need anything except your browser and ISP.

Well, you will have to sign up for the free trial service, and some sites do require you to download their software, but this material is free for the trial period. If you use a free fax service, there are programs to help you use it that are also free. *Free*. Don't you just love that word?

Sites and Features

There are a number of places on the Internet where you can go to fax, but let's start with those that are totally free—www7.fax4free.com/home.asp, www.gtfreemail.com, and www.zipfax.com.

Fax4Free.com

Signing up for the service with Fax4Free.com is free, as is every fax you send to anyplace in the United States, Canada, Australia, and Great Britain. The only drawback is that a few ads appear on the fax cover sheet, so folks know they are getting a free fax.

Except for the ads, however, this is one terrific service. Not only can you compose a fax online with word processing–like format capabilities, but you can also attach a document that is up to 250 Kb in size. So you can write a letter in Microsoft Word, for example, and fax it attached to the Fax4Free cover page. You can also specify as many recipients as you want for a fax, so you can broadcast a fax to a group, sending it to all of their fax machines at once.

NOTE Fax4Free also lets you receive faxes and voice mail messages over your own private phone number. More on that later!

GTFreemail

For free faxing to anyone in the United States and Canada, sign up for a free account at www.gtfreemail.com. This service offers free e-mail and faxing, an online calendar and address book, and even an expense register and a briefcase to store files online.

You won't be able to attach a document—just compose a plain text message. But for unlimited free faxing and other services, GTFreemail is a bargain!

ZipFax

To send a quick fax to anyone in the world, check out www.zipfax.com. When you get to the site, you have to scroll down past a lot of advertising, but about halfway down the page you'll find the section ENTER YOUR FAX HERE!

Enter the recipient's fax number, your name and e-mail address, the subject of the fax, and the text that you want to send, and click ZIPFAX it!

Pay-Per-Fax

If you find that you really like faxing from your computer through the Internet, you can sign up with one of the fee-based services. There are plenty of them.

The service at www.faxaway.com, for example, doesn't charge by the page but just according to the actual transmission time. Faxes to anywhere in the United States are just 11 cents per minute, and rates are available for most countries worldwide.

You can also register for fax service though home.netscape.com/qwest/fax/. An outfit named Qwest runs Netscape's Fax Center. They charge 15 cents per page, with a $2.95 minimum monthly charge that covers your first 19 pages faxed anywhere in the United States or Canada, but only for each month that you use the service. (International rates vary.) This means that if you do not send a fax during a month, you won't be billed for the $2.95.

Other fax services include

- ourworld.compuserve.com/homepages/pormesan/global/number/bar/distribution.htm
- info.ox.ac.uk/fax
- www.awa.com/faxinet/faxinet.html

When you use any of these services, check the directions very carefully. One thing to check with a potential service is how they handle busy signals and uncompleted faxes. Some charge for each attempt to send the fax, even if the fax does not go through.

31 Free Faxing Revisited

If you think you're spending too much for telephone service, then here's your chance to get even with a free fax telephone number. Anyone can send you a fax at that number, just as if they were calling your phone at home.

Get a Free Fax Line

Now this is something that amazes me. You can sign up for a FREE phone number for receiving faxes. The service receives the fax, and then e-mails it to you. That's right—the phone number is all yours.

Here's What You Need

In addition to your e-mail address, you have to agree to complete a periodic survey or questionnaire. That's it.

Sites and Features

If you already have a fax machine, or fax modem at home, then why would you need this service? Have you ever been awakened in the middle of the night by some incoming fax? Do you have to remember to turn on your fax machine or get your computer started to receive a fax?

With a free incoming fax service, you don't have to worry about all that. Your own private phone number is ready 24 hours a day, seven days a week to receive incoming faxes. When you're asked for your fax number when filling out a form or by some annoying salesperson, just give them your free one.

How can these companies supply this service for nothing? Surprise, surprise—the sites are advertising-sponsored. Your only obligation is to respond to a periodic e-mailed questionnaire and let the company share the information with its sponsors.

All of this is relatively painless—except for the person sending you the fax, perhaps. You see, the numbers assigned are not necessarily in your local area, so the sender may be charged for long-distance.

In this chapter, we'll look at three fax receiving sites—eFax.com, Callwave, and JFAX. You can also get fax messages from the sites discussed later in "Picking Up Voice Mail Online."

Receiving Services

We'll take a look at three such services: eFax.com, CallWave, and JFAX. All of these services give you a free number for receiving faxes. You can sign up for one or all, and it won't cost you a dime.

eFax.com   If you're not particular about where the fax number is located, you can sign up for a free fax number at `www.efax.com`.

Once you complete an online form that asks for your name, e-mail address, zip code, and some other information, you'll be given your private fax number. You will then receive your PIN number via e-mail. The fax number assigned depends on what they have available at the time. (For instance, the one I received is in Massachusetts even though I live in New Jersey.)

To access your account using your PIN number, follow these steps:

1. Go to `www.efax.com`.

2. Click the My Account button.

3. In the text boxes that appear, enter your eFax number and PIN.

4. Click Login. You'll see your user profile with your name and address. You'll also have options to change your PIN and specify a password to encrypt the faxes before they are transmitted to you.

5. Click Activity Log. You'll see a list of faxes that have been received and forwarded to you.

6. Click Logout when you're done.

When someone sends a fax to your number, eFax.com converts it into a graphic and e-mails it to you as an attachment readable by Kodak Imaging (this product comes free with Windows 98). You can also use a free program that will be sent to you by eFax.com, attached to an e-mail. Once you install the viewing program in Windows 95 or Windows 98, double-click the fax attachment in the e-mail message to display it in the viewer.

CallWave   If you want to tell folks you have a West Coast office, no matter where you are really located, you can get a fax number in northern California (in the 209, 530, 559, or 916 area code) by navigating to `www.callwave.com/ffn.html`.

Navigate to the site, complete the application, and you are on your way. Just warn friends and relatives that northern California may be a toll call, unless they are lucky enough to live in that beautiful part of the world. The faxes, like those from eFax.com, arrive as e-mail attachments in a format readable by Kodak Imaging.

Both eFax.com and CallWave offer additional services for a fee, and both reserve the right to discontinue the free number at any time. However, as of this writing they do not ask for any charge card information, and they provide the service for free.

JFAX You should also check out www.jfax.com for a free fax number. As with eFax, you get your own number and a PIN to access your account. You can also download a free fax viewing program. Faxes received by JFAX are sent to your e-mail address.

For a fee, you can also sign up for their Personal Telecom service that lets you select a personal number from over 90 cities worldwide, and send faxes from your computer or wireless device. There is a $15 one-time activation charge, a monthly charge of $12.50, and a charge for the actual fax transmission time. There is also a 25 cent per minute charge to check for e-mail using their toll-free telephone number.

32 Picking up Voicemail Online

Tired of telemarketers calling you at all hours of the day? Don't have an answering machine at home? Well, how would you like to pick up voicemail for free over the Internet?

Get Free Voicemail

You'll get your own private phone number that folks can call to leave you messages. To pick up your voicemail, just connect to the Internet and log on to your free voice mail account. You'll hear your voicemail messages directly from you computer's speakers. And depending on the service, you may also be able to call in from a phone anywhere in the world to get your voicemail.

Here's What You Need

Access to the Internet! To listen to voicemail messages online, you'll need a sound card and speakers.

Sites and Features

There are quite a few sites that offer free voice e-mail. Most require the caller to enter an extension to reach your particular voicemail inbox. In most cases, the telephone number assigned to you will not be local but in whatever area the service is located. Three companies—Audio Highway, Ureach, and MyTalk—give you a toll-free number to call, and a few offer local numbers for a fee.

OneBox, at www.onebox.com, is a good example of a service that helps you get voicemail over the Internet. Signing up for OneBox gets you an e-mail address as well as a telephone number and four-digit extension to get incoming voicemail and faxes. The caller dials the number and extension and can then either record a voice message or send a fax. When you log on to your Onebox account, you see the number of waiting voicemails, e-mails, and faxes:

Hi alan! Welcome to your Onebox!	
New Messages	**Account Information**
Voice: 1	Vacation Message: OFF
Email: 0	Storage Usage: 2% of 3 MB used
Fax: 0	

Click on Inbox to see the waiting messages. In this example, there is a voicemail message 8 seconds long:

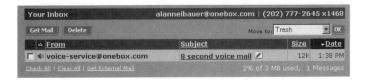

Click on the message to see these options and then click on the one that you want to use to listen to the voicemail:

[Listen to your 8 sec voicemail using Quicktime]
[Listen to your 8 sec voicemail in WAV format]

N O T E   Onebox also gives you a calendar and address book to use online.

You can also get voicemail and fax messages from these sites:

◆ www.deltathree.com

◆ www.ureach.com

◆ www.mytalk.com

◆ www.noticenow.com

◆ www.audiohighway.com

JFAX and NoticeNow deliver voicemail messages and faxes to the e-mail address you specify. You'll need to download a free program to listen to messages from JFAX, but NoticeNow sends the message to you in Real Player format.

With DeltaThree, you listen to the message from your DeltaThree account using their built-in player.

audiohighway, uReach, and myTalk accept only voice calls, not faxes, but can also report the caller's phone number for a callback. You listen to your voicemail online using either RealPlayer or Windows Media Player.

DeltaThree, JFAX, and NoticeNow are the only services that do not require the caller to enter an extension after they dial the assigned phone number.

33 If Ma Bell Could Talk!

Don't bother asking the telephone company whether you can make long distance calls to anywhere in the United States for free. After they got done laughing, they'd hang up the phone and charge you for the call.

Make Free Phone Calls

Using the Internet, however, you *can* make free phone calls. You can connect to any regular phone number anywhere in the United States. There are no long distance charges, no monthly fees, and no depending on your local or long distance phone company.

Here's What You Need

There are two ways to make free phone calls—over the Internet using IP telephony, and by getting a free phone-to-phone call just as if you dialed your phone yourself.

To make free five-minute phone calls to anywhere in the United States over your telephone, from www.speak4free.com, you'll need two phone lines in your home. You'll learn why soon.

Using Internet telephony, you use your computer's microphone and speakers as your "telephone," so you'll need a sound card, microphone, and speakers. While the sound quality is sometimes low and your voice can be difficult to hear, you can't beat the price. These systems actually work much better and sound clearer if you have a headset—one of those gadgets you fit over your head that lets you hear and speak without holding a telephone or leaning over to reach your computer's microphone.

If you like making calls from your computer, you make a better quality connection from a low-price service called Net2Phone. Calls to anywhere in the United States are as low as 1 cent a minute, with special rates to other countries. With Net2Phone, you prepay for the telephone time and then make your calls. You'll need to install a program which you can download from www.net2phone.com.

Sites and Features

The best deal in the world must be free five-minute phone-to-phone calls to anywhere in the United States. The company that performs this wonder is at www.speak4free.com. While the account and phone calls are free, you do need two phone lines in the house.

After you register as a member, which is free, here's how it works:

1. Connect to www.speak4free.com.

2. Sign in with your Speak4Free user name and password.

3. Enter the telephone number in your home that is not being used for your Internet connection.

4. Enter the telephone number you want to call.

5. Click the Submit button.

In a moment or so, depending on how busy Speak4Free is at the time, your phone line will ring. Pick it up to listen to a short (30-second) advertisement. When the ad ends, the number you are calling rings and you can talk for up to five minutes. About 30 seconds before the time is up, a message will play warning you that your time is almost up.

As soon as you click the Submit button, you can continue surfing the net, or even disconnect from your ISP. You do not need to be connected to Speak4Free while the phone call is in progress.

Voice Over IP

If you want to talk for more than five minutes, then consider making internet-to-telephone calls. You'll be able to dial any phone in the United States and speak for as long as you want, but using your computer microphone and speakers instead of your telephone.

There are a few companies that offer this service, but my favorites are www.dialpad.com and www.deltathree.com. Both services let you sign up and make phone calls for free.

After logging on to Dialpad, you can create a phonebook containing the names and phone numbers of persons you call. You can then either click on the phone number of a person in your book or use an on-screen numeric pad to dial your number. Speak as long as you want, and then click HangUp when you're done.

DeltaThree works about the same way, except you have to download and install their dialing program, called PC-to-Phone, shown in Figure 33.1. The program dials into the Internet and retrieves your other DeltaThree inbox information to show the number of faxes, e-mails, and voice messages that are waiting for you.

FIGURE 33.1 **Calling over DeltaThree**

NOTE When you first run PC-to-Phone, a box appears asking you to select your sound card. Choose your card from the list—it may be the only item listed—and click Done.

Enter the phone number you want to dial and then click Call. Use the Address Book button to maintain a list of frequently called numbers.

Another choice is www.phonefree.com. After you install their program, which you can download from their Web site, you can make free PC-to-phone calls. You can also use the PhoneFree program to make PC-to-PC calls, getting voice instant messaging to online friends who are also running the program.

The Net2Phone service (www.net2phone.com) charges for calls, but offers a better quality connection as well as Net2Fax service. It also allows you to send voicemail messages and connect to other computers with a PC-to-PC connection. You'll need to install their program, Net2Phone, which you can download from their site. The program is shown in Figure 33.2.

FIGURE 33.2 **Using Net2Phone**

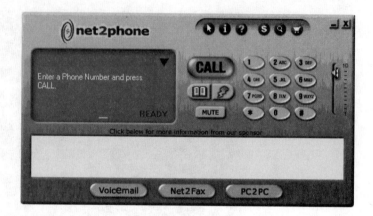

34 Don't Miss a Call Again

If you only have one phone line, your friends and relatives can get frustrated trying to get in touch when you are on the Internet. You cannot use your call waiting service, even if you pay for it, because the call waiting tone will confuse your modem and possibly disconnect your line. The solution, however, is not to go out and get that second phone line, but to sign up for a free Internet call waiting service.

Internet Call Waiting

An Internet call waiting service monitors your phone line when you are on the Internet. If another call comes in when your line is busy, it can take a message or signal you on screen with the caller's phone number, without knocking out your modem connection. When you're not on the line, you can use the service as a remote answering machine.

Here's What You Need

You need to sign up for the service over the Internet and give them the phone number on which you want Internet call waiting installed—it cannot be a cell phone or DSL line.

You then have to sign up for two services from your local phone company, although the Internet call waiting provider may be able to set up these services for you:

Call Forward Busy   Forwards incoming calls to another number when your phone is busy.

Call Forward No Answer   Forwards incoming calls to another number when your phone does not answer.

Depending on your local company and the Internet call waiting provider you choose, there may be an initial setup charge and monthly charge for these services from your phone company.

Here's how it works.

1. When someone calls you while you are online or not home, the call is forwarded to the Internet call waiting provider's phone. In most cases the number is toll free, so you or the caller does not incur any long distance charges.

2. The company then pops up a message on your screen letting you know that someone is trying to call and giving you the caller's phone number. You do not need to subscribe to the Caller ID service—that is handled by the provider.

3. Then, depending on the company, you can forward the call to voicemail, send a message to the caller, or reject the call.

Sites and Features

There are a number of places on the Internet to get call waiting, including:

◆ www.buzme.com

◆ www.callwave.com

◆ icw.sasknet.sk.ca/css

◆ www.internetcallmanager.com

◆ www.freeinternetaccess.net/realtime2.htm

As an example, let's look at the BuzMe service. BuzMe offers two levels of service: free and extended.

The free services give you call waiting with voicemail, popup notification, and caller ID when a call is received. You can choose to transfer the incoming call to your BuzMe voicemail or to reject it.

The extended service, which costs $4.95 per month, also lets you send a custom reply to callers when you are online or disconnect from the Internet and speak with the caller. The call is routed to your phone through the BuzMe line, and you get 60 minutes of free talk time each month.

N O T E In some cases, BuzMe will arrange to have Call Forward Busy and Call Forward No Answer set up and installed by your local company for free.

To sign up for the service, follow these steps:

1. Connect to www.buzme.com, shown in Figure 34.1

2. Click Sign Me Up.

3. Enter your telephone number.

4. Click Submit.

5. In the form that appears, enter your name, address information, and birth date. You can select to get e-mail notifications when voice mail is received.

FIGURE 34.1 BuzMe call waiting service

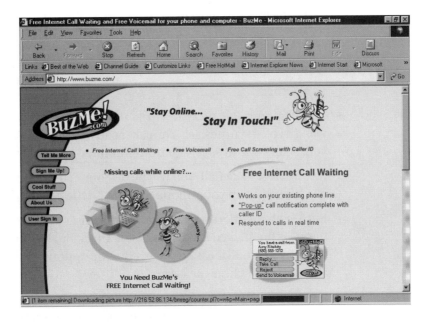

6. Select a numeric code that you'll use to manage your account and retrieve voice mail messages.

7. Select either the free or the extended service.

8. Click Submit

You will then be given directions for activating the account by calling a toll free number, downloading and installing the BuzMe software, and signing up for the call forwarding services, if BuzMe is unable to do it for you.

Once the call forwarding service is set up, when a call comes in while you are online, the caller is told that the system will attempt to contact you and is placed on hold. A window then pops up on your screen showing the phone number of the person calling.

If you signed up for the free service, you can either transfer the caller to voicemail or reject the call. If you select Reject, the caller is politely told that you are not available and is disconnected.

If you signed up for the extended service, you can also choose to reply to the caller or to take the call.

If you select Reply, a new window pops up with these options:

◆ Will Call You Back In

◆ Call Me Back In

◆ On My Way

◆ Other

These options let you type a brief reply to the caller that is played to them using a voice synthesizer. The caller can then leave a voice mail message for you, select one of several preprogrammed responses, or just hang up.

If you select Take Call, you will be disconnected from the Internet and you can then pick up your phone to speak to the caller.

BuzMe also works as an answering machine when you are offline. If your phone is not picked up in four or five rings, BuzMe answers the phone and takes a voicemail message. Using BuzMe options, you can record your own answering machine message.

Getting Your Messages　　If you are online when a caller leaves you a message, a window pops up giving you the option to connect to your BuzMe account and listen to the waiting voicemail. Just click Get Messages in the pop-up window and then click on the message you want to play.

You can also check for voicemail messages online from any Internet connection. Go to the BuzMe Web site and sign in to your account to access and listen to your messages, as shown in Figure 34.2.

FIGURE 34.2   Checking your BuzMe messages

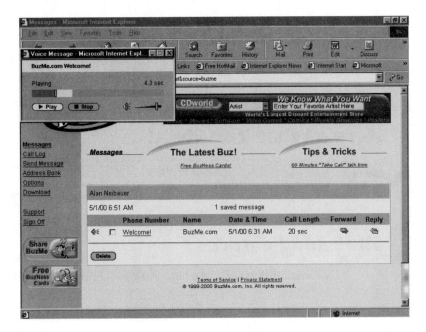

When you are not at home, or do not have access to the Internet, you can check your messages by telephone. Just follow these steps:

1. Dial your phone number.

2. Wait until BuzMe picks up the phone.

3. When the greeting message is being played, press the * button on the telephone dial pad.

4. Type your BuzMe numeric password, and then press the # key.

35   Finding Free Software

In this book's introduction, you learned how to download the programs mentioned in the text. The software mentioned here, however, is just a drop in the bucket, a needle in a haystack, a grain of sand on the beach (you get the point) compared to the software that's available on the Internet.

Download All Kinds of Free Software

There are literally thousands and thousands of programs out there for the taking. Some are excellent, some are average, and some just outright stink. You should not, however, judge a program by the way it is distributed. Many freeware programs are excellent—they do exactly what they are supposed to do, without bugs.

Here's What You Need

 You will, surprisingly enough, need access to the Internet. You should also have an unzipping program, such as WinZip, which you'll find on the accompanying CD.

Sites and Features

What kind of software can you get over the Internet? Almost anything:

Utilities	Browsers	Screen savers
Sample documents	Graphics	Educational programs
Games	Music and sound	Business programs
Device drivers	Web site tools	Operating systems

There are three general places where you can get software—collections, company home pages, and personal pages.

Collections These are services that catalog a number of programs. They usually offer a way to search for programs, tell you something about the software, and let you download programs. Most collections also rate programs. This way you know which are the most popular and dependable.

Home pages These are the sites maintained by the company that wrote or distributed the program. You can find these by searching the Internet or by following links from many of the collections.

Personal pages These are maintained by plain, ordinary people like you and me. Often, these sites have the owner's favorite programs and offer them to anyone who is interested.

As a general rule of thumb, download programs only from recognized collections and company home pages. Why? Unfortunately, there are some crazies out there. Some people just get their kicks by giving other people misery, and they spread programs with viruses. When you download anything onto your machine, think of it as giving control of your computer to whomever wrote the program.

The vast majority of software collections routinely test their offerings for viruses, so you can be relatively sure they are clean. Companies also test their software. Let's face it: they are letting you download, hoping you'll buy the product, so they want to make a good impression. But if you're surfing the Internet and you run across John Doe's Groovy Web site, you have no idea what you're going to run into.

With the necessary cautions aside, feel free to look for and download software. You can start with your ISP. Most ISPs offer links to software on their home page. Services such as AOL and CompuServe excel in the number of software products they offer and make their software easy to find. But the best collections of software can be found at the sites discussed below. These sites all offer a wide variety of programs. They are easily searchable and are grouped by category. Also look for software at Stroud's Consummate Winsock Apps List (`cws.internet.com/home.html`) and SoftSeek (`www.softseek.com`).

NONAGS

NONAGS gets its name by not nagging you on-screen with advertisements; it also specializes in software that follows a similar practice. It offers two types of services—free and paid.

Nonpaying members get access to a tremendous range of software. Paying members get access to many more bonuses, special downloads, and free e-mail with five addresses for a one-time, lifetime membership of $29.95.

NOTE   You can also sign up for the paid service and get a set of CDs containing most of the programs available on NONAGS.

When you navigate, you go through a series of steps to start getting files.

1. Navigate to www.nonags.com.

2. Click the Software Free Access icon to display a map of the world.

3. Click your part of the world to see a list of mirrors—sites that contain the entire NONAGS collection. A portion of this list is shown in Figure 35.1.

FIGURE 35.1 **NONAG file locations**

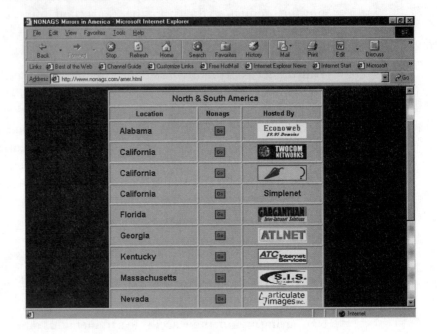

4. Click the GO graphic for the site that is closest to you to open the NONAGS home page.

The What's New section lists recently added or updated programs. The category in which the program is located is shown as a colored link.

Click the link to display programs in that category. You can also click any of the links on the left of the screen to navigate through NONAGS, or you can click the Search link to enter a search word or phrase for the program you want. The search shows a list of areas in which programs matching your search phrase can be found.

Click one of the links to list the specific files within it. The name of the program is shown first, followed by the date the program was last updated, a link to the company's home page, the name of the author, and a brief description. Below that is an icon representing the NONAGS rating, although not all programs are rated. To download a program, click its name (the one that appears above the date).

Winfiles.com

When you navigate to `www.winfiles.com`, a site that helps you find freeware or shareware products, click the Search Winfiles.com icon in what appears to be a Windows 95/98 window. Enter a word or phrase that describes the type of program you are looking for (such as graphics or virus), or enter the name of the program if you know it, and then click Find. You'll see a list of categories that contain files that match your search.

Click a category to display a list of programs. To the right of the program name is a description, the version number, the date and size of the file, the operating system it runs under, and any shareware registration fee. You'll also see any expiration date, whether it is a limited-time version, and whether it includes installation and removal routines. Below that are approximate download times. Under the description are links you can click to send an e-mail to the program's author or go to the author's home page.

Click the name of the program to start downloading, or click the home page link if you want to read more about the program and download it from the source.

Download.com

This site is run by a company called CNET. When you navigate to `www.download.cnet.com`, click one of the categories that interests you. You may then have to select from a subcategory to see an individual program listing.

You'll see the name of the program, a brief description, the operating system, its type of license, and other information about the program. Click the program name to see more information about the program, and then click Download Now to get your copy of the program.

Tucows

This site, pronounced "two-cows," offers a wide range of software organized by operating system. In the main window, www.tucows.com, you start by selecting your operating system, then your country, and then the mirror site that is nearest to you. You can then browse through programs by category, or search for a program by its name or keyword. When your search is complete, and you've selected the program in which you are interested, you see the name of the program, followed by its version number and revision date, its file name and size, the type of license, and the cost. You'll also see a link to the author's home page, any other operating systems it is available for, and a description.

Below the description is the Tucows rating, from three cows (OK) to five (excellent). Moo!

Supershareware

To access about 8000 shareware programs, go to www.supershareware.com. As shown in Figure 35.2, the site organizes programs by categories and features a selected Jewel of the Week.

FIGURE 35.2 **Supershareware collection**

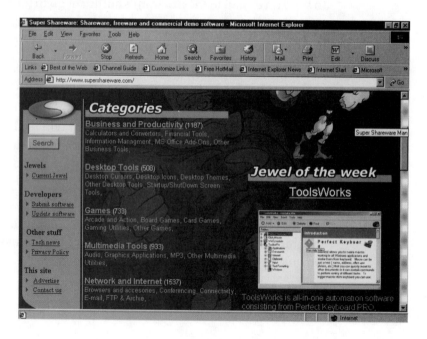

Under each of the major categories, such as Desktop Tools and Games, is a list of the program subcategories. Click a category to list all of the programs available for downloading in each of the subcategories.

Selecting Tech News on the left of the window, by the way, displays headlines and summaries of major technology-related news stories. You can click on the headline to go directly to the full story at its source Web site.

36 Get Free Books Online

When you're looking for a classic or something interesting to read, start by looking for it on the Internet. You can download free electronic copies of hundreds of books fairly easily.

Download the Classics and More from the Web

You can actually purchase books, the nonelectronic ones with real pages, from a lot of Web sites, as you'll learn in Section 59. But copyrights don't last forever, so many of the old classics can be freely distributed. Since printing, binding, and distributing costs money, you won't find free copies of books unless you're on the Internet.

Here's What You Need

You will need your Web browser, a connection to the Internet, and the sites listed in this chapter.

Sites and Features

You can download the complete versions of many of the best classic books (of course, you will also be able to find some that are not so classic but interesting anyway) directly into your computer. You can then read the book on-screen or print a copy of it to take with you.

Now reading a book on your screen is not as convenient and comfortable as curling up on the sofa with a good book. Reading a long book can be tiring and cause eyestrain. But, on the positive side, you can search the full text of the book to look for names, words, or topics that interest you. If you're a Sherlock Holmes fan, for example, you can search through all of the Sherlock Holmes stories for references to "bullet" to find out where Watson was really wounded. You can also search several versions of the Bible for references and citations.

NOTE If you don't want to read the book online, you can print out a copy and read it in the old-fashioned, conventional way.

Project Gutenberg

The best place to start looking for free books is at Project Gutenberg, www.gutenberg.net. This site has one of the world's largest collections of free books. In addition to Doyle and Shakespeare, you'll find Chekov, Balzac, Butler, Plato, Socrates, Ibanez, Barrie, Milton, and thousands of others. It has all six volumes of the Decline and Fall of the Roman Empire, the Warlords of Mars by Edgar Rice Burroughs, the Bible, the Book of Mormon, Roget's Thesaurus, Aesop's Fables, and the CIA World Factbook.

You'll also find historical documents, such as Lincoln's and Kennedy's inaugural addresses, the Gettysburg Address, the Mayflower Compact, Patrick Henry's Give Me Liberty Or Give Me Death speech, the United States Constitution, the Bill of Rights, and the Declaration of Independence.

Use the links in the Project Gutenberg home page to either search for a book, browse through the listings by author or title, or download a ZIP file containing the complete list of available books by author or title.

Use the search section on the home page to perform a simple search by author and by words in the book's title. Click the Search option on the left of the page to search by author, title, subject, or keywords. You can also specify a language and Library of Congress classification. After entering sufficient information to locate the book, click Submit Query.

If you'd rather browse, click the Browse option on the home page. In the screen that appears, choose whether you want to browse by author or title.

Choose the FTP site that is closest to you and click Select. You will then be able to see an alphabetic list of books by author or title.

Once you find the book you are looking for, click its title to download it. In most cases, you can choose to download a file with either the TXT or ZIP extension from options like these for Silas Marner by George Eliot:

- `smarn10.txt`—395 KB
- `smarn10.zip`—169 KB

ZIP files are smaller, but you have to unzip them before you can read their contents.

The Etext Archives

Another interesting site for free books is The Etext Archives at `www.etext.org`. This site offers documents in these categories: e-Zines (online magazines), politics, fiction, religion, and poetry. The collection isn't as large or varied as Project Gutenberg, but it contains some very interesting items.

You can also access the book collection formally held at `quartz.Rutgers.edu`.

There are plenty of other places on the Internet to get free material to read. Check out this one from Yahoo!: `dir.yahoo.com/Arts/Humanities/Literature/Electronic_Literature/Collections`.

37 Solve Downloading Problems

Can't find that downloaded file? Get knocked offline before you're finished? Join the club! Downloading can be a rewarding experience, but it can also be frustrating. You'll find some answers here.

Downloading Problem Solving

Downloading can be like eating potato chips. Once you start, it is difficult to stop. If you're not careful, you can forget to note the location where downloaded files are being saved or their file names. Then, when you want to run a program you've downloaded, you don't know where to find it. That's bad. In this section, you'll learn how to use free programs to solve your downloading problems. That's good.

Here's What You Need

 You need access to the Internet and a program to help you download software. You can either download one from the Internet, or use one of the two that are on the CD with this book: Download Assistant and GetRight.

Sites and Features

Within no time, you may find that you're downloading more and more programs. It is easy to get hooked on the convenience of getting software over the Internet, especially after you encounter the tremendous variety of material available. As a result, you may run into some problems. Downloading does have its downside, if you'll excuse the pun. Sometimes it gets difficult to find where you saved the downloaded program, and occasionally you'll get disconnected in the middle of downloading.

Even though the Save As box appears and asks for the name and the location of the downloaded file, it gets too easy to just click Save without making a note of the filename and location. I've done it, as have most folks in their downloading careers. Once the file is in, and you are offline, you realize you have no idea how to find it.

You can't search for the file using the Find feature because you don't know its file name. Sometimes, the name of the file has no apparent relationship to the name of the program. The alternatives are to start scanning all of your folders for something that looks right, or you could begin downloading the file all over again, and this time do it correctly.

The second big problem with downloading files, especially large ones, is the chance of getting disconnected in the middle of the download. There's something so frustrating about waiting for a 10-megabyte file to arrive, only to be disconnected.

No worries; you're in luck. There are scores of programs out there that can help. There are programs that help you organize your files for easy retrieval and automatically pick up where you left off if you are accidentally disconnected.

Some of the programs that you'll find include Download Wonder from `www.forty.com`; Download Butler from `www.lincolnbeach.com`; and Download Minder from `www.zedsoftware.com`.

If you do some searching in any software collection, you'll find dozens more.

Two helpful programs (Download Assistant and GetRight) are included on the CD with this book. Let's look at them a little more closely so you get the idea of how they can help. Both of these programs operate in the same general way. They monitor your online activity and wait for a file to be downloaded. They then become active, substituting their own download features for those of your browser. If you have a virus protection program installed, both of these programs can use it to scan incoming files for viruses.

Download Assistant

Download Assistant helps you keep track of your files by saving them in one of three groups of folders—Programs, Research, or Internet—all within the `C:\Program Files\IOLO` path. Each of these three folders is divided into other folders. For example, the `C:\Program Files\IOLO\Programs` path contains folders named Productivity, Games, Utilities, and Applications. You'll find the program on the accompanying CD or you can download it from `www.iolo.com`.

After you install the Download Assistant, the Configuration Wizard starts up. It scans your system for virus protection software and installed browsers. It asks you to choose which browser you want to use the program with and whether you want to scan downloaded files with your virus protection software. You can also choose to have the program automatically open each file after it is downloaded.

To use the program, start it first and then open your browser. Whenever you start to download a file, the Download a File window appears, as shown in Figure 37.1. The information in the Download Description, File Source, and Specify a Filename for this Download text boxes appears automatically. You can use the other options in the dialog box to customize how you want the file downloaded.

FIGURE 37.1 Download a File window in Download.

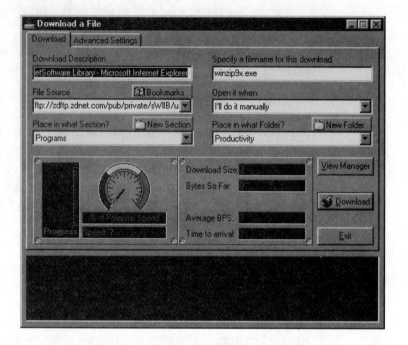

NOTE Each time you start the version of the program on the CD, you have to wait until the Continue Evaluation button is no longer dimmed before you can click it.

Advanced Settings tab Lets you choose to have Download Assistant automatically delete the file in 30 days, or asks if you want to delete the file if you have not opened, run, or installed the file in 10 days.

Place in what Section? Provides a selection of locations to which the file can be stored.

Place in what Folder? Provides a list of folders to which the file can be stored.

Open It When Either opens the program automatically after it is downloaded, or opens it only when you request it to be opened (choose between these two choices on the drop-down list).

Download button Begins the actual download. As the file comes over, you can watch its progress on the display to the left of the Download button. You'll see the total size of the file as well as the current number of downloaded bytes. This display also shows an approximate download speed and how much longer it will take. When the download is completed, a box appears reminding you of the section and folder.

View Manager button Takes you to the main screen of the Download Assistant (see Figure 37.2).

FIGURE 37.2 **View Manager**

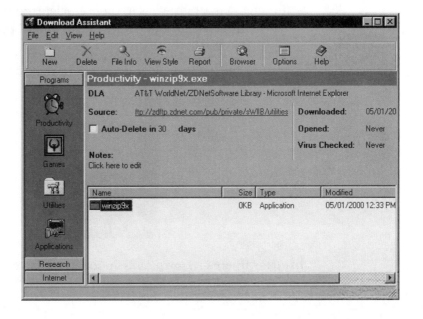

Along the left of the window are four groups. Click the group to display its folders, and then click a folder to list the files contained within it. In the main part of the window, you can select a file to see when it was downloaded, opened, and virus checked. You can also turn on the AutoDelete option. Use the menu bar to choose from these options:

New Creates a new section and folder.

Delete Deletes a section or folder.

File Info Displays the properties of the select file.

View Style   Lets you change the way files are listed.

Report   Lets you print or save a report summarizing your downloaded programs.

Browser   Launches your Web browser.

Options   Opens a dialog box for customizing the way the program looks and operates.

In addition to the options listed above, consider the following actions.

◆ To run a program from the Download Assistant, just double-click it.

◆ To delete a file, right-click it, choose Delete from the shortcut menu, and then choose to either move the file to the Recycle Bin or permanently delete it.

You can also control Download Assistant by right-clicking the icon in the system tray to see these options:

Turn off the Intercept Downloads option if you do not want the program to handle downloading chores.

GetRight

GetRight is a shareware program that can be downloaded from www.getright.com. In addition to its other functions, GetRight maintains a list of popular software collection sites. If there is a problem downloading a file, it can search for an alternate location from which to download it.

You can also set GetRight to download files at a certain time (such as when you're sleeping), hang up, and turn off your computer when it is done (if your computer offers that feature).

When you first install the program, it takes you through a series of screens to configure it for your system. The installation program then places an icon in the system tray. Use the icon to control GetRight features.

NOTE If GetRight doesn't seem to be working, right-click its icon in the system tray, click on Downloads, and select Start Automatic Downloading.

When you start to download a file, the GetRight Save As box opens. In this box, you should check the name of the file and choose a location. You can also use an FTP search to search for an alternate location. When you click Save, a progress window appears. This window shows the address of the program source and the location where the file is being stored. There is a running count of the number of bytes that have been downloaded, how much more time the download will take, and the speed at which it is downloading.

From the icon in the system tray, you can also open the Status box. This box shows the same basic information, but it shows it for all of the files that have been downloaded. The buttons on the toolbar are shown here:

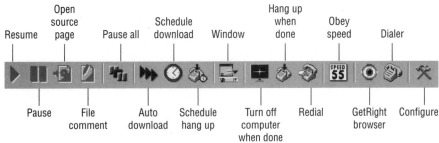

Use the toolbar and menu options to control and schedule downloads. The GetRight Browser, for example, lets you display the files in FTP or HTTP servers, in much the same way as Windows Explorer displays files on your disk. To see the files that are on the site, click the GetRight browser button on the toolbar. You can then download any file you see by selecting it and choosing Download from the File menu.

The Hang up when done and Turn off computer when done options are useful when you want to download files unattended. If you need to download a huge file, for example, wait until you're ready to go to sleep, click the Turn Off Computer When Done button and start the download. When you wake up in the morning, the program will be on your computer waiting for you.

38 Finding the Endless Supply of Free Stuff

The Internet is just full of free offers. Some are totally free; others have quite a few strings attached to them. If you have the time to surf, read all of the offers, and respond to them, do so. You can save quite a lot of money on the Internet—enough to pay for your monthly ISP charge!

Get Discounts and Samples Galore!

Manufacturers are always trying to find a way to get you to buy their products. Some do it in a way with which most people are familiar—coupons and free offers. Clip a coupon out of the paper, hand it to the cashier at the store, and get some money off in return. With the Internet, you no longer have to cut coupons from the paper. You can just print or download coupons, and get free merchandise of all types.

Here's What You Need

All you need is access to the Internet—and a printer to get copies of coupons and free offers.

Sites and Features

There are scores of sites offering coupons and free merchandise, but a few rise to the top. Supermarkets.com is a particularly good site. You should also check out www.priceline.com.

Web Bucks

We all have to shop for food, paper goods, and other household items. Coupons help by giving us money off products that we purchase. Some stores even double the value of manufacturer's coupons, giving you 50 cents off for a 25-cent coupon. Whether or not you clip and use coupons, however, you can get money back from your shopping trip at many of the larger supermarket chains by printing a Valu Page from `www.supermarkets.com`.

Here's how it works.

1. You print a page of money-back offers, called a Valu Page, which includes a UPC code for each market.

2. When you go shopping, before starting to check out, have the cashier scan the UPC code into their system.

3. For each item on the Valu Page that you purchase, you get a printed coupon called a Web Buck.

4. During your next shopping trip, you use the Web Buck coupons just like cash on any product you buy, whether or not that product is on the Valu Page.

So let's say the Value Page has an offer for $1.00 if you purchase a specific brand of cereal. When you check out, you'll get a $1.00 coupon to use on anything on your next visit—it's just like cash.

If you have a manufacturer's coupon in addition to the Value Page offer, it's even better. While you cannot use two coupons for the same product, you can use a coupon when you purchase the cereal, you can still show the cashier the Value Page offer, and you will still be able to use the Web Buck you receive on your next visit. So, a 50-cent coupon and a $1.00 Web Buck actually get you $1.50 off over two trips, or $2.00 off if your market doubles manufacturer's coupons.

Now, for the instructions to get your Value Page. Go to `www.supermarkets.com`. Enter your zip code and click the Click Here to Save button to see a list of participating supermarkets in your area.

Click the market that you use for shopping to see the total amount available in Web Bucks. You will also be able to customize your Value Page at this screen. For example, you can choose to eliminate baby and pet items, if you're not interested in these products. You can also enter your e-mail address, if you want to receive a weekly reminder to print out the Valu Page.

When you click Click Here to Save, the page appears with the market's UPC code and a list of items that are currently on special. Print the Valu Page, which is actually four or five pages long, and take it to the market on your next trip.

When you get your Web Bucks on that trip, store them in a safe location until you visit the supermarket again. You will then be able to use the Web Bucks like cash. You can also print out a new Value Page for that week to get additional Web Bucks for the items you buy.

N O T E Many supermarkets have their own home pages that include coupons and special offers. Try `www.our_market's_name.com`.

Priceline.Com

At Priceline you not only search for discounts, but you actually purchase products as well. The site, at `www.priceline.com`, earned its reputation as a great place to purchase discount airline tickets, but now also offers hotel rooms, rental cars, new cars and trucks, long distance calling, and groceries.

Here's how it works:

1. You search Priceline for the product you want.

2. You tell Priceline how much you'd like to pay for the product.

3. Priceline checks with its sellers to see if any will accept your offer.

4. If a seller accepts your offer, you then purchase the item online with your charge card. If the sellers reject your offer, you can increase it or just forget about it.

For example, to save money on groceries, connect to Priceline and establish an account. They will send you a membership card that you can use at any major supermarket. Then before shopping, log on to Priceline and go to the WebHouse section where groceries are available.

WARNING Most major supermarket chains accept the Priceline system, but you might want to call and confirm before ordering groceries.

Locate an item you wish to purchase—you may have to select two brands from which Priceline can choose—and select a category of price to pay— usually a range from 50% to 85%. If your offer is accepted, the price for the quantities that you ordered will be charged to your credit card and Priceline displays an order list with a UPC barcode.

Print out the order list and take it to your favorite supermarket. Separate your Priceline items, which you have already paid for, from your other items. The cashier will ring up the Priceline items separately at their regular prices, but they will not be charged to your account. When it comes time to "pay" for the items in the market, you scan your Priceline card and enter a PIN number printed on the order list.

For extra savings, you can still use coupons and store discount cards with Priceline items. Just give the coupons and discount card to the cashier when you check out. Within ten days, the credit for the coupons and any card discounts will appear with your Priceline account online, and will be deducted from your next Priceline purchase.

The Mothers of All Free Sites

You can spend countless hours scouring the Web for free offers, or you can go to one of the sites that has a collection of free offers and links to even more free stuff. A few of the hottest freebie collections are listed here:

- ◆ www.freestuffcentral.com
- ◆ www.gsmenter.com
- ◆ www.4free.net
- ◆ startsampling.com
- ◆ pages.ivillage.com/pp/xilamom

Two collections that are outstanding are at freeclutter.snap.com (snap.com) and www.free.com. At both of these sites, you can sign up for free samples of all kinds, and for special offers and promotions that don't require a single coupon. Just ask for the free stuff, sit back, and wait until it arrives in your mailbox.

At freeclutter.snap.com there are links to other collections of free offers, as well as 37 categories of items, from Baby Stuff to Wedding, many of which are divided into subcategories. Click on a category or subcategory to take you to a free offer or list of offers that you can sign up to receive. Clicking Clothing, for example, displays offers for free hats, T-shirts, socks, earrings, and more. Just click a link you're interested in and follow the instructions that appear onscreen to get a free sample.

For even more free stuff, go to www.free.com, mentioned earlier. This site has links to hundreds of other sites that offer free, or almost free, merchandise. Follow the link of your choice to sign up for free samples and other merchandise offers.

Enhancing the Internet Experience

The Internet is great, but it can always be better. In this part of the book, you'll learn how you can make the Internet faster, cut down on the advertisements, and share a single phone line and modem by networking your home.

39 Using Windows to Speed Browsing

No matter how fast your connection, sometimes it just takes time to download a Web site. Rather than waiting with nothing to do while a page comes in, wouldn't you rather read another Web page? This way, by the time you're done reading, the other site will be loaded and ready. You can even look at two or more sites at the same time!

Two Windows Are Better Than One!

If you are reading one site and you see a link you want to go to, you can start downloading the linked page while you finish reading. This trick makes it so you have another browser window open. One window will download its page in the background while you are reading the other. This has the added advantage of letting you return quickly to the original page when you're done reading the second.

Here's What You Need

You won't need anything other than your trusty Web browser. For extra browsing features, however, consider using a program called FourTimes, which you'll find on the CD with this book.

Sites and Features

The capability to use multiple windows is already built into Windows and the Web browsers designed for it (Microsoft Internet Explorer and

Netscape Navigator). If you are using either of these browsers, here is how to view more than one site at a time.

◆ In Microsoft Internet Explorer, press Ctrl+N or select File➢New➢ Window.

◆ In Netscape Navigator, select File➢New➢Navigator Window.

This opens another window with the same Web site; in this new window, navigate to the other site you want to display. Now each browser window will contain a different site, and you'll now see two items for the browser in the Windows taskbar. As the new page is downloading, click the button for the original page on the Windows taskbar and continue reading. The first site will continue to load even though its window is in the background.

As you can see, it is easy to switch back and forth between the two windows by clicking their buttons in the taskbar. You can also use standard Windows techniques to tile both windows so they are viewed at the same time, as shown in Figure 39.1.

FIGURE 39.1 Displaying multiple browser windows

NOTE Though you can have more than two windows open, this is not advised because you'll start stretching the resources of your system.

If the browser windows are not already full screen, just drag each by a corner to the size you want it. You can place them top-and-bottom, as shown in Figure 39.1, or side-by-side. Side-by-side windows do not work as well because you'll have to scroll too much to read their contents.

If the windows are full screen, click the Restore button on the right side of the title bar in the foreground window. This makes it a smaller window so you can access its corners to drag. Then do the same for the remaining full-screen window.

Four Web Sites at One Time

If you are feeling the need to take this technique to an even higher level, run a wonderful little program called FourTimes. You can download it from www.members.tripod.com/~fourtimes.

FourTimes lets anyone with Internet Explorer 4 and later (sorry, it doesn't work with other browsers) easily navigate through four pages at the same time (see Figure 39.2).

When you start FourTimes, you'll see four empty browser windows. Each window contains all the typical browser buttons. FourTimes may automatically connect to the Internet to download a default set of pages.

Just pick a window, enter the address of the site you want to display, and press Enter or click the Home button. Load a different Web site in each of the windows. You can even drag and drop links between panels. If you see a link you want to open, but you don't want it to replace the current page, just drag it to one of the other windows. FourTimes opens the linked page in that window.

In addition to the toolbar, FourTimes provides most of the common browser functions in its menu bar. You can use the View menu to access Internet Options and Preferences, the Tools menu to launch your e-mail and news programs, and the Favorites menu to add and organize bookmarks.

FIGURE 39.2   Reading four pages at once with FourTimes

The Four menu is something you won't have seen before, and it is really interesting. If you have a combination of pages that you use periodically, you can use the Four menu to designate them as a group. You can then quickly access all four pages by just selecting the group name.

You can create a group either by entering the address of each site or by loading each site's window ahead of time. For example, once you have one to four sites in the FourTimes windows, select Four ➢ Add to open this dialog box:

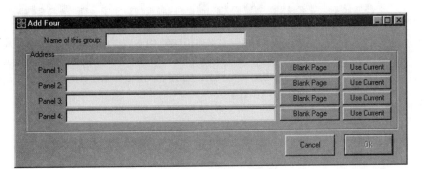

First, type a name for the group; then use any of these techniques to specify a Web site in each of the panels:

- ◆ Click Use Current to add the currently open site to the panel.
- ◆ Click Blank Page to make the panel blank.
- ◆ Type in the address of the site.
- ◆ Finally, click OK.

Using the same technique, you can create any number of groups, each with its own name and combination of up to four sites.

If you later need to change the group, select Four➤Organize to see a list of your group names in the Organize Four dialog box. Click the group you want to change and click Properties in the dialog box. Make any changes in the box that appears, and then click OK.

When you want to load the sites in a group, select Four➤Open. A bar appears down the left of the screen showing the group names. Just click the group you want to display. When you are finished with whatever changes you need to make, click the Back button on top of the bar to remove the group names from the screen.

40 Speed Up the Internet

Ever wonder what your computer is doing between the time you enter a Web site name and the time the page begins to appear on your screen? Get ready to find out!

Make Your Web Browsing Go Faster

When you enter the address of a Web site, you may notice a message in the browser's status line that explains that it is looking for the site. Knowing what the browser is actually doing while the message appears can help you speed up surfing.

Here's What You Need

In order to proceed, you will need your Web browser, an Internet connection, and FastNet99 or SpeedyNet, two handy programs.

Sites and Features

No matter how fast your modem, sometimes browsing the Web seems to take forever. If you already have the fastest modem available, and you don't want to go to the expense of a special phone line or cable modem, you can still speed up your connection.

Each Web site name is identified by an Internet Protocol (IP) address. The site www.microsoft.com, for example, is located at the IP address 207.68.131.62. When you type a site name into your browser's location or address box, the browser has to first find the IP address before it can actually go to that site.

NOTE If you know the IP address of the site you want, enter it into the browser instead of the URL to speed things up.

Windows 98/NT maintains a file on your disk containing the IP addresses and names of sites that you have visited on the Internet. The file is called Hosts (without any extension), and it is in the C:\Windows folder in Windows 98, and the C:\WinNT\System32\Drivers\Etc\Hosts folder in Windows NT. The Hosts file is a plain text file that you can open and look at with a word processing program.

If that file doesn't contain the IP address of a new Web site you are looking for, your browser checks a similar but much larger file at your ISP called a Domain Name Service (DNS) lookup. If the DNS file does not contain the IP address, one of several master DNS files maintained by organizations around the world is checked. Each of these steps takes some time.

To speed up the process of finding domain names, you can run one of several programs that let you manipulate the host list. Two such programs, FastNet99 and SpeedyNet, are on this book's CD.

FastNet99

FastNet99, which can also be downloaded at www.geocities.com/
TimesSquare/Stadium/1851, works in the background when your connection is idle. It looks up and verifies the IP addresses of sites in your Favorites
or Bookmarks lists. You can add IP addresses manually to FastNet99, if you
know them, and otherwise manage the host file. This program also verifies
each IP address to confirm that it is correct by going to the sites to make
sure the address is still valid.

Starting FastNet99 opens the window shown in Figure 40.1. To look up an
IP address from a domain name, follow these steps:

1. Click the Find IP option button.

2. Enter the Web site URL in the text box.

3. Click OK.

FIGURE 40.1   **FastNet99**

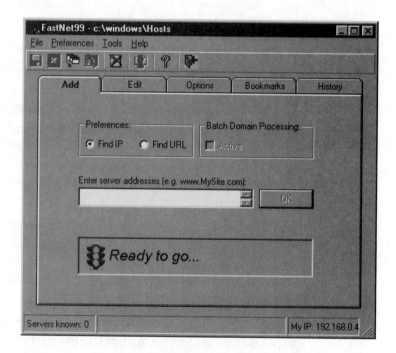

You can also locate a site name if you already have the IP address. To locate a site name from the IP address, follow these steps:

1. Click the Find URL option button.

2. Enter the IP address in the text box.

3. Click OK.

FastNet99 first checks the Hosts file (mentioned earlier) to see if the site is already listed. If it is, a message appears telling you so. Otherwise, FastNet99 connects to the Internet through your ISP and locates the information you are searching for. When the word Done appears in place of Ready to Go, click Save to add the information to the Hosts file.

The Edit tab in the FastNet99 window lets you view the entries in the Hosts file, verify that they are accurate, and remove duplicates.

Use the Options tab to fine-tune how FastNet99 works. For example, the Monthly Batch Function lets you have FastNet99 perform any of these four tasks at the start of each month:

Verify All Checks to make sure that all IP addresses are still correct for the domain names.

Scan Bookmarks Ensures that each entry in the Bookmark list has a valid IP address.

Scan History Ensures that each entry in the History list has a valid IP address.

Update Checks for a FastNet99 update.

To access this function, click the Options tab and then the Batch button. In the box that appears, select the tasks that you want FastNet99 to perform each month.

You can also use the menu bar and toolbar buttons to work with FastNet99. Click the Report button on the toolbar, for example, to display the report shown in Figure 40.2. The report shows the sites that you've added to or deleted from the host file and the sites that were verified, duplicated, cached, or renamed.

FIGURE 40.2 FastNet99 report

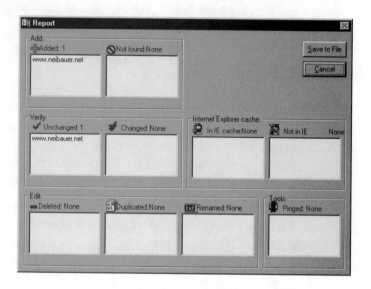

SpeedyNet

SpeedyNet also lets you manage the Hosts list using the interface shown in Figure 40.3. You can download it from www.comcen.com.au/~netwiz/ software/snet4.

To add an IP address, follow these steps:

1. Click the Add/Modify Server option button.

2. Enter the URL of the site.

3. Click Go.

Use the Import button in the SpeedyNet window to add the sites from your Internet Explorer favorites and Netscape Navigator bookmarks. View Site options displays the contents of the Hosts file so you can delete or verify specific entries. Use the Verify All button to verify the entire Hosts file.

FIGURE 40.3 SpeedyNet

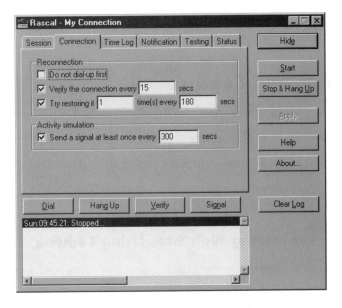

41 More Ways to Speed Up the Internet

In addition to DNS lookups that you learned about in the last section, there are all sorts of other ways to speed up your Internet experience.

Make Your Web Browsing Go Even Faster

Wherever you have creative minds, you'll find people trying to do things better and faster. There is no shortage of creativity on the Internet, so you shouldn't be surprised that there are plenty of ways to surf the Internet more quickly.

Here's What You Need

You will need your Web browser, an Internet connection, and LinkFox and ModemBooster, handy programs you'll find on the CD of this book.

Sites and Features

In this section, we'll look at two different approaches:

◆ Preloading pages onto your computer's hard disk

◆ Fine-tuning your modem and Internet settings

Programs to help you get started experimenting with each of these techniques are on the accompanying CD.

Preloading Web Sites Using LinkFox

The longest delays in browsing occur when you're waiting for a Web page to download to your computer. Rather than using multiple windows, which take up a lot of your computer's resources, you can preload a page into your computer's hard disk. This process is called caching. It is much faster to load a page into the cache file than into a hidden browser window. After you preload a site, the process of downloading will take almost no time at all. The information will just be loaded from the cache into the window later on.

LinkFox is a program that lets you select pages to preload into the cache. You can download it from www.hageltech.com.

After LinkFox is installed, you can start the program from the icon it places in your system tray, but it will start automatically when your browser connects to the Internet.

LinkFox can take three forms—a full window, a small window, or an icon on the desktop called a drop box.

To select a view, right-click the icon in the system tray and choose the view from the menu that appears. Right-click the LinkFox icon in the system tray and choose Options to select a default view.

Before reading a Web page in detail, scan the page and look for links that you would be interested in seeing. Drag the links from the Web page to the

LinkFox window or Drop Basket. Now, as you are reading the page, LinkFox downloads the linked pages to the computer's cache.

If you drag the link to the window, you'll see a small disk icon in the LinkFox window as the file is being downloaded and saved. A checkmark will then appear to indicate each page that has been successfully completed. If the site cannot be loaded, a red X appears next to its name.

When you're ready to read one of the pages, double-click it or select it and press Enter. (You can also right-click it and choose Open in New Window from the shortcut menu.)

If you drag the link to the Drop Basket, the chain image turns yellow as the link is downloading. It turns green when it is finished. If the site cannot be loaded, the chain turns red. To open a site, right-click the Drop Basket and choose either Show Full Window or Show Link List Only from the shortcut menu.

By default, the links are deleted from LinkFox when you exit the program. To retain a link so you can open the page at a later time, right-click it and choose Persistent Link from the shortcut menu.

Fine Tune Your Modem with ModemBooster

While we all take our modems for granted these days, a modem is a complicated device that should be treated with respect. ModemBooster knows how to treat a modem. The program fine-tunes your modem's settings, and the settings in the Windows registry that affect your modem, to get the most out of your Internet connection. You can download it from www.inklineglobal.com.

When you first install and run ModemBooster, it asks some questions about your ISP. You click the Auto Tune-Up option and then the Play button in the ModemBooster window. ModemBooster will dial into your ISP and disconnect several times as it analyzes your settings for the best performance. Depending on your ISP and modem, a thorough analysis using Auto Tune-Up could take one to two hours, so it is best to perform this when you have plenty of time to spare.

42 Monitor Your Connection

Keep an eye on your network connections to find the best time to get files and surf the Web. In order to do so, read the following information.

Keep Track of Your Actual Connection Speed

Even though your modem is advertised as 56K, it doesn't mean you're actually downloading and uploading that fast. By monitoring the actual connection speeds, you can determine the best time to connect and download files.

Here's What You Need

In order to do this, you will need your Web connection and Windows Dial-Up Networking or a program on the CD with this book.

Sites and Features

You can connect to the Internet using Windows Dial-Up Networking and still monitor your connection speeds.

 One of the easiest ways is to run a program designed to display a small window that reports connection speed as you work. DU Meter, on the CD with this book, or downloaded from www.hageltech.com, can perform this function. Running the program displays an icon in the system tray and a small box, as shown here:

The box stays in the foreground as you surf the Internet, showing the actual download time (for information coming to your computer) and upload time (information from your computer to the Internet).

Hide or redisplay the box by right-clicking the system tray icon. Right-click the icon and choose Manual Hide from the shortcut menu to remove the DU Meter box from the screen. Click the tray icon again to restore the box.

Choose Options from the shortcut to customize DU Meter. Use the Window Properties tab of the Options dialog box to adjust how the meter appears, how times are reported, and the color of lines on the graph. The Network Interface tab lets you choose what connections to monitor. By default, DU Meter keeps track of your modem and LAN connections. You can use the tab to specify watching one connection and ignoring the other.

The Graph Scale tab of the dialog box lets you set the upper limit of the scale—the maximum value of the y-axis. The options on the Graph Scale tab are

Automatic Scale Update   Adjusts the scale to accommodate the highest transfer rates.

Pre-defined Values   Sets the upper limit of the scale to the speed of your modem.

Manual Setup   Lets you specify the upper range.

Use the Notifications tab to have DU Meter warn you, or disconnect you, when the connection reaches a minimum value. The Ticker feature plays a sound when a set number of bytes is downloaded, giving you an audible representation of the transfer speed.

The Totals option on the DU Meter shortcut menu opens a box reporting the total number of bytes uploaded and downloaded. You can choose to reset the number to start counting from zero.

The StopWatch option lets you track the transfer rate over a specific period. Right-click the system tray icon and choose StopWatch. Click Start when you want to begin monitoring the transfer rate. Click Stop—which replaces the Start button—to stop the counter.

43 Get Help Connecting

The Dial-Up Networking feature of Windows is easy to use, but it has no frills. It dials your ISP, but that's all. You can get your dial-up connection to do a lot more with a little help from our online friends.

Make Connecting Easier

In It's About Time, earlier in this book, you learned how to keep track of your online time by using programs that you can download from the Internet. These programs acted as an intermediary between you and Windows Dial-Up Networking. There are all sorts of other programs that expand on Windows Dial-Up Networking.

Here's What You Need

You need your browser, your ISP, and some free or inexpensive software. Some of this software can be found on the CD that comes with this book; other products will need to be downloaded from the Internet.

Sites and Features

Programs abound that let you control your online sessions and help you connect more easily. In fact, you can set up these programs so you can connect through them rather than through Windows Dial-Up Networking. Instead of opening your browser, start one of these programs and connect through it to access its features.

Most of these programs offer a variety of functions that can be found separately in other software (such as Whois, Ping, and Trace Route). Like software that we have already discussed, these programs keep track of online time and cost and keep your connection alive. By using one of these programs, however, you get all of these features and more in one place.

Some of the more popular programs in this category follow:

Program	Download Location
Dunce	www.vecdev.com
CyberKit	www.cyberkit.net/
InterNet Anywhere Toolkit	www.tnsoft.com
Net Toolbox	www.nettoolbox.com
NetScan Tools	www.nwpsw.com
Network Toolbox	www.jriver.com/products/network-toolbox.html
Sam Spade	http://samspade.org/ssw/

We'll take a closer look at two such programs here—ConnectPal and Rascal.

Your Pal, ConnectPal

ConnectPal is a full-featured shareware program downloadable from www.connect-pal.com. Use it to work between you and the Windows Dial-Up Networking feature. For example, you can set ConnectPal to automatically start other programs when you go online. You can launch an e-mail program, a downloading helper such as GetRight, another timer or cost-tracking program, an FTP application, or a program such as Microsoft Word.

When you first start the program, you'll be asked to configure it using the dialog box shown in Figure 43.1.

Use the tabs of the dialog box to explore these functions:

Connection   Sets up user profiles with name and passwords.

Cost   Keeps track of free time and online charges.

Warnings   Sets warnings to occur at cost and online time levels.

Options   Customizes your online environment.

Mail Watch   Sets the program to automatically look for new mail and news messages.

Statistics   Shows records of online time, costs, and other calculations.

You first task is to set up a profile.

FIGURE 43.1   **Configuring ConnectPal**

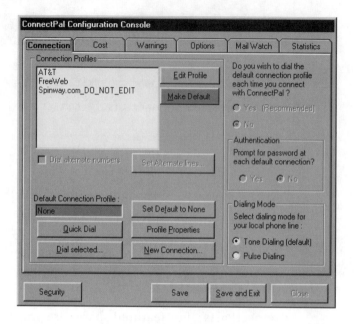

1. In the Connection profiles list, click the dial-up networking connection you want to use. If you need to create a new one, click New Connection to launch the Windows program that lets you create one.

2. Click the Edit Profile button to display this dialog box:

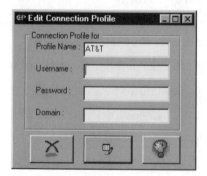

3. Enter your username and password. You must enter these in ConnectPal, even though you may have already saved them when using Windows Dial-Up Networking. ConnectPal uses the phone

number information from the Windows Dial-Up Networking profile but sends its own username and password when logging in.

4. Click the Modify button—the center button below the Domain text box.

5. If you have to change any of the settings in the dial-up networking connection, click Profile Properties.

6. Click the dial-up connection you want to use and then click the Make Default button.

7. Use the Options tab to customize other aspects of the connection. For example, you can choose to:

- ◆ Dial your ISP as soon as you start ConnectPal.

- ◆ Start up to five other programs when you connect.

- ◆ Display online time information when connected.

- ◆ Keep your connection alive using up to three different methods— simulating e-mail (Post Office Protocol—POP main), requesting a Web site (Ping), or downloading software (FTP).

- ◆ Redial if disconnected.

8. Click Save and then Close.

Once you configure ConnectPal for the first time, you'll see the main program window shown in Figure 43.2. To change the configuration later, click the C.C.C. button.

Use the Connect button to dial into the connection you established in the configuration as the default profile. Once you make the connection, you can start your Web browser, e-mail program, or any other application for which you want to use your Internet connection. The Speed button makes the connection without prompting for your username or password. The Launcher button lets you select up to 10 programs to launch manually.

If you make your Internet connection before starting ConnectPal, click the Scan button. ConnectPal will detect the connection, start timing it, and apply your selected options, such as launching additional programs.

FIGURE 43.2   **ConnectPal window**

The Net Tools button accesses four common Internet features:

Who is   Lets you look up the registered owner of a Web site.

Finger   Lets you check to see if a friend is online, if their ISP supports this feature.

Time   Lets you access Greenwich Mean Time.

Get Host   Lets you get the domain name of an IP address, and vice versa.

When you disconnect with ConnectPal, you'll be asked to confirm the action in this message:

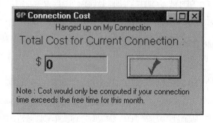

You Rascal, You

Another popular connection management program is Rascal, which you can download from www.basta.com. Rascal also acts as your dial-up connection and includes automatic reconnection and keep-alive functions. The Rascal window is shown in Figure 43.3.

Rascal uses the default dial-up networking connection, but before dialing, you have to click the Session tab and enter your username and password.

At the bottom left of the Sessions tab is the Dial button. Click this button when you want to connect to your ISP. After making the connection, you can start your Web browser or e-mail program.

FIGURE 43.3 **Rascal window**

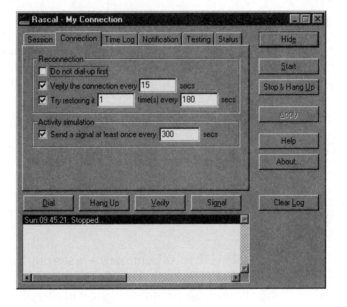

Use the Reconnect options on the Connection tab to determine how Rascal monitors and reacts to your connection status:

Do Not Dial Up First If you are disconnected, Rascal will not reconnect, but it will wait until you connect with some other programs before monitoring the connection.

Verify the Connection   This specifies at what intervals Rascal checks to see if you are connected or offline. This option must be turned on in order to use the Activity Simulation feature to keep your connection active.

Try Restoring It   This specifies how often Rascal will attempt to reconnect and the interval between attempts.

Use the Activity simulation setting to keep your signal alive by pinging the ISP at regular intervals. Enable the check box and then enter the number of seconds between pings in the text box.

N O T E   To manually send a ping to the ISP, click the Signal button. Click Verify to check your connection status.

Use the other tabs of the Rascal window to time your sessions and keep track of online costs, to play sounds when you connect and disconnect, to test Rascal by simulation connections and disconnections, and to display connection status information such as your ISP's address and name.

44 There's No Place Like Home

Most ISPs give you a home page—a starting location that your browser first opens when you connect to the Internet. You shouldn't feel locked into their home page if it doesn't give you everything you want. Some other ISP might offer more features—you can take advantage of them even if you are not a member.

Changing Your Home Page

ISPs try to offer a wide range of features on their home pages. Some of the items, such as links to support help, are for members only. However, most of the links in a home page can be used by anyone, whether they are members or not, so keep your eyes open for another ISP home page that is better for you. There are even home pages that aren't provided by ISPs.

Here's What You Need

You won't need anything special, except access to the Internet and the knowledge to set your home page, which is provided here. You set the home page within your browser. That's how it knows the page to open when first launched and where to go when you click the Home button on the browser's toolbar.

NOTE Some of the sites mentioned here have a link that will make it your home page automatically, but it is best to set the home page yourself to make sure it gets done right.

With Microsoft Internet Explorer, follow these steps when you want to change your home page:

1. Right-click the Internet Explorer icon on the desktop and choose properties. If you don't have an icon, try Start➤Settings➤Control Panel and open Internet Options. If the browser is already running, select Tools➤Internet Options.

2. In the General tab of the Internet Properties dialog box, shown in Figure 44.1, enter the address of the home page in the Address box.

3. Click OK.

With Netscape Navigator, follow these steps to change the home page:

1. Launch Netscape.

2. Select Edit➤Preferences to open the Preferences dialog box.

3. Click the Navigator tab if it is not already selected.

4. Enter the address of the home page in the Location text box.

5. Make sure the Navigator Starts With option is set to Home Page.

6. Click OK.

FIGURE 44.1 Changing the home page in Internet Explorer

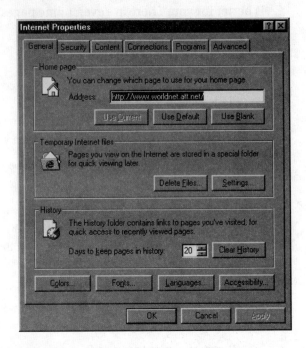

Sites and Features

In your search for the perfect home page, start by taking a look at the home pages for some of the nationwide ISPs, such as www.aol.com, www.att.net, and www.compuserve.com.

The AOL home page offers links to categories it calls Web Centers. Click the link for the category that interests you and then continue browsing.

The CompuServe home page offers links to categories, as well as links to top news stories, stock prices, weather, and sport scores.

NOTE Click Main Menu under the Member Benefits section to get to a special area for CompuServe members only. You'll have to enter your CompuServe user number and password.

You should also consider www.netscape.com. The site is not just about Netscape the company—it offers a series of links by category, called Channels, as well as the top news stories, stock quotes, weather, business news, shopping sites, and Web tools.

Next, look at the home pages of these popular search engines:

◆ www.lycos.com

◆ www.yahoo.com

◆ www.snap.com

All of these sites provide a great starting point for browsing because they offer a variety of links to popular topics and services. In fact, their categories are almost identical, and much like the ones shown for Netscape. There are still enough differences among them that you should take your time to explore each one. You never know what special feature you'll find.

Why do these sites offer so many features? The answer, as I am sure you have heard before, is advertising. The more hits the site gets, the more advertising revenue it can generate—sort of like free television. So it pays for a site to offer as many freebies and other enticements as possible.

There's so much possible revenue involved that there are sites that exist just to be homepages, such as www.homepageware.com.

When you log onto this site, you get a menu of current news links, as well as free and not-so-free offers, as shown in Figure 44.2. While most of the "free" offers are just that, you can't take all of the "free" offers too literally. Several links lead to sites and offers where some money is involved. The offers change periodically, so it pays to check back with Homepageware.com regularly.

Creating a Custom Home Page on Excite

A number of the home page sites let you customize them to match your interests and tastes. They do so by letting you select options to display or by indicating your local area or other personal information. They then store the information as a cookie on your computer, and access the cookie when you log on to the site.

An example of this is www.excite.com. Excite is one of the most popular search engines, and its home page offers a wide variety of links and services.

FIGURE 44.2 Homepageware's home page

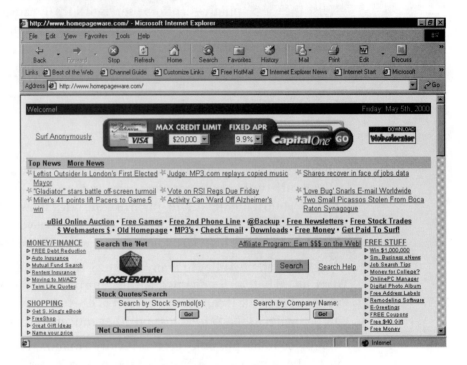

Most of the areas are labeled My, such as My Weather, My Stocks, My Sports, My Services, My Horoscope.

With My Horoscope, for example, you are prompted to enter your birthday, and then click Get My Horoscope. Excite adds the birth date to your cookie, so each time you log on, you get your personal horoscope.

For My Weather, you enter your zip code to get local weather conditions. For My Sports, My Stocks, and My Services, along with free e-mail and other features, you have to sign up with Excite, but membership is FREE.

Click the link Sign up at the top of their home page, then follow the on-screen instructions. You'll be asked to choose a user name and password and to enter your e-mail address, birth date, and zip code. Once you enter them, you'll be welcomed personally whenever you log on, you'll get local weather and your horoscope each time you connect to the site, and you will be able to change My Sports and My Stocks.

To customize your Excite home page, click the link Page Settings at the top of the page. You can then choose from these options:

◆ Select Content lets you select the information that appears in each section of your start page.

◆ Move Content lets you determine the number of columns and where information appears on the page.

◆ Change Colors lets you pick a color scheme for the page.

◆ Your Greeting lets you change the welcome message that appears on the top of your start page.

◆ Password lets your password protect access to your page.

◆ Time Zones lets you select the time zone and choose either a 12- or 24-hour clock.

◆ Refresh Rate lets you determine how frequently the information on your page is updated, with options from every 5 minutes to every hour, or no refresh at all.

◆ Member Services lets you review the benefits of Excite membership.

Excite isn't the only service that offers a personal home page. AT&T WorldNet, Netscape, Yahoo!, and many others let you create custom home pages once you sign on or become members.

Surfing the EZ Way

As another alternative to a home page, you can run the EZSurfer2000 Portal that you'll find at www.ezsurfer.net. The program makes its site your home page.

The program actually installs most of the graphic elements of the home page on your hard disk. When you launch your browser, Windows connects to your ISP, quickly loads most of the home page from your disk, and then downloads any new EZSurfer features from its Web site, www.ezsurfer.net.

Just click any of the topics shown in the EZSurfer screen to get information or navigate to other locations.

45 Browsing Offline

After you wait for a site to come onto your screen, it is really a shame to keep your phone tied up while you read it. The solution is to read the Web page after you've hung up the phone; this is called offline browsing.

Freeing Up Your Phone Line

One way to read a Web page offline is to print a copy of it and then read it after you've disconnected. The only problem is that you can waste a lot of paper and time printing. That's when you download the site. You can then read the Web site even after you've disconnected from the Internet.

Here's What You Need

You need a free or inexpensive program you can download from the Internet or find on the CD with this book.

Sites and Features

Downloading the site lets you view it in your browser when you are offline, exactly as it appears when you are online. You can also use programs that let you download more than one level of information. Each level represents the pages that the links on the original page would display. When you disconnect, you can then browse though the site offline.

Before we look at the programs that can perform this magic, let's look at how you use your Web browser offline.

The quickest way to read a Web page offline is to display it when you are online and select File➤Save As. In the dialog box that appears, set the location where you want the file stored on your disk—the desktop is the easiest place to access it—and click OK.

When you are ready to read the page offline, just find the Web page file using Windows Explorer or use the My Computer icon on the desktop. Double-click the page to open it in the browser, which will remain offline.

You can also start your browser but cancel the connection so it does not dial in. The last downloaded copy of your home page might appear, or some message will appear saying that the site cannot be displayed. Next, choose Open from the File menu. In the box that appears, click Browse and locate the Web page you want to open. Double-click it to open it in the browser window.

NOTE Using the Save As command only gets the information that you see on the screen. There are often files associated with the Web site that you'd need on your disk to view the site offline exactly as it appears online.

The Programs

There are hundreds of programs that can download Web sites for offline browsing. We were fortunate enough to get four for inclusion on the CD—SurfSaver, Zip Up The Web, Leech, and BlackWidow. For other programs, go to any of the software collections and search for the word "download."

NOTE The BlackWidow program is described in this book's Introduction as part of the Internet Tool Pack.

SurfSaver This is one great program. With SurfSaver, you can choose to download an entire site for offline browsing, including all of its graphics and multiple levels of linked pages. You can download it from www.surfsaver.com.

After you install SurfSaver, when you find a site you are interested in, right-click it to see these options in the shortcut menu:

♦ SurfSaver Save

♦ SurfSaver Quick Save

♦ SurfSaver Search

Choose SurfSaver Quick Save if you just want to save the current page, without any linked pages, to a default folder maintained by the program. You can later view the page with the SurfSaver Search option.

Choosing SurfSaver Save, however, opens the dialog box in Figure 45.1. Use the options on the left of the dialog box to select the folder where you want to store the page offline. Two folders are provided by default—Archive and askSam—but you can use the buttons under the title bar to create and organize additional folders.

FIGURE 45.1 SurfSaver

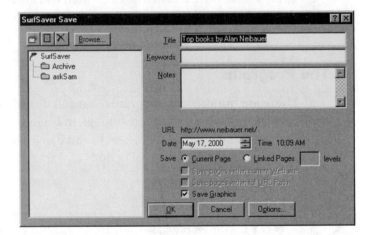

Use the Save options on the right to save just the displayed page or linked pages up to a specified level, and if you want to save the graphics displayed on the page. If you choose to save linked pages you can also select from these options:

Save pages within current Web site Saves pages just in the current domain

Save pages within full URL path Saves pages which are in or under the current URL path but not in the root domain.

When you want to view a saved site offline, start your Web browser but do not connect to the Internet. Right-click within the browser window and choose SurfSaver Search. In the SurfSaver Search dialog box that appears, you can search for a site using keywords, the title, a full text search, or by the date the site was saved. You can also click List All to display all of the sites you saved in a window as shown in Figure 45.2. Just click the site in the list at the bottom of the window to view it on the top.

FIGURE 45.2 Browsing offline with SurfSaver

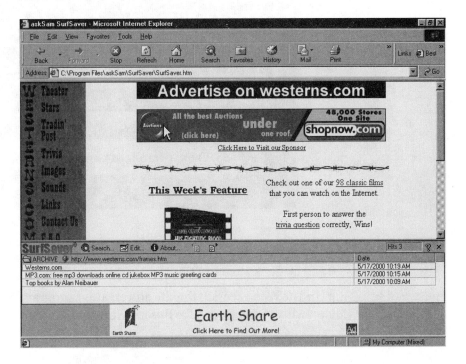

 Zip Up The Web This handy program doesn't let you download levels of a site, but it is easy to use and very kind to your disk space. Zip Up The Web, which you'll find on the CD, or which you can download from www.zipuptheweb.com, saves a copy of the selected site as a compressed, self-executing program on your disk.

When you start Zip Up The Web, it dials your ISP and launches your Web browser. (The first time you start the program you have to go through the free registration process.) You'll then see the dialog box shown in Figure 45.3.

Then follow these steps:

1. Enter the address of the site you want to download in the first text box.

2. Enter the location and name of the resulting files on the second text box.

FIGURE 45.3 Zip Up The Web

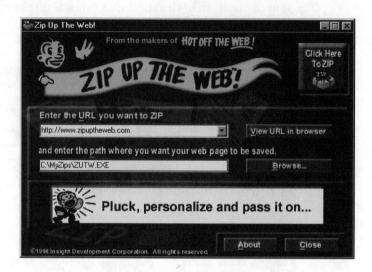

3. Click View URL in Browser if you need to confirm the site.

4. Click Click Here to ZIP.

Zip Up The Web accesses the site and creates a program file in the My Zips folder, which will appear like this in Windows Explorer:

The file contains all of the text and graphics of the Web site, but it is compressed to take up as little disk space as possible. Because the file is actually an executable program, just double-click the file to display it in your Web browser.

Leech

The program Leech takes another approach to offline browsing. You can download it from `www.aeria.com/products/ leech/leech.htm`. The Leech window with a downloaded site is shown in Figure 45.4.

FIGURE 45.4 Leech

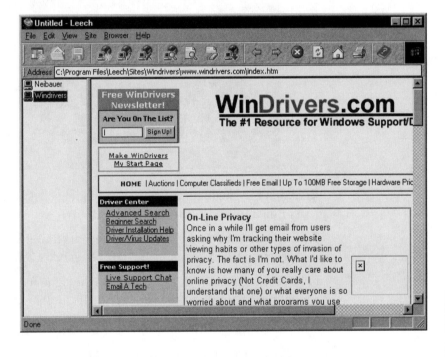

To download a Web site, follow these steps:

1. Select New from the Site menu, or click the New Site button.

2. In the box that appears, enter the URL of the site you want to download, give the site a name, and click OK.

3. Click the icon on the left that represents the site and then choose Leech from the Site menu or click the Leech button. The program connects to the Internet and downloads the site, showing its progress in a box such as this:

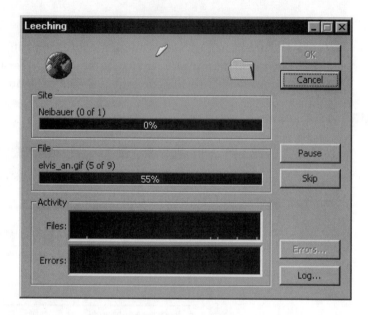

4. When the site is completely downloaded, click OK. You can now disconnect from the Internet.

5. Click the icon on the left that represents the site and then choose View from the Site menu and click Leeched Content.

You'll see the site in the large window on the right, just as if you were viewing it online in your Web browser. In fact, the toolbar in the Leech window, shown here, also contains browser buttons to surf the Web.

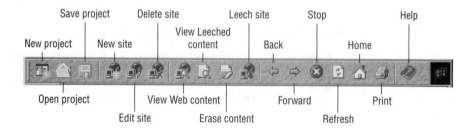

Leech organizes downloaded files in projects. A project is the collection of sites shown on the left of the Leech window. Rather than list every site that downloads at one time, for example, you can group the sites into projects. Use the New project, Open project, and Save project buttons to work with your project files. Whenever you want to view one of the sites offline, start Leech, open the project containing the site, click the site on the left, and then click the View Leeched content button.

All of the Leeched sites are stored in the `/Program Files/Leech/Sites` folder. You can always access a Leeched site directly from its folder on your disk.

46 Staying Alive and Online

Most ISPs won't let you keep the line tied up for extended periods when you're not doing anything online. After some set number of minutes of inactivity—no browsing on your part—your ISP may disconnect you, or flash an on-screen message letting you know that you'll be disconnected in so many seconds.

Don't Let Your ISP Cut You Off

You may be called away from your computer while online, or just get preoccupied doing something else. If you have to stay online during periods of inactivity, then here are some solutions.

Here's What You Need

You need your Web browser and Connection Keeper.

Sites and Features

While some users may consider this an annoyance, it is actually a very considerate policy to other users who are trying to get online. With unlimited service, it would be tempting for a user to stay online all day so they wouldn't have to encounter a busy signal. This practice just causes busy signals for others.

NOTE While programs that keep your connection alive are handy, be considerate of other users and disconnect if you'll be idle for any length of time.

With that said, if you have to go away from your computer for a short time, and you need to remain online, there are plenty of programs to help you. These programs work by either pinging your ISP at regular intervals, or by sending requests for nonexistent or random Web sites. Your ISP thinks you're online and doesn't start the disconnect clock.

Connection Keeper

You'll find one such program, Connection Keeper, which you can download from www.gammadyne.com, is shown in Figure 46.1.

Before you walk away from your computer, or fall asleep online, just start the program. It works in the background, sending queries for Web sites at either random or regular intervals that you control from the Query Interval list.

You can choose to have it ask for a nonexistent site or for random sites from a built-in list. Use the Sites tab to review the list or to add others. If you choose random sites, you can also select from these options:

Read Entire Page Downloads the entire page from the random Web site. With this option turned off, the site is just opened and closed but is not actually downloaded.

Report Errors Displays an on-screen message if an error occurs when a random site is being called.

Max Query Time Is the time the program waits for a query to be completed.

FIGURE 46.1 Staying alive online with the Connection Keeper

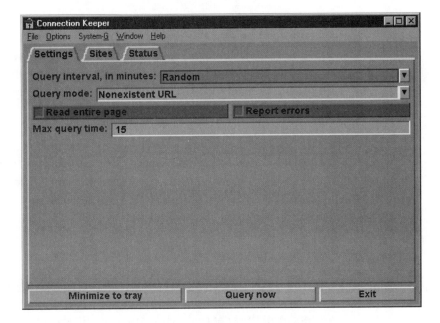

If your ISP still disconnects you with Connection Keeper running, reduce the Query interval time, or click the Status tab and turn on the Auto-Reconnect option. With this option on, Connection Keeper will redial your ISP when you are disconnected.

Some other programs that will keep your connection alive are Stay Alive from www.tfi-technology.com and Auto-IP Publisher from www.lakefield.net/~smiller/autoip.

47 Trace Your Steps

Where does your computer go to get to that Web site? Your signals bounce around from computer to computer to bring it to you. Find out where your computer has gone!

Follow the Computer's Route

When you travel from your house to Grandma's, or to any other place for that matter, you make a lot of stops and turns along the way. So does your computer when you send it off to fetch a Web site. The Internet is really a whole bunch of computers linked together, so you can track down the route your computer takes to get from one point to another.

Here's What You Need

 All you need is your Web browser and free programs that come with Windows. For even more features, use TJPing or Ping Plotter, both of which are included on the CD with this book. You may also download other shareware programs.

You also need to know a little about the way information is transported around the Internet.

Information is transmitted through the Internet in packets of data. The packets travel through a series of computers called Internet Protocol (IP) routers until they get to their destination. Every computer is connected to the Internet, and so every Web site has an IP address. The address is a series of numbers, something like 135.145.64.39, that uniquely identifies it. Your own computer has an IP address as well.

Tracing programs work by sending several small packets of information called echo records, or pings, through the Internet. The ping includes a Time To Live (TTL) number. Each site that handles the message is supposed to decrease the TTL number by 1 before sending it on to the next site. When the TTL gets to 0, the site sends back a signal to the source that includes its IP address, and the time the round trip took as measured and displayed in milliseconds (1/1000 of a second). The lower the time, the better your connection.

The first ping the trace program sends includes a TTL number of 1. When the message gets to the first router, it subtracts 1 from it, sees that the number is now 0, and sends back a response. Your computer then sends another packet with a TTL of 2. This packet gets as far as the second router, which sends back a response with its IP address and time.

The pings continue until they are received and returned by the destination you specified. The TTL used to reach that site represents the number of "hops" the route takes. The round trip time (RTT) to this site is the actual time to the Web site.

By reporting each of the IP addresses that receives the pings, you get a complete picture of the route taken through the Internet.

Programs that send pings through the Internet will not wait forever for a response, so they have a time-out time. A time out means that after so many seconds the program gives up and stops.

Sites and Features

To get to a Web site, your browser has to hop from computer to computer until it reaches its destination so it can display it on your screen.

It's interesting to see the route your computer takes to get to a Web site. The number of stops it makes along the way and the places it goes might amaze you. But more than that, tracing the route can show you where some bottlenecks occur.

Ping and Tracert—Free with Windows

Windows comes with two free programs for tracking the route to any Web site: Ping and Tracert. You run these programs from the DOS command line rather than from a window, but they are easy to use.

The Ping program sends four pings to the Web site you specify so you can compare the response time for each. To use Ping, follow these steps.

1. Select Start➤Programs➤ MS-DOS Prompt to open a DOS window.

2. Type ping, then a space, and enter the name of the Web site you want to go to. The command would appear like this: `ping www.att.net`.

3. Press Enter.

The program will dial into your ISP, if you are not already connected, send pings to the site specified, and display the results. (See Figure 47.1, from my computer to `www.att.net`, my ISP.)

FIGURE 47.1 Pinging a Web site

The Tracert command sends out three packets and measures the time it takes to get to each IP address along the way. To use Tracert follow these steps:

1. Select Start➣ Programs➣ MS-DOS Prompt to open a DOS window.

2. Type tracert, then a space, and enter the name of the Web site you want to go to. The command would appear like this: `tracert www.sybex.com`.

3. Press Enter.

The program will dial into your ISP, if you are not already connected, and send pings to trace the route. Figure 47.2 shows the trace from my computer to `www.sybex.com`. It shows the time it takes for each of the three packets, and the name and IP address of each stop.

NOTE To make Tracert go faster, add –d after the command so the name of each site is not reported, just the IP address.

FIGURE 47.2 Tracing the route to Sybex

```
MS-DOS Prompt                                              _ □ X
Auto          □ 📋 📋 🔲 📋 🖨 A

C:\WINDOWS>tracert www.sybex.com

Tracing route to www.sybex.com [206.100.29.83]
over a maximum of 30 hops:

  1    152 ms    142 ms    177 ms  199.70.67.39
  2    168 ms    155 ms    160 ms  1.philadelphia-06-07rs.pa.dial-access.att.net [1
2.78.210.1]
  3    261 ms    193 ms    169 ms  199.70.127.21
  4    195 ms    163 ms    200 ms  br2-a350s6.n54ny.ip.att.net [12.127.11.101]
  5    149 ms    193 ms    185 ms  gr1-a3100s1.n54ny.ip.att.net [192.205.31.245]
  6    148 ms    180 ms    152 ms  204.70.10.146
  7    271 ms    235 ms    268 ms  corerouter1.SanFrancisco.cw.net [204.70.9.131]
  8    226 ms    238 ms    301 ms  core2.SanFrancisco.cw.net [204.70.4.201]
  9    252 ms    243 ms    262 ms  border7-fddi-0.SanFrancisco.cw.net [204.70.158.5
1]
 10    298 ms    269 ms    358 ms  wlinet-sf.SanFrancisco.cw.net [204.70.161.70]
 11  wlinet-sf.SanFrancisco.cw.net [204.70.161.70]  reports: Destination net unr
eachable.

Trace complete.

C:\WINDOWS>
```

Running TJPing

Rather than work with the DOS command prompt, you can use the freeware program TJPing to trace a route and more. You can download it from www.topjimmy.net/tjs.

TJPing provides several useful functions:

PING Sends a signal to let you know whether the site is valid and can be reached. It also tells you the RTT and the TTL—the time of the round trip and the number of hops.

TRACE Traces the route the IP packets take to get to the site.

LOOKUP Finds the site's name if you enter its IP address, and vice versa.

Start the program to see the window in Figure 47.3. Type the name of the site or its IP address, and click the function you want to perform.

By default, the trace option shows the IP address and round trip time, but not the name of each router.

To display the names, and set other options, click the Set Options button to open the Options dialog box. If you want to display the site name along

FIGURE 47.3 TJPing

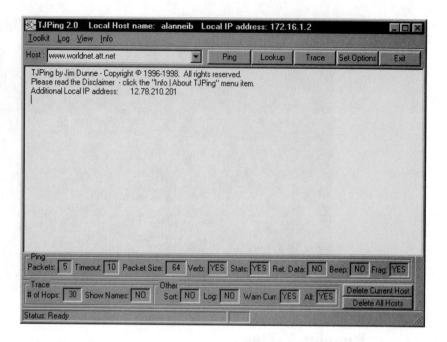

with its IP address when tracing, turn on the Show DNS Names check box. You can change the number of packets sent with a ping, the time-out period, and other options.

Plotting with Ping Plotter

Another tracer program is Ping Plotter, which you can download from www.nessoft.com/pingplotter.

To speed up the tracing, Ping Plotter actually sends out packets to the first 35 servers in the route—all at the same time. Ping Plotter, with a trace to my ISP, is shown in Figure 47.4. It not only shows the IP address and name of each router, but it also shows the average and current times of the pings in a timeline graph next to the hop list, and in a graph of time along the bottom. The program continues to run, updating the times until you click Stop so you can monitor the speed of your connection over a period of time.

FIGURE 47.4 Ping Plotter

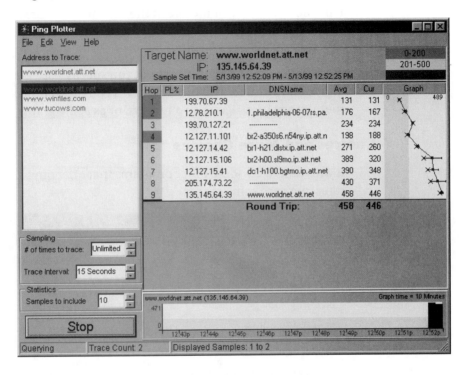

You can customize what appears on the timeline chart, adding the minimum and maximum times, by right-clicking the chart and choosing options from this menu:

You can also right-click the chart at the bottom of the window to select other time periods, ranging from 1 minute to 24 hours.

Graphing with Neotrace

For the most graphic picture of the Web, run Neotrace. This program shows the route traveled, using icons to indicate the type of site at each spot. If the destination of a particular path is a site in Germany, a German flag is used to denote the type of site or its location.

You can download Neotrace from www.neoworx.com. Start the program, type the IP or name of the site in the Host to Trace box, and then click the Trace button on the toolbar along the left of the window.

A newer version of Neotrace is being developed that shows the route on a map. When you install this version, you specify your zip code or your longitude and latitude. The program gives you the option of displaying the route as a map, as icons, in a text list, or as a line graph.

Choices and More Choices

If you want to try some other programs that offer ping and trace route features, here are some more:

Program	Download Site
DeEnesse	www.cyberspacehq.com/deenesse
net demon	www.netdemon.net
NetScan Tools	www.nwpsw.com
Network Toolbox	www.jriver.com/index.html
Sam Spade	samspade.org
CyberKit	www.cyberkit.net

48 Cover Your Steps

Big brother is watching! As you surf the Net, someone may be keeping track of the sites that you visit. It may be your ISP, your employer, or your organization. But whoever it is, they may have a complete record of the places you surf.

Keeping Your Path Private

It is no fun being watched. Even if you don't visit any "questionable" Web sites, you may want to keep your path hidden from prying eyes.

Fortunately, there are ways to prevent the Internet snoops from following you around the Net.

Here's What You Need

All you need is a handy program called PrivateSurfer that you can download from www.cdrsoft.com. The program works in conjunction with the PrivateSurfer Web site to act as a proxy server. It intercepts and encrypts your Web requests so your ISP only sees a request to the PrivateSurfer Web site.

The trial version of the program on the CD works for 30 days.

Sites and Features

Using PrivateSurfer couldn't be any easier. Just install and run the program to automatically start its secure mode feature. Secure mode encrypts all of your browsing activity to hide it from the prying eyes of your ISP or system administrator. You can always turn off secure mode by right-clicking the PrivateSurfer icon in the system tray and choosing Non-Secure Web Traffic. Choose Secure Web Traffic from the same menu to return to secure mode.

To see what information is being passed on to your ISP, select Network Snoop from the PrivateSurfer icon to open the box shown here:

Pull down the Snoop on list and select what you want to display in the box:

Request From Browser   Shows the actual request your browser is making to access a Web site.

Request from Internet   Shows the encrypted request that will be seen by your ISP.

Reply to Browser   Shows the information being sent to your browser to be displayed.

Reply from the Internet   Shows the encrypted information that will be seen by your ISP.

N O T E   For a Web-based solution to safe surfing, try `www.anonymizer.com/3.0/index.shtml`.

49   Busting Those Ads

You're looking at Tripod.com or some other site, and a second window pops up on your screen with an advertising message. You click its Close button to remove it, but before you blink another pops up in its place. They appear almost as fast as you can close them.

Kill Those Pop-Up Windows and Annoying Ads

So much of the stuff on the Internet is free because advertising supports it. You pay for those free Web sites by being subjected to windows that pop up with advertising. Pop-up windows are getting to be about everywhere, but you can strike back!

Here's What You Need

You need your Web browser and a free or inexpensive program you can get from the CD or download from the Internet.

Sites and Features

Internet advertising is probably here to stay, just the same as commercials on television. With a TV, you can turn down the sound, run to the kitchen for a snack, or change the channel. But what can you do if the pop-up windows and other Internet ads get to you?

Plenty!

There are programs that are designed to keep these annoying ads from annoying you.

KillAd

If you want to get rid of the pop-up windows while you're browsing, try KillAd. This program monitors your browser for extraneous windows and closes them. You can download it from `www.wplus.net/pp/fsc`.

KillAd places an icon on your system tray. Double-click the icon to toggle the function on and off. It is off when the icon appears dimmed. When KillAd is turned on, each time a pop-up appears, it quickly disappears—if you blink you'll miss it altogether. You can also hold down the CTRL key to temporarily disable the program. Right-click the icon for this menu:

Select Watch to toggle the program on and off. Use the Play Sound option to control the sound played when a pop-up window is closed.

The default action that KillAd takes on windows depends on its settings. Select Terminator Mode, however, to kill all pop-ups regardless of the settings. To see how the program is set up, and to customize it, select Advanced Options from the shortcut menu. You'll see the dialog box in Figure 49.1.

FIGURE 49.1   **KillAd options**

When the Hide option is not checked, pop-up windows are moved to the background rather than closed. Enable Hide to completely remove the windows from your screen and from the Windows Taskbar.

The Wait for caption change option tells KillAd not to close the window until its title bar is complete.

Turn on the Kill listed pop-ups only option if you only want to close windows maintained in the list. If you turn this option off, KillAd considers a pop-up to be any browser window that opens in addition to the main browser window. Turning off this option may cause problems if you're using links that are supposed to open a second or third window.

To change the list of sites, click Edit list. A Notepad window appears in which you can delete, edit, or add sites.

The Skip maximized browser windows option is useful when you do not want to close windows to linked sites. If you are running with your browser maximized and it opens another window, this window will also be maximized. Choosing the Skip maximized browser windows option prevents KillAd from automatically closing the new maximized window that appears.

Use the Kill every browser window smaller than option and the Don't kill browser windows bigger than option to fine-tune which browser windows are closed. The three buttons next to the size boxes perform these functions:

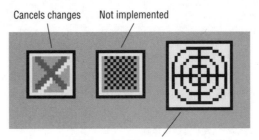

When a pop-up window appears, it is often given the keyboard focus. This means that any keys you press affect the pop-up window, not the original window you were viewing when the pop-up appeared. Use the options in the Restore focus section to prevent this. When set at Online (once), the focus is restored to your original window as soon as the pop-up appears. When set at Offline (always), the focus is restored each time the pop-up tries to take the keyboard focus.

The Enabled browsers section determines which Web browsers the program monitors. The Pre-kill extra delay option lets you delay the closing of a pop-up window. Increase this setting if KillAd causes errors.

Rather than edit the URL list from the Advanced Options box, you can add a pop-up to the list by dragging it. When the pop-up appears the first time, right-click it and choose Add Pop-up to see this dialog box:

Select the list you want to add the pop-up to—Kill list or Don't kill list—then drag the Finder Tool to the pop-up window, release the mouse button, and click Add.

To quickly see how many ads the program saved you from watching, point to the icon in the system tray. A box appears showing the number of windows killed, ignored, and being watched. For more information, choose Show Statistics from the shortcut menu to see a box such as this:

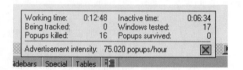

This box reports the amount of time you've had the program running and inactive, as well as the number of pop-ups per hour for your Internet session.

CrushPop 2000

CrushPop 2000 is another useful program that prevents pop-up windows of all types from appearing. You'll find a copy of the program on the CD, or you can download it from megasolutions.hypermart.net.

Right-click the CrushPop 2000 icon on the desktop to access these options and make sure that the Enable Crushing option is selected:

When a pop-up window appears, it will be removed from the screen. To see a list of all of the pop-ups and windows that were open when CrushPop 2000 was running, select Manage Pop-ups to open the window shown in Figure 49.2. To ensure that a pop-up listed in the Crushable Windows list is removed, select it and click the Crush button to add the window to the Crushing List.

FIGURE 49.2 CrushPop 2000

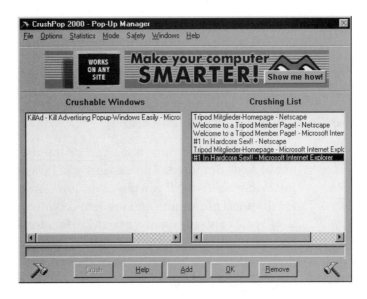

If you want CrushPop to remove just selected windows, select Control by Crushable Window List from the Mode menu. The program will now just automatically crush windows that you've added to the Crushing List.

CrushPop 2000 is a comprehensive program with a wide range of options. For example, select Use Authorization Checking from the Options menu to require a password to run the program.

50 Share Your Phone Line

If your computers are networked, more than one person in the house can use the phone line to surf the Internet on the same Internet account with only one modem. The software may even be free, depending on your version of Windows.

Don't Wait Till the Line Is Free

Just consider the benefits. With one phone line and one modem, everyone on your home network can access the Internet at the same time, browse different locations, download files, and send and receive e-mail. You don't need a second phone line or a second ISP account.

Here's What You Need

You'll need at least one phone line, one Internet account, and two or more networked computers. The network can be a peer-to-peer network using just Windows 95/98. If you have Windows 98 Second Edition, the software for sharing a phone line and modem is built-in. If you have an earlier version, you can get inexpensive software for modem sharing—there are even two such programs on the CD with this book.

Sites and Features

To share a phone line and modem you have to be networked, which in itself involves some money. But network "starter kits" that let you connect two computers cost less than just one month of a second phone line and second Internet account. So once you are networked, you get to enjoy the benefit of sharing a phone and modem all year around.

The computer that contains the modem that you'll be sharing is called the host. The other computers on the network that will be using that modem are called the clients.

Now, in addition to being networked, to share a modem you need the following things:

◆ You need to set up something called TCP/IP on your computer, but it is included with Windows.

◆ You need Internet sharing software, which is included in Windows 98 Second Edition.

◆ You need to install the software and make some minor adjustments to your Internet browser.

Setting Up the Host Computer

If you are networked, chances are TCP/IP is already on your computer. So let's start by checking to make sure it is there.

1. Select Start➤Settings➤Control Panel➤Network, and Configuration tab, if it is not already displayed.

2. If you see a listing in the list box for TCP/IP followed by the name of your network card, click Cancel. Otherwise, install TCP\IP by following these steps.

    1. Click Add, then select Protocol in the box that appears.

    2. Click Add in that dialog box. You'll see a list of hardware manufacturers on the left and protocols on the right.

    3. Choose Microsoft from the list on the left, and choose TCP/IP from the list on the right.

    4. Click OK twice, and then select Yes to restart your computer.

Next, if you have Windows 98 Second Edition, you can set up Internet sharing without any additional software. You do have to install Internet Connection Sharing, however, because it is not installed automatically with Windows 98. Just follow these steps on the host computer. (You do not have to install Internet Connection Sharing on the client computers.)

1. Insert the Windows 98 Second Edition CD in your CD drive.

2. Select Start➤ Settings➤ Control Panel➤Add/Remove Programs in the Windows Control Panel and click the Windows Setup tab.

3. Select Internet Tools and then click the Details button to see a list of the items in the Internet Tools category.

4. In the Components box, turn on the Internet Connection Sharing check box and click OK twice. Windows installs the feature and then starts up the Internet Connection Sharing Wizard.

5. Read and follow the instructions in the Wizard dialog boxes, clicking Next after each. At one point, you'll be asked to insert a disk in your floppy disk drive so Windows can create a program to configure the client computers for sharing.

6. Click Finish at the final Wizard dialog box, and then select Yes to restart your computer.

Setting Up Client Computers

That's all you need to do to the host computer. The next steps involve the clients. You should set up TCP\IP on each of the clients so they get their IP address automatically.

Follow these steps on each of the client computers:

1. Select Start➤Settings➤Control Panel➤Network.

2. Select the TCP/IP listing for your network card and click the Properties button.

3. Click the IP Address tab and select the option Obtain an IP Address Automatically.

4. Click the WINS Configuration tab, and confirm that the Use DHCP for WINS Resolution option is selected.

5. Click the Gateway tab, and confirm that the Installed Gateways list is empty.

6. Click the DNS Configuration tab, and select the Disable DNS option.

7. Click OK three times, and then select Yes to restart your computer.

The client computers are now set up for TCP/IP. The final step is to set their Internet browsers to connect over the network rather than dialing in. That's the purpose of the floppy disk you made on the host computer with Internet Connection Sharing.

1. Start the host computer and use it to connect to the Internet.

2. Insert the disk into the floppy drive and run the program Icsclset.exe on that disk to start the Browser Connection Setup Wizard.

3. Click Next until the last Wizard box appears and then click Finish.

You're now ready. As long as the host computer is turned on, any of the client computers on the network can connect to the Internet. If the host is already connected, the other computers just connect without having to dial in. If the host is not connected to the Internet, a client computer will actually dial in through the modem on the host to initiate the network's connection.

WinGate and RideWay

You can still share a phone line and modem if you do not have Windows 98 Second Edition. There are lots of programs, most of them shareware, which can provide the same features as Microsoft's Internet Connection Sharing feature. The CD with this book includes two such programs, WinGate and RideWay.

You install WinGate on all of the computers on the network. The first dialog box of the installation program asks whether you are setting up a WinGate Server (another name for a host) or a WinGate Internet Client. Choose the WinGate Server option on the computer you want to use as the host, and choose the Client option on the other computers.

The version of WinGate on the CD is a 30-day trial version for use by up to six computers at one time. When you install the program, you'll be asked for a license name and license key.

For the license name, enter Sybex. Enter it exactly as spelled, with the uppercase S, and remaining letters lowercase.

For the license key, enter the following exactly as it is shown:

AA6285939E998D1AA35A2B66

For more information about using WinGate, check out the program's help system, or go to www.wingate.com on the Internet.

To use the RideWay program, install it only on the computer you're using as the server, making a note of the server's IP address. On the client computers, you need to go to the Control Panel, open Network, and then double-click the listing for TCP/IP followed by your network card. On the DNS Configuration tab of the dialog box, enter the IP address of the server at the DNS Server Search Order text box. Finally, you have to set up your Web browser to access the Internet through the network. You'll find detailed instructions for doing this with the RideWay program, or at www.itserv.com.

51 Safety in Surfing

Once you start networking and sharing computers, you open yourself up to a whole can of worms, bugs, and viruses. You never know who, or what, is lurking out there, so surf safe and stay secure.

Don't Wait till It's Too Late

Take some preventive steps now before you run into those denizens of the Internet dark world. Spending a few minutes, and maybe dollars, in advance can save you hours and lots of dollars later on.

Here's What You Need

You will need to use the security settings built into your Web browser, or a program that provides additional levels of Internet security. The security features of your browser are a good place to start, but they are limited. As an alternative, consider downloading or purchasing a more complete security solution. You'll find one such program, Lockdown 2000, on the CD with this book.

You might also want to prevent other users of your computer from accessing your ISP account. Rather than have to enter your ISP password every time you connect, however, you can use a nifty little piece of hardware that you'll learn about soon.

Sites and Features

The first place to start is by looking at the security features built into your Web browser. With Microsoft Internet Explorer, for example, right-click the Internet Explorer icon on your desktop and choose properties, or open Internet Options in the Windows Control Panel. Click the Security tab to see the options shown in Figure 51.1.

FIGURE 51.1 Setting security in Internet Explorer

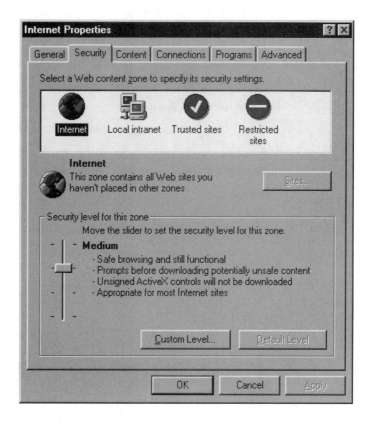

At the top of the box are icons representing four zones:

Internet   Determines security setting for all sites not in another zone

Local Intranet   Determines security settings for Web pages on your network

Trusted Sites   Determines security setting for Web sites that you know are safe to surf

Restricted Sites   Determines security settings for Web sites that you do not trust

The general technique is to select a zone and then drag the slider in the Security level for this zone section to the level of security that you want. Moving it up to the top sets security to High. This provides the most security Internet Explorer offers, but many Web sites may not display properly at this setting.

It is usually recommended that you leave the setting for the Internet zone at Medium, the Trusted zone at low, and the Restricted zones at high.

If there is a Web site that you know to be safe, for example, add it to the Trusted zone by following these steps:

1. Click Trusted Sites.

2. Click the Sites button.

3. In the box that appears, type the address of the trusted site and click Add.

To add a potentially hazardous site to the Restricted Sites zone, follow these steps:

1. Click Restricted Sites

2. Click the Sites button.

3. In the box that appears, type the address of the trusted site and click Add.

Security Software

For greater levels of security, however, consider a separate program. One program to consider is the Norton Internet Security Suite, a set of programs designed to prevent security problems. You can learn more about the program at www.symantec.com.

Another excellent alternative is to download the free program ZoneAlarm, from www.zonelabs.com. ZoneAlarm denies access to your computer by hackers on the Internet as well as by others on the network and prevents Web sites from obtaining information about you through requests to your system. It also controls which applications on your computer can access the Internet, preventing programs known as Trojan horses from accessing rogue Web sites without your permission. You can also turn on an Internet Lock that automatically prevents access to the Internet after periods of inactivity.

You'll find a copy of another security program, Lockdown 2000 on the CD with this book, or you can download it from lockdown2000.com. Shown in Figure 51.2, the program scans your computer for Trojan horses, lets you control access to your computer from other Internet and network users, and has the TraceRoute and Whois features built in.

FIGURE 51.2 Lockdown 2000

Access Approved, Mr. Bond

Finally, if you share your computer with other users, you may want to prevent them from accessing your Internet account or Web sites that require you to enter a user name and password. One way to prevent access is to not have your passwords maintained on the computer. The only problem is, you'll need to enter your password each time you connect to the Internet or try to log on to a members-only site. This may not be too inconvenient, if your passwords are easy to remember, but some ISPs and sites use a strange mix of letters and numbers that are not easy to remember and enter.

The solution is a little device that comes right out of science fiction or the latest spy thriller—the U.are.U Fingerprint Recognition System (www.digitalpersona.com). I just love this thing. In fact, even if you don't care about security at all, this is a great device to have on your office desk. Just watch your coworkers' faces as you use it.

U.are.U is a small device that plugs into your computer's USB port and that contains a small scanner just the size of your fingertip. You easily program the device to recognize any or all of your fingerprints, as shown in Figure 51.3.

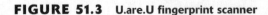

FIGURE 51.3 U.are.U fingerprint scanner

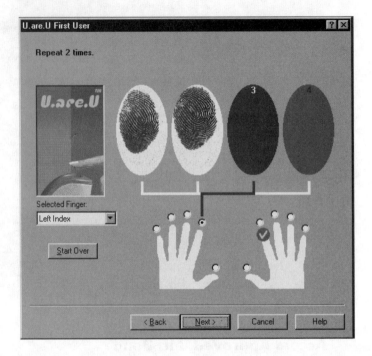

You then configure the device so your fingerprint is required to start your computer in place of typing a password. When you try to log on to the Internet, for example, a message appears telling you to put your finger on the U.are.U sensor. The sensor scans your fingerprint and only inserts your ISP password if the scanned print matches one that you programmed into it.

You can program the device to insert a password any time when one is required. You can use it to control access to your e-mail or entry to member-only Web sites that you want to keep away from your children or others in the household or office.

Some models of U.are.U also include a feature called Private Space. Private Space is an encrypted folder on your hard drive, network server, floppy drive, or removable drive. The file can only be decrypted by your fingerprint authorization.

52 The Ultimate Upgrade

No matter what software you run or which ISP you have, your Internet speed is limited as long as you have a dial-up telephone account. There's just so much speed that you can tweak out of the phone line, and then you have to cross your fingers and hope for the best, which sometimes just isn't enough.

Broadband Internet to the Rescue

The alternative to a dial-up Internet account is broadband Internet. Broadband means some medium through which lots of information can travel at very fast speeds. As far as the Internet is concerned, broadband means either a Digital Subscriber Line (DSL) or a cable modem and ISP.

NOTE You can also sign up for an ISDN line with your phone company but it is slower and more expensive than the other alternatives.

Here's What You Need

Both DSL and cable modems must be plugged into an Ethernet network port. So to use either of these high-speed solutions you'll need some sort of Ethernet network connection on your computer.

In most cases, the company that you purchase your Internet service from can install an Ethernet network card at the same time they install and set up the modem. You'll have to pay for the service, of course. The other option is to purchase and install an Ethernet adapter yourself before getting the service. Your best bet is to purchase an Ethernet adapter that plugs directly into your computer's USB port, so you won't have to open your computer and deal with installing a card.

If you have a home network and already have Ethernet adapters, you'll need a second one on the computer where you want to install the modem. All of the computers on the network will be able to share the high-speed connection using the Internet connection sharing that you learned about in Section 50.

You'll also need a little extra money. As you will soon learn, broadband Internet accounts cost more than dial-up access, usually about twice as much. If you spend a lot of time on the Internet downloading files or viewing videos, however, the extra money may be well worth it.

Sites and Features

The two great things about broadband Internet are the speed and the fact that you are always connected.

Let's look at speed first. Regular dial-up accounts are limited to a maximum of 56 Kbps, although most connections are considerably slower. Depending on your area's telephone system, you may never connect at more than about 28 Kbps regardless of the speed of your modem. DSL connections can be anywhere from 128 Kbps to 4 Mbps, and cable modems between 500 Kbps and 20 Mbps. At these speeds, downloads that took hours over a dial-up account take just minutes, and watching videos over the Net is like watching a movie on television.

Second, with broadband Internet you are always connected to the Internet. As soon as you turn on your computer, you are connected. You do not have to dial-in and wait until you don't get a busy signal.

Sound too good to be true? Well, there are problems. Neither DSL nor cable Internet is universally available. There are lots of places that have neither service available, and it may be some time—if ever—until both are as ubiquitous as the modular telephone plug.

Still, prices for broadband Internet are coming down, and both are becoming increasingly available.

Let's take a brief look at each type of broadband Internet.

NOTE Call your local cable television provider or telephone company to find out about DSL and cable Internet availability and costs.

DSL Internet

DSL Internet uses special telephone lines and equipment, and your home must be within a certain distance, usually a few miles, of the local telephone company's facility where DSL is available.

The phone company will have to install a special telephone jack, a DSL modem, an Ethernet card (if you do not have one), and maybe some other equipment to make your phone system compatible.

Installation generally costs from $100 to $500, and the modem can cost up to $400, although many DSL companies will rent the modem to you for a monthly fee. If your local phone company offers DSL Internet, you may get a package deal for the monthly line, and ISP charges for about $40 to $50. Other companies that provide DSL connections generally charge around $40 to $50 per month just for the connection, in addition to the cost of your ISP service.

You can use the same DSL line for both the Internet and telephone calls at the same time, so you do not need two phone lines.

Cable Internet

With cable Internet, the Internet connection is made through the same coaxial cable that brings the television signal into your home. Speeds vary between 500 Kbps and 20 Mbps, although about 1 Mbps is most common.

Unlike DSL, you do not have to be within any special distance of your cable operator, but cable Internet is still not available every place that has cable television.

Installation usually costs less than $100, not including an Ethernet adapter, if you need to buy one, and the cost of the cable modem. Monthly charges are usually about $30, and you can often pay for the cable modem with a monthly rental fee.

The speed of your Internet connection depends on the number of other subscribers in your area who are online at any given time, because everyone in the neighborhood, and possibly surrounding neighborhoods, shares the same cable.

Web Sites, Free or Easy

So far, you've been dealing with Web sites as an observer. Now it is time to be more of an active participant. In this chapter, you'll learn how to work with Web sites on a different level. You'll learn how to get files from Web sites, find out who owns a site, and get free Web sites for yourself. You'll also learn how to store files in those free Web sites and how to sign up for your own personal domain—www.you.com!

53 Grab Web Site Files

Ever see a neat graphic or hear a sound file when viewing a Web site? You can download those graphics, sounds, and individual files from Web sites; it is as easy as browsing.

View and Download the Contents of Web Sites

You've already learned that you can download entire Web sites for offline viewing. Sometimes, however, you're not interested in the entire site; instead you are just interested in a graphic, sound, or other file that's on the site. Rather than bringing over the entire site for offline browsing, you can identify the individual components that make up a Web site and get only what you need.

Here's What You Need

The only things you need are your Web browser and a program that you'll find on the CD, or download from the Internet.

Sites and Features

Being able to grab selected files from a Web site means you can build up a great library of graphics, sounds, and other files that you find interesting. We'll take a look at two programs that help you do this, one of which, Web Leech, you'll find on the CD with this book. Both of these programs give you a view of a Web site much different from what you see with your browser. Rather than displaying the page as a graphic, they show the objects that are linked to the page.

As with offline browsing, you can select the number of levels of linked objects to display. You can view just the links on the site's home page or the objects that are contained on the linked pages. You can then download any object that you see listed by either clicking it or dragging it onto your desktop. Remember, most of the files you'll find on Web sites are the property of the site owners. While you can use programs to download files, you cannot use the files commercially yourself. Get permission if you want to reproduce or otherwise use a file from a Web site.

Using Link Explorer

Link Explorer lets you view Web sites in a Windows Explorer–like interface. You can download it from www.lightman.com/linkexplorer.

Using Link Explorer, you can begin downloading files from a site. While it is downloading, you can continue browsing other locations. You can also schedule a file to be downloaded at a specific time. Here's how:

1. Start Link Explorer after you install it.

2. Type the Web address of the site you want to explore and press Enter. You could also use your Web browser to locate the page and then copy and paste its address into Link Explorer. The linked objects of the site will be listed on the right of the Link Explorer window, and the folders on your computer will be listed on the left.

3. Use the folder list on the left as you would Windows Explorer. Open the folder where you'd like to place the objects you'll copy from the site.

4. Drag a file from the right side of the window to the open folder on the left. You can also click the Download button in the toolbar, and then choose a location in the dialog box that appears. The evaluation version of Link Explorer on the CD will not allow you to drag and drop multiple files or load and save lists of links.

As the file is being downloaded, you can launch your browser and surf the Web. The icons on the status bar of the Link Explorer window display your progress. From left to right, the icons report

- ◆ Number of tasks remaining to be completed.
- ◆ Number of files you've scheduled to be downloaded at a later time.
- ◆ Number of completed downloads.
- ◆ Number of failed downloads.

Double-click an icon to see details of the tasks and downloads.

NOTE A download may fail if you try to get a file from a site that requires a user name and password. You'll find this most frequently when trying to download MP3 music files.

To schedule a download for a later time, follow these steps:

1. Click the file on the right, and then choose File↘Download Later.

2. In the dialog box that appears, select the location where you want to store the file, and then click Save.

3. Double-click any of the icons in the status bar.

4. Click the clock icon in the status bar to open the Tasks window.

5. Click the Timer button to open this dialog box.

6. Set the time and date and enable the Timer active check box to start downloading.

7. Click OK.

On the other tabs of the Task Manager, you can change the order in which pending tasks are downloaded, delete tasks that are pending, open downloaded files, and retry those that failed. The Activity Log displays and reports the details of Link Explorer's actions, including why a download failed.

The Easy Search button on the Link Explorer toolbar gives you access to a multimedia search engine for MP3 and other sound files.

Pull down the top list and choose the search engine you want to use. Enter a keyword or phrase to identify the music you're looking for and then click OK. Link Explorer will locate sites containing matching files and display them on the right side. You can then attempt to download files by dragging them to a destination folder.

Using Web Leech

Web Leech is a similar program to Link Explorer, but it uses its own interface for viewing files. You can find Web Leech on the CD or download it from www.voodoo-software.com.

When you run Web Leech, you'll see a listing of the files on the Web site on the right, and files on your hard disk on the left. To download a file, select it in the list on the right, and then click the Copy button.

There is a also a new version of the program, called Web Leech 2, that has an Explorer–like interface similar to that of Link Explorer. Check out Web Leech 2 at the voodoo-software site.

54 Who Owns That Web Site?

Most Web sites have a link to send e-mail to the sponsor or Webmaster, but some don't. If you want to know who's responsible for a Web site—either because you love it or hate it—find out who is in charge.

Find Out Who Runs What

All Web site domain names (the xxxx.com moniker) must be registered with a company called InterNIC. The registration includes the name and address of the organization holding the domain, a phone number, and sometimes the names of the responsible individuals.

Here's What You Need

You'll need your browser, your ISP, and some free or inexpensive software from the CD in this book or downloaded from the Internet.

Sites and Features

InterNIC has thoughtfully provided a function called Whois that will report the basic registration information if you give it the domain name.

To access Whois, you need to navigate to a Web site that offers free domain name lookup, or you will need to use a free or shareware program, many of which can be downloaded on the Internet or can be found on the accompanying CD with this book. Whois is very simple to use—just type the domain name and let it do its thing.

Two sites on the net that offer domain name lookup are www.domainsearch.com and www.domains-registered.com/domain_name_lookup.htm. At sites like these, you enter the domain name you are looking for and choose the domain type. The domain will be looked up and you'll see the name, address, phone number, and other information about the registered owner of the domain.

There are also plenty of programs that you can get that offer the Whois feature. For example, you can download a Whois program from `www.cix.co.uk/~net-services`. Many general dial-up networking utility programs also contain the Whois function. ConnectPal, a program included on the accompanying CD, is no exception. This program is covered in more detail in Section 43.

To use the downloaded program, just type the domain name in the Host text box and click Go. Enter the domain name without the "www" prefix—just `Microsoft.com` or `Corel.com` will work. The program dials into your ISP, if you are not already online, connects to InterNIC, and reports the registered owner of the domain.

55 Free Web Sites

This is one of the best bargains of all time! More and more people are getting their own sites on the Web, so why not you? Most ISPs offer Web sites to their members, but they can be difficult to set up and use. With free Web sites, you don't even need an ISP, just access to the Internet.

Make Your Web Presence Known

Just think of it. For free, you'll have a place on the Internet to make your opinions known, and you'll also be able to share information with friends, relatives, and complete strangers. You can advertise a product, ask for information, or just have a place to learn about Web site design. What a bargain.

Here's What You Need

All you will need is access to the Internet. You can set up your own Web site from the local library or from any other place where you can connect to the Web.

Sites and Features

First of all, what distinguishes these free Web sites from the ones you can create with an ISP?

ISP	FREE
You must be a paying member.	You don't pay a thing.
You can have sophisticated, multiple page sites.	You may be limited to a set number of pages.
You can build your Web site using any Web-creation software.	You may have to use the site's program to create your Web page.
There won't be any advertisements on your site unless you put them there.	There may be advertisements on your site that you didn't put there.

Given those distinctions, free Web sites are great, even if you already have a site through your ISP. You can use these free sites for your children, or for temporary information that you want to make available. You can put personal information on the site that you would not place in your business site, or vice versa. And while some of the free sites limit you to just a few pages using their own special software, others are just as good—if not better—than most ISPs.

Just to emphasize a point, you can create a free Web site even if you do not have an Internet account. You just need access to the Internet. Once you create the site, it exists on the service's computer, so anyone with Internet access can access it. What if they want to send you e-mail? No trouble—just get a free e-mail account.

There are plenty of places where you can create a free Web site. I will discuss three sites in this section, but there are at least a thousand more, so don't feel limited to these.

Some serve a special geographic area, such as www.chez.com, which limits its members to those in France. Others are aimed at certain themes or groups. The site www.henterprises.com/webucat, for example, is devoted to school home pages. For a list of free Web site offers around the world, look up uk.zarcrom.com/freehome.html.

Because some of these sites require you to use their own software, you are also limited to their design choices. Therefore, you cannot use a program such as Front Page and then upload the site. There are exceptions, however—some of the sites just give you a block of space and you're on your own. We'll look at those types of sites later.

If you create a free Web site using any service, make sure you record the site address and your password, along with any other registration information you enter.

TreeWay.com

This is a great site because you can use the site for just about anything. You design up to eight pages using interactive forms on-screen. You don't have to know anything about HTML or uploading. You can also get a free e-mail account.

Navigate to `www.treeway.com` to see the site shown in Figure 55.1, and then click the Free Site graphic. You'll be taken though the process of registering as a TreeWay.com member and getting a TreeWay.com e-mail address.

FIGURE 55.1   **TreeWay.com offers free Web sites.**

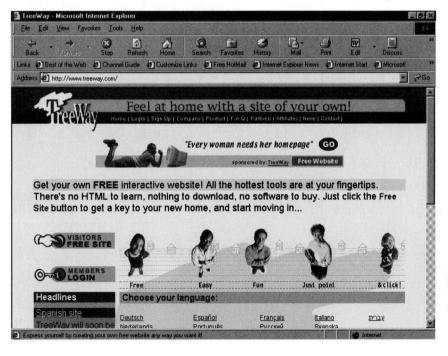

Once you sign in, you're taken through a series of screens in which you design your Web site by adding text and selecting design elements and themes. Each theme consists of a series of graphics that appear on your site. You can also choose an overall layout. You can even add multimedia elements; for example, you can play music tracks that you select or let viewers see a fashion show while they visit your site.

You can easily add and delete pages, change the layout, and add graphics and text. TreeWay.com doesn't clutter up your site with any advertisements, as shown in Figure 55.2. That's a small price to pay for the free service. The address of your site is `my.treeway.com/your-member-name`.

FIGURE 55.2   **Free home page on TreeWay.com**

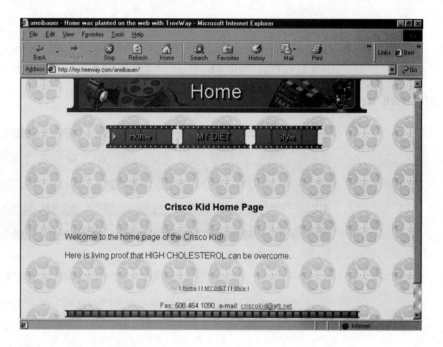

MyFamily.com

This service is aimed at family-oriented sites, hence its name! All of the sites created through it use a standard format; you add your own information. Navigate to `www.myfamily.com`, enter your first name, your last name and your e-mail address, and click the link Create My Site. You'll be taken through several screens in which you enter information about yourself and invite other family members to join your site.

NOTE Another great place to create a family-oriented Web site is at www.familyshare.com. You can create a Web site in a few minutes, share photographs and news, and invite family and friends to join. The service is free!

The focus of MyFamily.com is to offer a meeting place for family members and family information. You invite family members to join the site, give them permission to view it, add information, and upload files and pictures that they want to share with other family members. A typical site under construction is shown in Figure 55.3. Sites are private—your invited family members must log on to it.

FIGURE 55.3 Site under construction at MyFamily.com

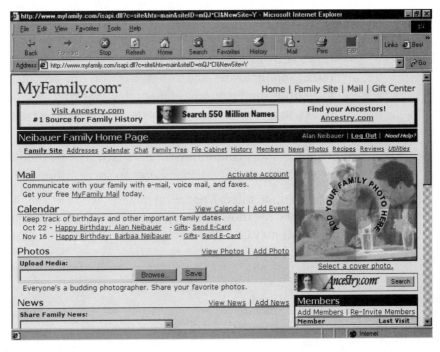

Tripod

If you want a little more freedom in creating a Web page, try www.tripod.com. Tripod gives you 50 megabytes of free storage space, which is more space than many ISPs give paying members. It also allows you to create pages on-line using their software, or upload Web pages you create using any Web creation software.

When you get to Tripod, click Sign Up Now for Free Homepages on Tripod. You'll be taken through a number of screens where you enter your name and e-mail address, and select a member name and password.

Tripod offers four basic options for creating sites:

Site Builder Lets you create a complete site by selecting options and entering text.

Freeform Allows you to enter the HTML code that creates a page.

Trellix Web Lets you download and use a free program that helps you create a complete Web site.

Microsoft Office 2000 Lets you create a Web folder that will be used when you create a Web page using tools provided in Microsoft Office 2000.

If you're a beginner, you can use the Site Builder option to create some rather sophisticated pages. In fact, the option lets you select a templated form from among dozens of examples. It also lets you add counters, guest books, maps, local weather reports, and other elements to customize your site.

Tripod is a very community-oriented site. It offers additional features and provides forums where members can share information and experiences.

While Tripod offers a powerful range of features and plenty of storage space, it does show a pop-up ad and some advertising at the top of your site. This may be a drawback, because it makes your site look like a commercial one.

56 Storing Documents Online

Most ISPs make it easy to get a basic Web site. But once you've added the standard "Here's My Home Page and Welcome To It" page, then what? You're now ready for more interesting things.

So You Have a Web Site. Now What?

Even if you don't want a Web site at all, you can use your space to store and share documents of all types. Just think of free Web sites as a little extra disk space that you can access from anywhere on Earth.

Here's What You Need

You need to have a Web site established on your ISP's server, or sign up for a free service that lets you store documents of all types online.

First, find out from your ISP whether you can upload information directly, using File Transfer Protocol (FTP). If not, you're stuck using their own programs for creating your Web site. If they do let you use FTP, ask them for the following information: host name or IP address for using FTP, your user ID, your password, and the initial directory, if you need it.

The host name or IP address refers to a specific computer at the service provider's site. It is not the address of your ISP's home page. It may be the IP address of the computer where your actual Web site is stored, or a general location where all of the ISP member sites are kept (such as upload.att.net, or something like that).

The User ID and password may be the same as the ones you use to log on or the ones you use to send and receive e-mail. It is also possible that a special ID and password are assigned specifically for Web site management.

The initial directory is used when you are uploading to a general ISP site, because it identifies your specific area. For example, with AT&T Worldnet, every user accesses their home page starting with the site upload.att.net.

The initial directory, however, is their user name, which tells AT&T where to put the files when they are uploaded.

If you do not have a place to store files with your ISP, you can sign up for free storage space through a number of Web sites. These sites give you storage and an easy-to-use interface for uploading and retrieving files.

Sites and Features

Most ISPs help you create a simple Web page by taking you through a series of menus and dialog boxes. The information that you enter and select is used to create the Web site.

You may have some other program that you'd like to use to create a Web page, such as Microsoft Front Page (which comes with Microsoft Office) or Trellix (which comes with WordPerfect Office). Perhaps you'd rather create a Web site using one of those programs rather than by using the step-by-step method provided by the ISP.

Or maybe you don't want a Web site at all! Should all that free Web site space go to waste? Not at all. You can use your Web site—whether provided by an ISP or one of the free Web sites offered by other companies—for many other purposes:

◆ Store pictures that you want to show friends or relatives. Rather than e-mail your picture to everyone on your list, you can place it on your Web site. This way, all of your friends who have access to the Internet can see the picture.

◆ Hold documents that you want to share with others. Do you have a document that you want to send to someone else? Rather than e-mail it, put it on your Web site so others can download it when they are ready.

◆ Distribute software. Written an interesting computer program? Found a freeware program that you'd like to share? You can put either on your Web site as well.

◆ Back up files for safekeeping. You know that very important report that you've been writing? In addition to saving it on a floppy for safekeeping, store a copy on your Web site. Then, even if a spaceship flies over your house and zaps every disk in the place, you are still protected.

◆ Make a file accessible from any location. Do you work at home and in the office? While on the road and on vacation? If you have Internet access at every location, don't bother carrying around a bunch of floppies. Store your working documents on your Web site and just download them from there when needed.

The trick to all of these features is uploading. Uploading means to copy files from your hard disk to your Web site. You may be able to upload files using online programs provided by your ISP. But that means getting online and going through a series of menus to make it happen. If your ISP allows you to send via FTP, then you're in luck, because there's plenty of free and inexpensive software to help you.

With an FTP program, you are connected to two computers at once—yours (called the local computer) and your ISP's (called the remote computer)—and you can move files between them in either direction. Moving a file from your computer to the ISP's is called uploading. Moving a file from the ISP's computer to your own is called downloading.

First of all, Windows comes with an FTP program that doesn't cost you an extra dime. There is a price to pay, of course. It is not the easiest program to use because it runs strictly from the DOS command prompt. See, DOS isn't really dead at all, just dormant.

The exact sequence for using FTP depends on your ISP, but it could go something like this:

1. Click Start➤Programs➤MS-DOS Prompt.

2. Type **FTP**, a space, and then the address of the site.

3. Press Enter. Windows will dial into your ISP. If it does not, try connecting to the Internet first, and then go to the MS-DOS prompt and run FTP.

4. At the prompt, enter your user name and press Enter.

5. At the prompt, enter your password and press Enter.

6. Type **binary** to transfer non-text files, and press Enter.

7. Type **Interactive Mode Off**, to turn off the interactive mode.

8. Type **CD**, a space, and the name of the folder where you want to add the files, and press Enter.

9. Type **put**, followed by the path and name of the file, and press Enter.

10. Type **bye** and press Enter when you want to quit the FTP program.

It is a lot of typing, and there are plenty of chances to screw up and enter the wrong command. It actually isn't that difficult, though, as long as you know the routine. But if you're not interested in the routine, then there's a perfect solution. Get yourself a free or inexpensive FTP program. Most of the programs are available for downloading and use a graphic interface. That means you upload files by clicking or dragging rather than by using a long series of DOS commands.

There are literally hundreds of FTP programs out there. Here are just a few:

◆ FTP Serv-U, which you can get from www.deerfield.com.

◆ FTP Explorer, listed with www.download.cnet.com.

◆ FTP Commander, at www.vista.ru.

◆ Crystal FTP and CuteFTP, at www.download.com.

Using WS_FTP

We'll take a close look at a great program called WS_FTP. The program comes in two versions, standard and Pro. The standard program is free if you use it non-commercially, and it can be downloaded from www.ipswitch.com. The Pro version is not free, but it has lots of extra features, including two interfaces and the ability to synchronize sites. The limited-time trial version WS_FTP Pro is available on the CD.

WS_FTP gives you a visual interface for uploading programs, so you don't have to worry about DOS commands. You can even rename, delete, and copy files on your Web site—just as easily as if they were on your own hard disk. It's like working remotely on your ISP's computer.

Figure 56.1 shows the opening dialog box of WS_FTP Pro. The folders represent popular sites for downloading software and other information.

Just double-click the site you want to go to. You'll learn later how to download files from a site.

Since we're interested in uploading programs for now, your first task is to create a listing for your Web page. Here's how:

1. Click the folder where you want to store your connection (usually My Sites).

2. Click New in the WS_FTP Sites box to open the New Site/Folder dialog box.

FIGURE 56.1 Select a site in WS_FTP Pro

3. Type a name for the site—something like My Site at isp.com is fine—and then click Next.

4. In the box that appears, type the host name or IP address of the upload site—you'll need to get this from your ISP—then click Next.

5. In the box that appears, enter your User ID and your password; then enable the Save Password option.

6. Click Finish. Your FTP site will now be added to the list in the WS_FTP Sites box.

If you need to specify an initial directory, however, you have to do so before connecting to the site. Click the site name in the list and then on the Properties button. In the dialog box that appears, click the Startup tab to see the options in Figure 56.2. In the Remote Site Folder text box, type your user name or folder name, then click OK.

Now, to connect to your site, select the site name and click OK. WS_FTP will connect to the Internet through your ISP and log on to your Web site for access. You'll see a list of the files on your site in the box on the right, as in Figure 56.3. The list on the left shows the files in the current folder of your computer.

FIGURE 56.2 Setting the initial remote directory

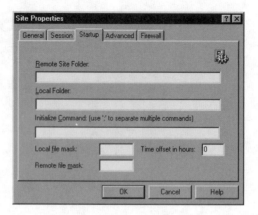

FIGURE 56.3 Access a site with WS_FTP

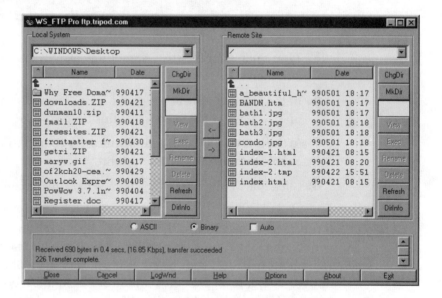

To upload files, you have to list them on the left. Click ChgDir, enter the path where the files are stored on your disk, and then click OK. On the list on the left, click a file, and then hold down the CTRL key and click any other files that you want to move to the Web site. Finally, click the button that has the icon of a right-pointing arrow to copy the files to your site. As the files are transferred, you'll see a status report in the bottom window and a progress box on the screen. When the files are uploaded, click Close and then Exit.

WARNING Always click Close before exiting and wait until the file list on the right is empty.

Downloading Files by FTP You can use programs such as WS_FTP to download as well as to upload files. Using the classic interface, click the file you want to download on the right of the screen, and then click the button that has the icon of a left-pointing arrow. Using the Explorer interface, just drag the file onto your desktop or into a folder on your disk.

Accessing Web Site Files If you want to share a photo by posting it on a Web site, just give people the site address. For example, if your site is members.myISP.com/~myname, and the picture is party.jpg, anyone can see the picture by pointing their browser at members.myISP.com/~myname/party.jpg.

With documents, programs, zip files, or any other file that the browser cannot display automatically, the browser will display the familiar box asking whether you want to open or save the file. Just click Save and then OK to download the file to your computer.

When you place a file on the Internet, remember that it is accessible to anyone who can get to that address. If you want to keep a file private, you can password protect it in a couple of ways.

◆ Some ISPs let you password protect your site. This means you can designate a password that must be entered before the site can be seen.

◆ You can use a program such as WinZip to compress the file with a password. A person must have the password to unzip the file.

Online File Storage Services

You do not need space on your ISP's computer to store your files online. As an alternative, take a look at www.idrive.com.

This free service, shown in Figure 56.4, lets you store an address book on-line and create photo albums that you want to share with friends. Its greatest benefit, however, is that it gives you unlimited space to store anything you want from the Internet (such as graphic and music files) and 50 megabytes of space for your own personal files such as documents and spreadsheets.

Use the site to save backup copies of important documents, or working copies of files that you want to be able to access from any place where there is a connection to the Internet. It also provides a drop box—a temporary storage area that holds files sent to you by other i-drive users.

FIGURE 56.4 **Your home at i-drive**

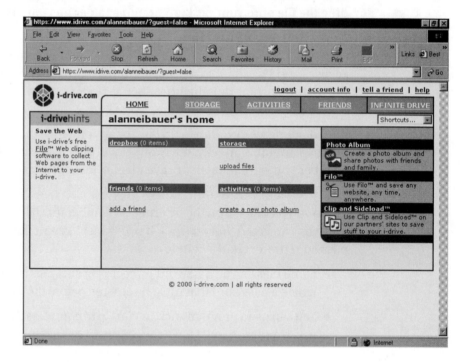

This site also provides you with two downloadable programs. Filo lets you save Web pages directly to your i-drive space, and Clip and Sideload lets you save files, such as music and videos, from partner sites.

To upload a file to your storage area, log on with your user name and password, and click the upload files link in the Storage section of your page to open your storage area, shown in Figure 56.5. The storage area is organized into four areas, although you can create additional folders:

Dropbox   Files sent by other users

Filo   Saved Web sites

Private   Uploaded documents you do not want to share

Shared   Uploaded documents you will share with others

FIGURE 56.5   Storage area

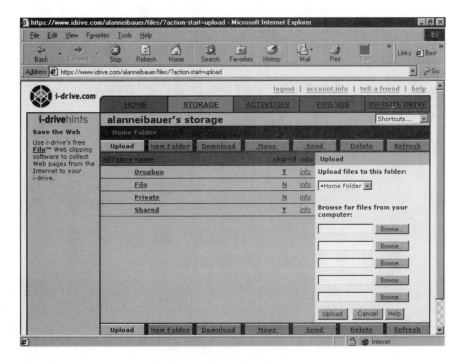

Pull down the Upload Files to This Folder list and choose the folder where you want to place the file. Then enter the path and name of the file on your computer, or use the Browse button to locate the file. You can upload up to five files at one time. Finally, click the Upload button to copy the file from your own disk to your storage space at i-drive.

When you want to download a file, log on to i-drive and click on Storage on your home page. Click on the folder to which you uploaded the file to see the folder's contents. Select the file you want to download to your computer and click Document. You can also click on the filename itself to open the file. Clicking on a graphic, for example, will display the graphic in a browser window.

There are plenty of other free storage sites. Sign up at www.xdrive.com for up to 100 megabytes of storage and a program that installs your online storage area as a virtual disk drive on your computer. You can then use My Computer or Windows Explorer to copy a file to the virtual drive, uploading to your Internet storage area. Also consider www.driveway.com for up to 25 megabytes of secure online storage.

57 Pass the Pictures, Please

Sometimes you don't want to bother with a whole Web site; you just want a place to share pictures—and no other types of files—with a few friends. The Internet to the rescue!

Online Photo Galleries

Lots of the free Web sites that you learned about earlier give you a place to post photographs. But displaying and sharing photographs is just one part of what they do, not their *raison d'etre*. If you're interested primarily in sharing photographs, then go directly to the places that specialize in it.

Here's What You Need

To share photographs on the Internet, you need some way to get your photographs into digital form. This means that you'll need to have a scanner or digital camera, or have your photo developer supply your pictures on a disk or CD.

Once your photos are digital, you can sign up for one of the free services on the Internet—www.photopoint.com and www.photoloft.com.

Sites and Features

Both PhotoPoint and PhotoLoft are great places to share photographs, but the site I like best is www.photopoint.com.

Why?

Because you don't have to go through FTP or use any special software to upload photographs. Once you sign up for a free Photopoint account, just e-mail a photograph as an attachment to photos@photopoint.com. The company stores the photo in the album based on your e-mail address.

Log on to the site and sign up for the account, giving the e-mail address from which you'll be uploading photographs and some basic address information. PhotoPoint will e-mail you a confirmation along with your password.

When you access your account, you'll have a standard set of albums ready to store photos, as shown in Figure 57.1, but you can create additional albums and assign passwords to keep them private as needed. The listing for each album shows the number of photos included, their total size, whether

FIGURE 57.1 **PhotoPoint albums**

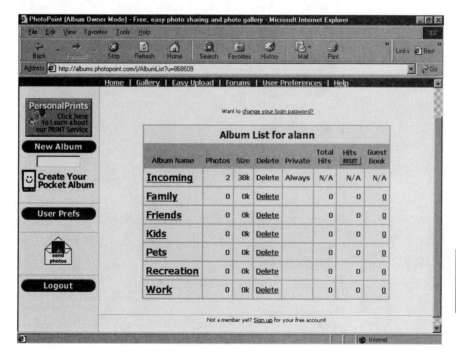

the album is private (password protected), and the number of times the album has been viewed by others. The list also shows the number of hits since you last reset the counter using the Reset button and the number of persons who have signed your guestbook. The guestbook feature lets those who view your album leave you a personal message.

Photographs you e-mail to photos@photopoint.com are stored in the Incoming album. Click on Incoming to see its contents, as shown in Figure 57.2, and then move or copy a photograph to another folder using these steps:

1. Select the check boxes under the photos you want to move or copy.

2. Pull down the list on the left above the Move and Copy buttons and select the album where you want to place the photo.

3. Click Move to remove the photo from Incoming and place it in the selected album, or click Copy to leave the photo in Incoming but make a duplicate in the selected album.

FIGURE 57.2 Contents of an album

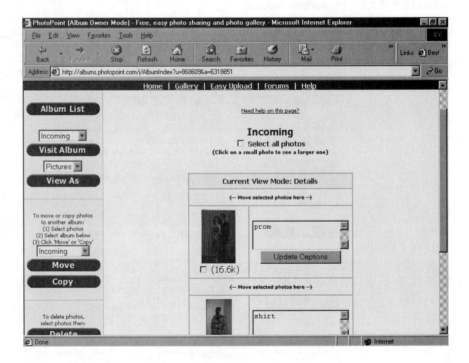

NOTE To customize a photograph displayed in an album, click it. In the screen that appears, you can choose to rotate, resize, crop, sharpen, blur, and flip the photograph.

To upload a photograph while you are online, click the Send Photos icon on the left of the window. PhotoPoint opens your e-mail program and starts a new message already addressed to photos@photopoint.com. Just attach the files and click the Send button.

You can also upload up to ten photographs at one time from within PhotoPoint. Click the Easy Upload button on a PhotoPoint screen, and in the dialog box that appears, specify up to ten photographs to upload to your Incoming album. Click Upload Now.

To share your photographs, just tell people to visit the PhotoPoint home page and look for the Visit Albums box:

They just type your e-mail address and click visit to access all of your folders except Incoming and those you have designated as private.

You can also provide access to an album by sending someone its address or including a link on a Web site. You can use a similar technique to link the album to an item you have for sale on Ebay or another online auction.

From the album window, click the Get HTML button on the left (you'll have to scroll the screen to see it). The screen that appears lists the HTML tags that access the album in four ways:

♦ As a URL link such as albums.photopoint.com/j/
  AlbumIndex?u=868609&a=6318851

♦ A clickable line of text that accesses the album

♦ A PhotoPoint logo

♦ A logo designed specifically for Ebay auction items

Just copy the HTML text for the type of link you want, and paste it into an e-mail, Web page, or eBay item description.

58 Get Your Own Domain

You can join the ranks of the world's largest companies and educational institutions by having your own name on the Internet.

Sign Up As YOU.com

Having your own domain on the Internet is easy and not that expensive to achieve. While it costs more than a free Web site, to be sure, your own domain will really establish your presence on the Internet.

Here's What You Need

You need access to the Web and about $70.00. The money reserves your domain name with one of the organizations that registers Internet domain names. With most of the organizations, such as the Internet Network Information Center (InterNIC), the initial fee covers you for two years—you then pay a smaller fee annually after that. If you want to actually have a Web site at your own domain, you'll need to pay a monthly Web hosting fee.

Registering your own domain just means reserving the name (me.com, for example) so no one else can claim it. It does not actually put a Web site on the Internet. I was a little late in my own case, for example, and my cousin reserved www.neibauer.com before me, so I had to reserve www.neibauer.net.

When the Internet first started, having a domain meant that you had a computer called an Internet Server connected directly to the Internet. If you connect to the Internet through an ISP, then you're not directly connected, so in addition to registering your domain name, you have to find someone to either park or host your site.

Parking means that your domain name will be associated with an actual place on the Internet—an IP address—that is on someone else's Internet Server. When you park a domain name, the site will be empty except for a message or graphic reporting that there is nothing there. There are companies that will park your domain name for free.

Hosting your site means that you actually have space on the server's computer to place your Web page. This is rarely given away free. Most ISPs that give you a Web page and companies that offer free Web pages will not let you do it under your own domain name. So to actually use your site, you need to find a company that will host your site for a monthly charge. That's not a problem because there are plenty of them. Many of them will also handle the task of registering your domain name at the same time—you still have to pay the initial fee, of course. Having your site hosted on someone else's server is called having a *virtual domain*.

Hosting fees range anywhere from about $5.00 to thousands a month, depending on the amount of disk space and the services provided. Getting a small Web site for a few pages, for example, will certainly cost less than a large corporate Web site. But in addition to the amount of space, the rates vary according to the Web site features you want to use. It will cost you more, for instance, if you want to sell your products online using a secure order entry system that accepts credit card sales. The rates also vary according to the number of e-mail addresses available at the site.

NOTE In addition to the monthly hosting charge, you'll still need to belong to an ISP, have access to the Internet one way or the other, or pay someone to manage your site for you.

Sites and Features

If you just want to reserve your domain name rather than actually have a site, you can find companies that will help you process the registration form and park the site on their server. For example, check out `www.domainvalet.com/index.html`.

DomainValet will register your domain name for you and park your site for no charge beyond the registration fee. They will even host your site for free, with up to 20 megabytes of space, although they will insert ads on the top of every page. Why do they do it for you? They hope that you decide to have them host your site without the ads at a later time. If you choose another host, you can transfer your domain name to it.

If you actually want to have a Web page on the site, then you need to have it hosted. There are literally thousands of Web-hosting sites.

The first place to start looking for a hosting company is with your ISP. Some ISPs offer the service for an additional monthly charge. If yours doesn't, or you think they charge too much, then search the Internet for the terms "website hosting" or "web hosting."

N O T E You can get Web hosting for free from www.bizland.com, but your site will carry some banner advertising.

Getting Your Own Domain

To show how easy it is to get your own domain, we'll use the hosting service www.11net.com as an example. This Web hosting service offers low monthly rates and will handle the chore of registering your own domain name. Signing up takes less than five minutes, and you don't even need a charge card! In fact, you'll find my own domain, www.neibauer.net, hosted by 11Net.com.

If you want to have your own Internet domain hosted by 11Net.com, just follow these steps.

1. Connect to the Internet and navigate to www.11net.com. As you can see, hosting starts at $6.99 per month.

2. Click the Sign Up icon to start the process on the form (see Figure 58.1). The company offers two levels of service. Plan 1 is $6.99 a month for 60MB of space and three e-mail accounts. Plan 2 is $14.99 a month for 100MB of space and 10 e-mail accounts. With Plan 2, you can also get detailed statistics about traffic to your site, and you can use a secure method of getting information, such as charge card numbers, if you sell a product.

NOTE Having your own CGI-BIN (Common Gateway Interface Binary) means that you can run custom programs, or scripts, that you maintain on the Web server.

3. On the sign up form, select either Plan 1 or Plan 2, and then scroll the page down to continue with the form.

4. Choose whether you want Front Page support. Front Page is a popular program from Microsoft that lets you create Web sites. If your hosting company supports Front Page, you can keep your site up-to-date automatically from within the Front Page program. If your site does not support Front Page, you have to transfer files to it using FTP. Some companies charge extra for Front Page support—11Net.com doesn't.

FIGURE 58.1   11Net.com's sign up form

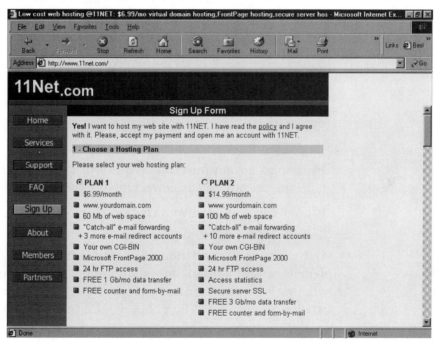

5. Select the type of URL. You can sign up for a virtual domain (`www.yourname.com`) or for it to be hosted under 11Net.com (`www.yourname.11net.com`). If you sign up for a virtual domain name, you choose to have 11Net register it for you for a two year fee of $64, register the name yourself, or transfer an existing domain to the 11Net.com server.

6. Click Check Here to see whether the domain name you want is currently registered.

7. Select a login name. You'll use this name to log on to the site to upload files, using either an FTP program or Front Page. The company will later assign you a password.

8. Enter your name and the address to be used by 11Net.com for billing, as well as your domain registration.

9. Enter a question and answer that you can use to retrieve your password if you ever forget it.

10. Select either a 6-month or 12-month payment period. There's a $20.00 setup fee if you choose six months that is waived if you sign up for a year.

11. Choose to pay by charge card, or click Let Us Know if you want to use some other payment method.

12. Specify how you heard about 11Net.com. (In the Please Specify if Other text box, type **Alan's Book**. Thanks!)

13. Click Next. You'll see a summary of your answers to the sign up form.

14. If there are any mistakes on the form, click your browser's Back or Previous button and correct them. Otherwise, click Submit.

15. You can now enter your credit card information and submit the form for processing.

Wait a few minutes and then check your e-mail. You'll get an e-mail explaining some important information about your hosting account along with your login password and a temporary URL to use until the domain registration is approved. Print a copy of the e-mail for your records.

When 11Net.com sends you its e-mail, it also sends your completed domain application to InterNIC. Within two weeks you'll be officially notified that your registration has been approved. Until then, you can start building your Web site at the temporary URL assigned by 11Net.com.

That's it. You're now on the Internet with your own domain!

E-Mail

Most hosting services offer e-mail accounts along with the Web site. If you register www.myname.com, you can have mail sent to me@myname.com.

Some hosts provide an actual e-mail server. Depending on the host, you can use a program such as Outlook Express or Eudora to send and receive e-mail through the server, or you can send and receive e-mail by connecting to their site on the Internet.

Other hosts offer e-mail forwarding. With 11Net.com, for instance, you get either 3 or 10 e-mail addresses, depending on which plan you select. You use the 11Net.com form, shown in Figure 58.2, to create the e-mail accounts and to designate where the mail is forwarded. Any e-mail received by your domain will automatically be forwarded to the address specified, without the sender's being aware of it at all.

FIGURE 58.2   Creating e-mail accounts in 11Net.com

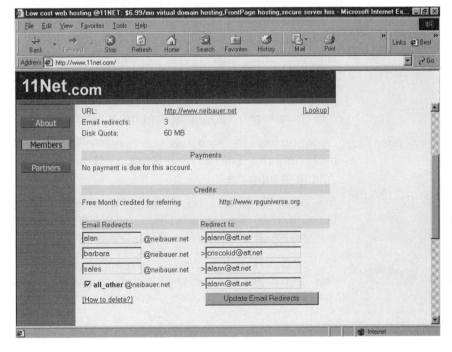

Putting Up Your Web Site

Now that you have your own domain, you have to upload your Web page to it. You can have as many pages and files on the site as will fit, but your initial page must have a special name, depending on the hosting company.

The file name is always some variation of either `index.htm`, `index.html`, or `default.html`. Depending on the hosting company the name may be case-sensitive. If your host requires the file `index.html`, as does 11Net.com, you cannot name it `Index.html` because the case of each character does not match. With some hosts the case does not matter, so you could name yours `INDEX.HTML`, `Index.HTML`, or `index.html`. The extension also matters. If your host requires htm, do not use html.

When someone navigates to your site, they automatically see the index file that you uploaded to the site. If you just signed up for a domain and did not install a site of your own, there will be a standard index file placed there by the host. It will probably be some message that the site is under construction. You have to design and upload your own index file containing all of the files and graphics to your host site (remember to check and make sure you are using the right case).

There are plenty of ways to design a Web page. Programs such as Microsoft Word and Corel WordPerfect let you create a Web page as easily as if you were writing and formatting a document. You can save the document in HTML format and name it Index.htm or Index.html.

Other programs, such as Microsoft FrontPage and Trellix, let you create Web sites of multiple pages linked together. You might already have some program that lets you create an HTML document, or, if you don't, you can find shareware programs all over the Internet.

Once you have the Web page or site created, you have to upload it to the host computer. You can do this using FTP or the FrontPage program, if your host supports it.

In Section 56, "Storing and Sharing Documents," you learned how to upload information to a free Web site using FTP. You use the same technique to upload pages to your own virtual domain.

Using WS_FTP, which comes on the accompanying CD, you can upload your Web page or site using your domain as the host name, and your login name and password.

NOTE Check with your host for the proper directory for your Web site files.

Counting Hits

You may want a hit counter on your page. This simply counts the number of times a Web page has been accessed.

If you are using Microsoft FrontPage, and your host supports it, you can add a hit counter by just selecting Insert➤Component➤Hit Counter from the FrontPage menu bar. Otherwise, you'll need to insert one or more lines of HTML instructions into your Web page.

The easiest way to create a hit counter is to ask your hosting company if they have a built-in counter program. If they do, they can give you the HTML line that you can insert into your page where you want the counter to appear.

With 11Net.com, for example, all you need to do is enter a line like this:

```
<img src="http://www2.11net.com/cgi-bin/count.cgi?neibauer"
align="absbottom">
```

NOTE The www2 part of the command varies with the specific server you are assigned in 11Net.

This line of HTML accesses a hit counter maintained by 11Net.com, inserts the counter into your Web page, and keeps a running count of the number of times the page is accessed.

NOTE You can have a different hit counter on each page of your site to see how often specific pages are accessed. Just use a different name (in place of "test" in the sample) on each page.

If your host does not maintain a built-in hit counter, you can access free ones made available by other companies. Check out these sites for free counter programs:

- `www2.freestats.com`
- `counters.qpt.com`
- `www.fastcounter.com`
- `www.digits.com/create.html`

Plenty of Options

As I said, there are thousands of hosting services out there. In addition to 11Net.com, take a look at `www.hostingsolutions.net`.

NOTE There is a different company at `www.hostingsolutions.com` that offers plans starting at $9.95 for 25MB of space up to $49.95 for 1250MB of space; this company will park your domain for free.

Hosting Solutions offers several levels of personal and business plans. Personal plans range from $9.95 per month for 5MB of space to $14.95 per month for 10MB. The plans include free domain registration—of course, you're still responsible for the registration fee.

Their business plans range from $19.95 to $149.95. The business plans provide additional storage space, maintain mailing lists, and feature business needs for online commerce.

All of the plans at Hosting Solutions also include a certain amount of network traffic and a number of e-mail accounts.

Network traffic measures the amount of activity on your site—the number of accesses and the amount of data that's moved in and out each month. The business plans provide for more traffic than the personal plans. Traffic beyond what is included in the plan incurs additional charges. The personal plans, for example, allow for 1GB or 3GB, while the business plans range from 5GB to 30GB per month. Additional traffic costs $1.00 per 100MB.

The POP mail accounts mean that you can check your mail, using programs such as Outlook Express, from any computer that has Internet access. The number of accounts depends on the plan, from one account for personal plans up to 75 for the most costly business plan. Additional e-mail accounts cost $5.00 per month for every five accounts.

The Bottom Line

There are a lot of choices on the Internet for hosting your own domain, so take your time and shop around. Your choice should depend not only on price but also on the services offered. If you're creating a family Web site, for example, you may want a host that offers an e-mail account for each member of the family, either on an actual server or forwarded to your ISP.

You may not need some of the more sophisticated services that are typical in business accounts (such as security for online purchases and CGI scripts). Just make sure that the amount of space provided is sufficient for your purposes. Most personal sites can easily fit in 5MB of space, unless they include many high-resolution graphics and special effects.

So what's the final cost of having your own domain on the Internet? It is a maximum of $70.00 for two years if you create your own Web page and find a company that offers free hosting.

If you have to pay for hosting, you can find companies that charge $5.00 and up. The most typical hosting charge ranges from $15.00 to $25.00 per month, but you can do better if you shop around.

Based on a $15.00 monthly hosting charge and the registration fees, your domain will cost about $215.00 per year. If you pay $20.00 per month to your ISP, your total annual Internet bill is about $455.00. That's not that much to pay for a presence on the Internet equal to that of the Fortune 500 companies.

 Of course, you have to get people to visit your site. The best way to promote your site is to register it with the major Internet search engines, such as Yahoo! and Excite. Go to each search engine and look for a registration link that you'll usually find near the bottom of the site's home page. As an alternative, you can register your site with a number of search engines at one time using the program Submission Wizard. You'll find a copy of the program on the accompanying CD, or you can download it from www.exploit.com.

Buying and
Selling Online

There are a lot of free things on the Internet, but there are a lot of good things to buy as well. You can find all sorts of items that can be delivered right to your door, and at great prices. The Internet is also a great place to sell things, whether you have a business or just want to clear out that old junk from the attic.

59　The World's Largest Bookstores

Without ever leaving your home, you can access the world's largest selection of books for sale. "So everybody already knows that," you say. But did you know that you can get hard-to-find, out-of-print, and antique books as well?

Order Any Type of Book Online

Remember that great book you had when you were a child? Do you collect books and paraphernalia about the Civil War or some other subject? Because of the global nature of the Internet, you can locate hard-to-find books on virtually every subject.

Here's What You Need

All you need is access to the Internet and a credit card that hasn't expired or exceeded its limit.

Sites and Features

First, to buy current books, check out one of these sites:

- www.amazon.com
- www.fatbrain.com
- www.barnesandnoble.com
- www.borders.com

Each of these sites has an easy search function for finding the book you want, and each features current best sellers right on their home page. You can also try the home pages of most publishers for book and ordering information. You just might be able to purchase directly from the publisher at a discount.

Searching Many Stores with AddALL

Rather than search through the individual stores, you can search several stores at one time. By navigating to www.addall.com, for example, you can enter search criteria into a form and search 40 bookstores at the same time.

NOTE You can also use AddALL to search for music and to sign up for free, Web-based e-mail.

Here's how to use the form:

1. Pull down the Shipping Destination list and choose the country or region where you want to send the book.

2. If shipping in the United States, select the state in the State list.

3. Choose the currency in which you want the prices displayed.

4. Pull down the Search By list, and select how you want to search the bookstores. The options are Title, ISBN, Author, and Keyword.

5. In the text box to the right of the Click to Find button, enter the search text—a title, ISBN number, author name, or keyword.

6. Click the Click to Find button.

You'll see a list of books meeting your search criteria. Click a book title to compare the pricing and availability at various online bookshops. To order the book, click Buy It to the right of your selected source.

To look for used, rare, and out-of-print books, click the Click Here link next to the Searching for Used Books? prompt that's below the addall.com form. In the form that appears, enter your search criteria. You can also designate the binding (all, hardcover, or paperback), whether you want a first edition or a signed copy, and the price range. Click Find the Book to get a listing of online sites that have that book listed in their catalogs, along with their asking prices.

Searching with BookFinder.com and Bibliofind

The Web site at www.bookfinder.com also lets you search for new, used, rare, and out-of-print books using a similar form. The results appear in a separate table for each online store.

Many of the search companies include www.bibliofind.com as one of their search sites for used and out-of-print books. You can also go to that site directly to look for books yourself. At bibliofind, you can maintain a personal "want list" of books you are looking for.

Bibliofind maintains a database of books in a large number of bookstores. The results of your search are displayed as a list of books, each preceeded by a check box.

Enable the check box next to each entry for books you want to order, or click the Seller's link to read more about the seller. Click the price of a book to display the price in many of the world's currencies. If there are more books than can be listed in one page, click the More Titles button at the bottom of the list.

If the book you are looking for is not listed, you can scroll to the end to display the Personal Want List form. Enter information about a book you're looking for and click the Place on Want List button. The list is available to Bibliofind's member stores, and you'll be notified if the book is located.

Once you've enabled the boxes for the books you want to purchase, click the Add to Shopping Basket button at the bottom of the list. You'll see a screen summarizing your order. Click the button labeled Place Order to enter your address and charge information, and to process the order. At this screen, you'll also have a chance to empty your shopping basket if you change your mind.

60 Buying at Internet Auctions

Auctions such as eBay and Amazon can give you the same thrill as a real, live auction house, but from the comfort of your home or office. The auction at eBay, for example, may have over 1.5 million items up for grabs at any one time. You'll find something for every collection, both old and new merchandise, and some real bargains.

Making Sure You Win

The trick to getting what you want is to win the bid at a price you think is fair, and then actually get what you paid for. Some folks get carried away with the spirit of competition and end up paying more than they want—and often more than the object is worth.

Here's What You Need

All you will need to get started is access to the Internet and an e-mail address. Of course, when you start bidding, you will also need to dig for your checkbook.

Sites and Features

There are plenty of online auctions, but the granddaddy of them all is at www.ebay.com. Amazon and other companies have their own auctions, but eBay seems to get the greatest number and variety of items for sale.

If you're not familiar with online auctions, here's how they work. People with stuff to sell and people who want to buy things register with the auction by giving their e-mail address and usually their name and mailing address. Registration is free. The sellers list items for sale. The listing includes a short description of the item, a minimum bid, and often a photograph of the item for sale. The description also states who pays the shipping charges—usually the buyer. The seller pays a small listing fee, usually under a dollar.

The auction is then started for the item for a set number of days—7 to 10 is about the average. Some auctions even let the seller select the number of days.

People who may want to buy the item leave a bid on it by filling out a form. You can check back regularly to see how the auction is going, and who has the current high bid.

Most auctions send a daily e-mail to the seller with the current high bids on their items. Buyers may be notified if they are outbid on an item, giving them a chance to submit a higher bid.

eBay and other auctions have proxy bidding. This means that you can leave the highest amount that you are willing to pay for the item. The auction house will post your bid as either the minimum bid or one dollar above the current winner. If someone bids higher than you do, it raises your bid, but not above the maximum that you set.

For example, suppose you see an antique that you are interested in. It has a $10.00 minimum bid and you can leave a maximum offer of $20.00. If no one else has yet bid on the item, your bid is recorded for just $10.00. If someone else has already bid at $10.00, your offer is shown as $11.00.

Each time someone outbids you, the auction raises your bid to make it the highest until it reaches your maximum. Of course, you can always manually make a larger offer if you really want the item.

When you win a bid, you and the seller get in touch with each other via e-mail. The seller will tell you the shipping charges; you then send them a check or money order, and they send you the item. There are also escrow services available. These charge a small fee to the buyer but allow them to pay by credit card. Until the merchandise is received, the funds are not released to the seller, who must agree to use the escrow service. See www.iescrow.com for more information on escrow services.

All in all, online auctions are a great way to buy interesting items that you may not be able to find locally.

Pick Your Items Wisely

Before bidding on an item, make sure it is what you want to spend your money on and that the seller is reputable.

Read the description carefully, and if there is a picture, look at it closely. If you have any questions, send an e-mail to the seller. Most auctions give you the e-mail address of the seller along with the item. If it is not listed, you can get it easily. With eBay, for example, every item shows the seller's eBay registration name. Sometimes the name is their e-mail address, so all you need to do is just click it to send them an e-mail. Other times, you'll need to click their eBay name and enter your own eBay name and password to obtain the seller's e-mail. If the seller does not respond to you at all, think twice about making a bid.

Look for similar items by other sellers. Auctions let you search by keyword or by category. With millions of items for sale, it may take some time, but you'll get a clearer picture of an item's worth.

In fact, included on the CD with this book is the program eBay Crawler. While you are in eBay's own search facilities, you can open eBay Crawler on your screen. The eBay Crawler screen is shown here:

To search using eBay Crawler, enter a keyword for the item; select the way the list is sorted, the auction type, and what you want to search for; then click GO. The program will connect to eBay by launching your Web browser, if it is not already online; it will then display the search results in the eBay window.

Check the feedback rating of the seller. The feedback rating is the way the auction site keeps everyone honest. After completing a transaction, the buyer and seller can leave a comment about each other—either positive or negative.

In the screen that describes the item for auction, you will see a number following the seller's name. This number represents the feedback rating, which is roughly the number of positive comments minus the number of negative comments. A large feedback number indicates that the seller is active and has completed a number of transactions successfully.

Click the feedback number to read all of the comments, looking for negative remarks from unhappy buyers. Just bear in mind that it is impossible to please everyone all of the time, and some folks just can't be pleased at all.

Winning Strategies

When you find an item you want to bid on, don't jump into it with your maximum bid. Use some of these techniques to help get the item at the right price.

Check the date and time the bidding for the item ends.   It will be shown along with the auction listing. If you will be available at that time, you'll be able to get online and follow the bidding so you can make a last-minute high bid before anyone else can outbid you.

Don't be the first to bid on an item.   There are some folks who just love the competition. They may not bid on an item if they don't think anyone else is interested in it. So wait until the last possible moment to show any interest with your first bid, or with raising a previous bid on the item. If you wait until the end, you might get in when everyone else is offline.

Don't be the only bidder on an item.   If you see the item going off auction without a bid, don't be the only bidder. Wait until the auction is done, then contact the seller by e-mail and ask if they are still interested in selling it. You may be able to purchase the item for the minimum bid, or even less, directly from the seller.

If you do not get the winning bid, send a note to the seller asking whether they have any additional or similar items. They just might, and you can negotiate with the seller yourself.

61 Clear Out Your Attic

Selling stuff at online auctions is the other side of the coin, and it can be lots of fun and profitable. You probably have things around the house, stuck in closets, the attic, or the garage that you no longer need. That stuff can bring in a lot of money through online auctions.

Make Money Online

We know. Before our recent move, my wife and I sold hundreds of items that we just didn't want to move—furniture, clothing, books, small appliances, knick-knacks of all types, and even an old car, my cherished 1958 right-hand drive Morris Minor convertible.

Here's What You Need

You'll need to register with one of the online auction companies and have things to sell. For items to sell just look around the house or shop at local flea markets and house sales.

Items sell best when you post a photograph of them with the auction. For that you'll need to scan a photograph or take a photo with a digital camera. You can also cut out and scan a picture of the item from a catalog or instruction booklet, but an actual photo works better.

Even though the buyer pays the shipping cost, you should select items that are easy to pack up. Things that fit in a United States Postal Service (USPS) priority envelope, United Parcel Service (UPS) envelope, or a small box are the best. Items such as skis and pieces of furniture are the most difficult to pack and ship. So, you'll need a supply of envelopes and boxes, shipping tape, and packing material. You'll have to pack the item and then take it to the Post Office or call UPS for a pickup.

If you don't want to pack and ship items yourself, you can pay a local store to do it for you. In most areas you'll find a Package Plus, Mail Boxes Etc., or similar store. For a fee, they will pack the item and have UPS pick it up at their location.

If you become an active online auction seller, you will soon need a space or room in the house as your packing and shipping department, and you'll start begging friends for their empty boxes.

Sites and Features

There are lots of online auctions—Amazon and Yahoo! to name two—but eBay (www.ebay.com) is the best place to sell things. eBay is the most popular and has the greatest number of items for sale and the most buyers looking for bargains and interesting items.

Registration is free, but you'll have to give your credit card number to pay for listing and sales fees. Here's how eBay works for the seller.

You pay a small fee to list an item. The fee is based on your starting bid price:

Starting Price	Listing Fee
Up to $9.99	$0.25
$10.00 - $24.99	$0.50
$25.00 - $49.99	$1.00
$50.00 and up	$2.00

When your item sells, you pay a percentage of the sales price, called the *final value fee*. There is a three-tiered system that decreases in percentage in inverse proportion to the price of the item.

Percentage	On Amount
5%	On the first $25
2.5%	On the amount between $25.01 and $1,000
1.25%	On any amount over $1,000

For example, suppose you sell an item for $50. To calculate the fee, take 5 percent of the first $25 ($1.25), then 2.5 percent of the remainder ($0.63). The total final value fee is $1.88. If you set the starting price at $15, your total eBay charges are $2.38.

N O T E There are some special charges for placing a reserve price on an item and for selling real estate.

On eBay, you can include a photograph of your item, but you have to first place the photograph on a Web site. You can upload the photo to the Web site you maintain at your ISP, or you can place it in PhotoPoint or some other service. Make a note of the URL address of the photograph, or the link that displays it.

Then, to sell an item at eBay, first go to www.ebay.com, register as a member and follow these steps:

1. Click Sell at the top of any eBay page.

2. In the form that appears, choose the category that your item falls under and click Continue to open the Sell Your Item form.

3. Enter your eBay user ID and password.

4. Type a title for the item, up to 45 characters.

5. Choose the subcategory for the item.

6. Type a complete description of the item.

7. Enter the address where the photograph of the item, if any, can be found.

8. There are now a series of optional items for which there are additional charges.

◆ Select whether you want to pay an extra fee to place the photo of the item in a special location called the Gallery. It costs $0.25 to place the photo in the Gallery or $19.95 to have it appear as a featured gallery item.

◆ Choose to boldface the item title for $2.00.

◆ Choose to feature the item on the eBay home page for $99.95.

◆ Choose to feature the item in its category for $14.95.

◆ Choose to highlight the item with a special gift icon for $1.00.

9. Enter your city and state.

10. Choose an optional region in which to list the item. Choose a region only if you are selling an item that you'd like to make available for inspection.

11. Specify your country.

12. Select one or more payment methods that you will accept. The options are Money Order/Cashiers Check, Personal Check, Visa/MasterCard, COD, Discover, American Express, and Other. You can also choose See Item Description if you want to explain acceptable payment methods in the item description. If you select a credit card method, you must have your own resources to process credit card payments or select to use the Billpoint option.

13. Select if you will accept Billpoint online payments. Use Billpoint when you want to accept credit card payments but cannot process the payments yourself. The buyer charges the item through Billpoint, which then forwards the money to you. Billpoint charges the buyer a small fee; there is no charge to the seller.

14. Specify whether you will accept escrow payments, and whether the escrow charges are to be paid by the buyer or the seller.

15. Specify whether you will ship items only to the United States, or to any country worldwide, or to specific regions.

16. Designate who pays for shipping. The options are Seller Pays Shipping, Buyer Pays Fixed Amount, Buyer Pays Actual Shipping Cost, and See Item Description.

17. Enter the number of items you have for sale. If you have more than one of the item but want to sell them all to the same high bidder, enter 1 here, and then specify the quantity in the title and description. If you enter more than 1 here, eBay assumes you want a Dutch auction, in which multiple high bidders each get one item. There are special rules and fees for Dutch actions, so you should check out the eBay help system.

18. Enter the minimum bid.

19. Choose the length of the auction—3, 5, 7 (the default), or 10 days.

20. Specify an optional reserve price. A reserve price is the minimum you are willing to accept for the item. You will not be obligated to sell the item if the high bid is lower than the reserve, but eBay will charge you the final value fee anyway.

21. Select if you want to make this a private auction, in which the names of bidders are not revealed.

22. Click Review.

A page appears showing your eBay account balance, a summary of the details of the auction, and the total fees to be charged to your account for this item. Click your browser's Back button if you have to make any changes, or click Submit My Listing to place the item up for auction.

NOTE If you click Back, you will have to reenter your password at the top of the form.

A confirmation page appears with the item's auction number and a link to its auction page. You can use this number to keep track of your auctions and eBay charges. eBay will send you an e-mail confirming the auction and giving the link. Click the link to see the item and to add it to your Favorites or Bookmarks list for quick access.

When the auction is over, you and the high bidder, if anyone has bid on the item, receive confirmation e-mails. eBay protocol suggests that you get in touch with each other via e-mail to complete the transaction.

62 Hard-to-Find Collectibles

eBay and other online auction houses aren't the only places to locate antiques and collectibles. There are plenty of online sources, both commercial and private.

It's All in the Search

Locating items is really an exercise in searching the Internet. It can be time-consuming, but it is usually well worth the effort. As your search abilities improve, you'll be able to locate items more quickly, and you'll build up a Favorites or Bookmarks list.

Here's What You Need

You'll need access to the Internet and some time to search in order to use the tips provided here. Using the program Collectibles Organizer Delux will help you get started.

Sites and Features

When you're searching for a hard-to-find item, use all of the techniques that you learned about in Section 5, "Supercharge Your Searches." Unfortunately, even the best search techniques can result in thousands of items being listed, especially if you use multiple search engines.

Collectibles Organizer Deluxe

The best place to start is by using the program Collectibles Organizer Deluxe. You can download it from `www.primasoft.com/iebook/collbook.htm`.

Collectibles Organizer Deluxe is a database management program that you can use to organize information of all types. It comes with two built-in databases, CollectData and WebResources. The CollectData database, illustrated in Figure 62.1 is ideal for storing information about items in your own collection.

FIGURE 62.1   Collectibles Organizer Deluxe item database

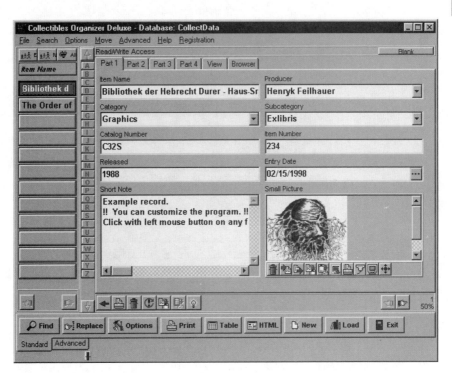

The WebResources database is designed for listing online sources of antiques and collectibles, and it includes a number of built-in listings, as shown in Figure 62.2. To select the database to display, click the Load button at the bottom of the Collectibles Organizer Deluxe window, choose the database from the dialog box that appears, and click Load.

Use the tabs on the top of the form to open additional pages of information. You can also click the Browser tab to access the Internet, displaying Websites directly on the Collectibles Organizer Deluxe window.

Although the program comes with a number of interesting sources, you can add your own as you find them. Click the New button at the bottom of

FIGURE 62.2 Database of Web resources for collectors

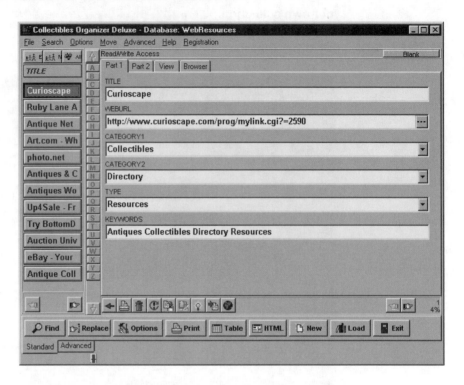

the program window to open a blank page. Enter the information about the site, selecting from the Category and Subcategory lists.

NOTE Before purchasing an item online, look up the prices of similar items on eBay and other auctions to judge its value.

When you install Collectibles Organizer Deluxe, you'll also get the program PrimaSoft Organizer Designer. Use Designer to modify or create Collectibles Organizer Deluxe databases. Designer, for example, lets you customize the entry forms and import information from other database programs, including Dbase, Microsoft Access, and Paradox.

63 When You Wish Upon a Star

Do you hate getting gifts that you just don't want? Sure, it is nice that people remember your birthday, anniversary, and other occasions, but wouldn't it be better if they gave you something you could actually use?

Creating an Online Wish List

Brides do it all the time with a gift registry. They make a list of the things they need and then just point their friends and relatives in that direction. Well, you don't have to be a bride to create a gift registry or wish list online. You can personally select items that you'd like to have, and then make the list available to everyone. When a person selects an item from the list, they pay for it, but the company ships it to your address. Slick.

Here's What You Need

You'll need access to the Internet, and you'll need to register your name, address, and the items that you'd like as gifts. You don't need to divulge your credit card number because you won't be paying for anything.

There are quite a few sites that offer a free gift registry service, including

- www.wishlist.com
- giftregistry.yahoo.com
- www.ewish.com
- www.wishworld.com
- www.giftregistrysuperstore.com
- findgift.com
- www.netgiftinc.com

There are also sites that are designed for special occasions. The service at www.yourweddingregistry.com, for example, is designed for bridal registries, while expectant parents can register at `pregnancy.about.com/msubregistry.htm`.

You can also register at many retailers' home pages, such as `www.toysrus.com`, `www.jcpenney.com`, `www.target.com`, and `www.macysbridal.com`.

Sites and Features

All of the sites work about the same. At `www.wishlist.com`, for example, you register for a free list, "window shop" at over 400 merchants, and just click Add to WishList when you locate an item you'd like for a gift.

Yahoo!, however, is one of the world's most popular online portals because of the wide range of services that it offers. The Yahoo! Shopping service (`shopping.yahoo.com`) features hundreds of stores and thousands of products. Through its gift registry service at `giftregistry.yahoo.com` you can create two types of gift registries:

◆ A public registry will be listed in the directory so that any person on the Internet can search to locate your wish list.

◆ A private registry will not be listed in the directory, and can only be accessed by other Yahoo! members that you designate.

To create a gift registry in Yahoo! just follow these steps:

1. Go to `giftregistry.yahoo.com`.

2. Click Create a Registry to open the form shown in Figure 63.1. If you have not yet signed on to Yahoo! with your user name and password, you'll need to do so now and click the Sign In button.

3. Enter a name for the registry.

4. Pull down the Occasion list and select one of the options:

FIGURE 63.1   Creating a registry at Yahoo!

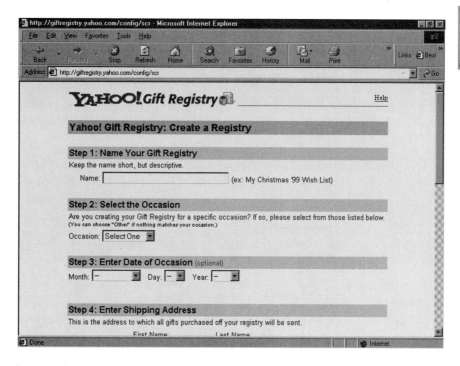

Copyright © 2000 Yahoo! Inc. All rights reserved.

5. Enter the date of the occasion.

6. Fill in your complete shipping address—buyers will see just the city and state.

7. Choose to create a private or public registry.

8. Click Accept to see your gift registry page, as in Figure 63.2.

The next step is to add items to your registry by following these steps:

1. Click Shop for Items on your registry page and then click Begin Adding Items Now at Yahoo! Shopping.

2. Use Yahoo! Shopping to locate an item you are interested in and add it to the merchant's shopping cart.

FIGURE 63.2 Yahoo! gift registry

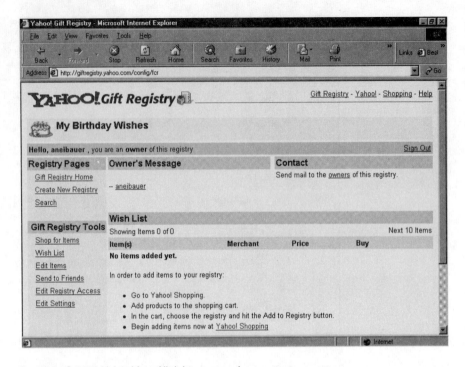

Copyright © 2000 Yahoo! Inc. All rights reserved.

3. In the shopping cart, click the Add to Registry button. Not every merchant currently supports the registry feature, so the button might not appear in every shopping cart. Your registry wish list appears with the item inserted.

4. Click Keep Shopping if you want to add additional items.

NOTE To make changes to your registry, return to the Yahoo! Shopping home page and click **Create or View a Gift Registry** to see the list of your registries. Click the registry you'd like to edit.

If you created a public registry, tell friends and relatives to go to giftregistry .yahoo.com, enter your name or Yahoo! ID, and click Search. The person does not have to be a Yahoo! member to select registry items.

If you created a private registry, you have to invite other Yahoo! members to access it. Just follow these steps from your registry page:

1. Click Send to Friends to see the Invite Someone to Join form.

2. Enter the e-mail address or Yahoo! ID of the person you want to invite.

3. Enter a personal message to include in the invitation.

4. Click Send.

The person receives an e-mail inviting them to join, with a link to your registry. When they click the link and sign on to Yahoo!, your page appears with all of your items listed.

Once a person accesses your registry, they can choose an item and click Buy Now to purchase it. They will have to enter their credit card information to make the purchase, but the merchant will send the purchases item to your shipping address that is on record with the registry.

64 Online Investing

While the market has its ups and downs, there's money to be made in stocks and mutual funds. Certainly there's some risk involved, but the rewards can be substantial. Use your computer and the Internet to buy and sell stocks, and to track your investments.

Buying and Selling Online

The Internet has put a lot of pressure on the traditional stockbroker. Trading through the Internet is fast and easy, and much less expensive than using a traditional broker. On the Internet, you can buy and sell stocks for as little as $5.00 per trade. Try getting that from your broker!

Here's What You Need

You'll need access to the Internet, and you'll need to register with an online brokerage. You may have to provide a credit card number, send a check as a deposit for your trades, or establish credit through your bank or current broker, if you have one. On the CD with this book, you'll find two programs to help you track your investments once you get set up.

Sites and Features

If you are just looking for stock quotes—before you place an order or just to check your portfolio—look on the home pages of most ISPs. Usually they offer an investing link, and this is a good place to start. Many ISPs, such as AOL, CompuServe, and AT&T WorldNet, let you maintain a database of your stocks for instant tracking. When you log on to the investing area, you'll see the updated values of your stocks. At AT&T WorldNet, for example, your portfolio is maintained free by the Thomson Investors Network, which offers these features:

- ◆ Real Time Quotes
- ◆ Portfolio Tracker/Flash Mail
- ◆ First Call Center
- ◆ Stock Center
- ◆ Mutual Fund Center
- ◆ Investor Education Center
- ◆ Help

All of the major search engines have links to investing information. Over at Yahoo!, click the Stock Quotes link to search for a quote using this form:

Copyright © 2000 Yahoo! Inc. All rights reserved.

NOTE You can go directly to the Yahoo! stock quotes site at `finance.yahoo.com`.

Enter the symbol for the stock in the first text box, and choose the extent of information you want in the drop-down list. The options are Basic, DayWatch, Performance, Fundamentals, Detailed, Chart, and Research. Then click Get Quotes.

If you don't know the symbol, click Symbol Lookup or go to `finance.yahoo.com/1`. In the box that appears, enter the name of the company and click Lookup. You can also click Alphabetical Listing for a list of companies.

From the Excite.com home page, enter the symbol in the Get Quotes box in the My Stocks section, and click Go. Click Find Symbol to find the stock's symbol.

At Lycos, go directly to its stock quotes and information page at `investing.lycos.com`.

Most of the major stock brokerages have their own sites for getting account information and placing buy or sell orders. You can get the lowest commissions, however, from firms that specialize in online trading. At Brown and Company (`www.brownco.com`), you can purchase stocks for as little as $5.00 per trade, and options for as low as $10.00 per trade.

To place orders at deep discounts on commission, try these sites:

A. B. Watley, Inc., `www.abwatley.com`

Accutrade, `www.accutrade.com`

Ameritrade, `www.ameritrade.com`

Brown and Company, `www.brownco.com`

E*trade, `www.etrade.com`

The Net Investor, `www.netinvestor.com`

TradeOptions, `www.tradeoptions.com`

Vanguard, `www.vanguard.com`

If you are concerned about the dependability of online trading, check out `www.sonic.net/donaldj`. At this site, you'll find ratings for online discount brokers based on customer feedback. The ratings are updated twice a month.

There are a lot of other investing and financial sites on the Internet. For investment advice, for example, check out The Motley Fool (`www.fool.com`). You can apply to get a free credit report online from `www.consumerinfo.com`.

You should also check with your bank for online banking information. Many banks let you transfer funds and pay bills over the Internet or by using programs such as Microsoft Money, Managing Your Money, and Quicken.

To make online investing even easier, we've included on the CD four programs that will keep your portfolio up to date:

◆ Personal Stock Monitor from `www.dtlink.com`

◆ QuotesNow from `www.quotesnow.com`

◆ StockTray from `www.emtec.com/stocktray`

◆ WebTicker from `www.spaeder.com`

65 E-Commerce

The ultimate in online commerce is to run your own store. Don't bother going into the office or running the storefront from 9 A.M. to 9 P.M. Just stay home and watch the orders—and money—flow in from the Internet.

Open Your Own Online Store

If you run a retail or wholesale business, or are thinking about starting one, then consider opening a store online. You can run it part time or as a sideline, to supplement your storefront or mail order business, or as a full time income producer.

Here's What You Need

Running an online store is a lot like setting up your own Web site. Instead of information about yourself or your hobbies, however, you post descriptions of items for sale. Buyers can select items from your site, adding them to a shopping cart. When they are done shopping, they "check out" by giving their shipping and billing information.

To run an online business, you need an e-commerce site. This is an Internet location in which you can display a catalog of items for sale and accept orders and payments. The best way to get started in online retailing is to join a service that provides the Web space and all of the sales tools that you need. The best e-commerce services will also process credit card sales for you or sign you up for a merchant account with a credit card processing company.

Sites and Features

There are two general types of online stores—those that let you sell your own merchandise and those that supply the merchandise to you.

If you already have a product for sale, either something you manufacture or purchase wholesale, you can create a store to sell it. You'll need to handle your own inventory and shipping.

You can also create a store to sell products provided by the service you join. In this type of site, you primarily select the category of merchandise you want to sell, add your own name to the store, and promote the site as if it were your own. The service maintains the inventory, ships orders, and collects payments. It sends you a commission for all items purchased in your store.

Let's take a look at both types of online stores.

Earning Commissions

Opening up an online store to sell other people's merchandise is a great way to get started in e-commerce. You don't have to worry about inventory, shipping, or collecting money—just sit back and watch the commissions roll in. Of course, to make money with any type of online store, you have to gain exposure. You have to promote the store and get people to go to it and purchase products.

One of the easiest and fastest sites for creating such a store is at www.vstore.com. At Vstore, you create a complete customized store in just a few minutes using thousands of products that Vstore makes available.

You earn a commission from all sales made through your store. The commissions vary between 2 percent and 25 percent, depending on the product, and there are no charges or fees you have to pay, even for credit card payments. Vstore sends you a commission check every 90 days.

Your fiscal relationship with Vstore is as an independent contractor. Vstore does not withdraw any funds for income tax, and must report to the Internal Revenue Service all Vstore members who earn $600 or more in commissions. It is your responsibility to report income and pay the appropriate taxes.

Follow these steps to create a Vstore business:

1. Go to www.vstore.com.

2. Click the link Open your store.

3. Select the category of store you'd like to open. The options are

   ◆ Books

   ◆ Electronics

   ◆ Fan club

   ◆ Gifts and holidays

   ◆ Health, beauty, and wellness

   ◆ Movies

   ◆ Music

   ◆ Specialty

   ◆ Sports and outdoors

   ◆ Superstores

   ◆ Toys and hobbies

   ◆ Video games

NOTE You are only allowed one category for a store, but you can open up to 10 different stores under the same account, each selling a different category of merchandise.

4. Select a subcategory. In most cases you can choose to include all of the subcategories in the same store. If you choose books, for example, you can select to sell all types of books or just a certain subcategory such as computer books or fiction. Vstore displays the

number of products available in that category and the range of commissions.

5. Click Next.

6. Choose a template for the overall look of the store.

7. Select a color theme.

8. Select the typeface for the store text.

9. Click Next.

10. Enter a personalized store name up to 20 characters, such as Carmen's Computers or Harold and Daughters.

11. Enter a store slogan up to 45 characters, or accept the default suggested by Vstore.

12. Designate the Internet address of the store. You have to enter a directory name and select the domain. For example, my own store is `www.neibauer.vstorecomputers.com`. I entered **Neibauer** as the directory name and chose vstorecomputers from a pull-down list of domain options.

13. Enter a custom home page title.

14. Enter any text that you want to appear on the home page.

15. Enter information that you want to appear in the About section of the store.

16. Enter a URL of a page that you want linked to the store. For my page, for example, I linked back to my 11Net Web site, `www.neibauer.net`.

17. Click Next.

18. Enter your account information, including your email address, password, and the address to which you want your commissions mailed.

19. Read the agreement between you and Vstore and select Yes, I Accept.

20. Click Next. A "congratulations" message appears, giving the address of your store.

21. Click View Your Store to see how it looks. A sample Vstore is shown in Figure 65.1.

FIGURE 65.1 Personalized Vstore

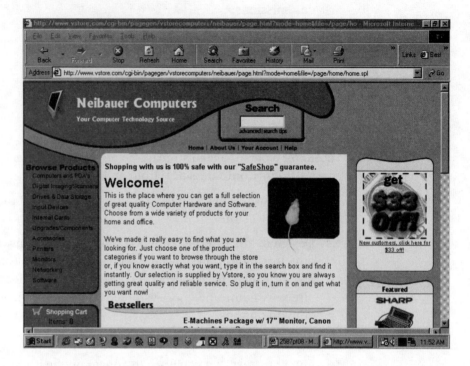

You can make changes to your store or get current sales and commission reports by selecting Manage Your Store from the Vstore home page. In the screen that appears, enter your email address and Vstore password and then click Sign In.

Selling Your Own Products

If you have your own products to sell, then you'll want to open an online store that features just them.

Yahoo!, one of the most popular sites on the Internet, gives you two ways to run an online business with your own merchandise. You can use a feature called Order Manager to run a Yahoo! auction business, or you can open and run an online store.

Neither is free. Order Manager for auctions costs $29.95 per month. The fees for an online store depend on the number of items you want to offer for sale. A small store of up to 50 items costs $100 per month, a large store of up to 1000 items costs $300 a month, and an unlimited store is $300 for the first 1000 items, plus $100 for each additional 1000 items.

There are additional fees involved for obtaining a credit card account and processing credit card payments. Yahoo! has an arrangement with a company called Bank One to provide credit card services to its Order Manager clients and store owners. Bank One charges an initial $250 setup fee, plus a $45 monthly charge. There is a also a charge of 30 cents for each transaction as well as a percentage of each charged amount, depending on the card you select.

Because running a business and getting a merchant account involves up-front costs and a financial commitment, Yahoo! offers a free 10-day trial period for starting an online store. During that period, you create your store and learn how to manage it, but you won't actually be able to sell any products.

N O T E There is no trial period to use Order Manager for auction sales.

To take advantage of this free trial offer, start with these steps:

1. Go to `store.yahoo.com/`.
2. Click How It Works in the Getting Started section of the page that appears.
3. Click Test Drive in the Take a Test Drive section.
4. Enter your Yahoo! user ID and password, and click Sign In to open the Create Your Own Yahoo! Store Account form.
5. Enter a one-word ID that will identify the store.
6. Enter the full name you want for your store.
7. Click Create to see the member agreements.
8. Click I Accept and then click Continue.
9. Click Start the Tour.

You will now be taken through the step-by-step process of creating a store. Just follow the instructions that appear on the screen for adding items and setting up your store's appearance.

After 10 days, Yahoo! will notify you that you need to convert your trial store into an actual store. At this point, you have to provide credit card information to charge your fees, and you can sign up for a Merchant Account to accept credit card payments.

Getting Help

While a lot of the information on the Internet is interesting and fun, much of it can be downright helpful. When you have a question about almost anything, you can usually find an answer—or a place to go for an answer. You can always just type a keyword or two in any search engine and go from there. For some hints on how to find help on some specific matters, read on!

66 Driving Lessons— Making the Most of Your Drivers

Windows is driven by software drivers. To get your modem, monitor, mouse, and other peripherals working together as a computer, Windows needs special files, called drivers, for each peripheral. Some of the drivers are built right in to Windows, and some come with the disk packaged with the peripheral.

Get the Latest Drivers

If you are having problems with part of your computer, you may not have the latest drivers installed. Over time, the companies that make computer hardware improve and refine their drivers for optimum performance. There may be updated Windows 98 drivers specifically designed for a piece of hardware made before Windows 98 came about. Using the Internet, you can get the latest drivers, as well as news about your hardware, to keep that computer of yours humming.

Here's What You Need

All you need is access to the Internet—and enough disk space to store downloaded drivers.

Sites and Features

The first place to look for the most recent drivers is on the home page of the company that made your hardware. Most manufacturers provide a library of drivers for all of their hardware, along with installation instructions and other information. Also look for a section on frequently asked questions (FAQ) to learn from the experiences of others.

If you have a Zoom modem, for example, go to www.zoom.com and look for modem drivers. You can usually find the company's Web site address in the manual packaged with the software. If not, try www.companyname.com (substituting in the name of the company, of course), or do a search for the company's name in any search engine.

If you have Windows 98 and Microsoft Internet Explorer 5 or later, you can check for updated drivers and other Windows files automatically by following these steps:

1. Select Windows Update from the Start menu. Windows dials into your Internet provider and begins a process of checking for newer files and recommended additions. Go directly to the site at any time at windowsupdate.microsoft.com.

2. When the site opens, click the link Product Updates. You'll be asked to wait as it customizes the update process for your computer, and then you'll see programs in these categories of updates:

   ◆ Critical Updates

   ◆ Picks of the Month

   ◆ Recommended Updates

   ◆ Additional Windows Features

   ◆ Fun and Games

   ◆ Device Drivers

3. Click the check boxes for the items you want to update and then click Download.

Microsoft may not have all of the device drivers for your hardware. Rather than go to each manufacturer's site, you can try several sites that specialize in links to the latest drivers from the major, and some minor, players in the Windows hardware field.

WinDrivers (`www.windrivers.com`), for example, has direct links to the driver sites of hundreds of manufacturers. You can also search for drivers. By clicking Advanced Search on the WinDrivers home page, you can search by company name or device category, as shown in Figure 66.1.

FIGURE 66.1   Finding device drivers at WinDrivers.com

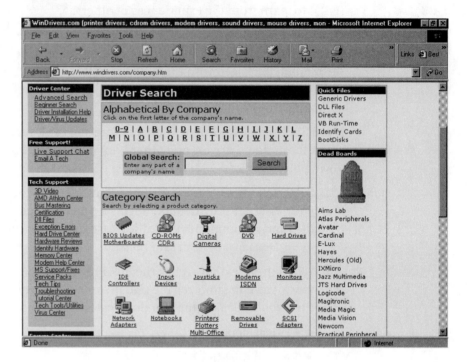

You can also locate generic drivers, run-time files, boot disks, and other common files. You can also find drivers by the device's Federal Communications Commission (FCC) ID number, which is stamped on almost all pieces of computer equipment.

N O T E   If you're still having trouble finding your driver, click **Beginner Search** in the WinDrivers home page for detailed information.

Another excellent source for drivers is Drivers HeadQuarters (`www.drivershq.com`). On the first screen that appears, click the graphic of the wizard for a list of the categories of drivers shown in Figure 66.2. Click a link to access a listing of manufacturers, from which you can locate the drivers you need. You can also download a free program, Driver Detective, that will identify the current drivers on your system, as well as their version and manufacturer.

FIGURE 66.2   **Drivers at Driver Headquarters**

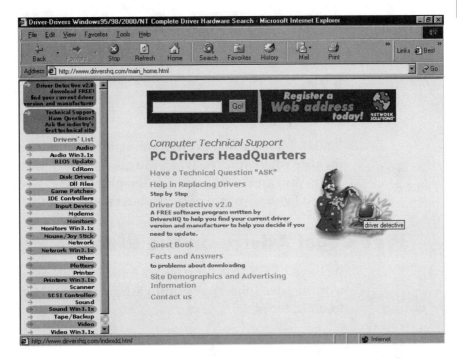

NOTE   If you still can't find your driver, you can sign up for a free membership in DriverGuide.com (`www.driverguide.com`), which takes you step-by-step through locating and installing the driver you need.

If you want to look for updates to programs as well as for drivers, you can try the program CatchUP. Installing the program associates CatchUP as a helper application to your browser. To upgrade your software, go to the site catchup.cnet.com and click Software Updates. CatchUP identifies your software programs and drivers, and then searches the Internet for upgrades.

67 I'm Going to Call My Lawyer! But before I Do

The law is a very complex thing with various interpretations, depending on the state where you live. When you need a lawyer, nothing beats finding one in your area, sitting down, and explaining the issues. But a good place to start fighting your legal battles is on the Internet.

Free Legal Advice on the Web

While you can't go to court via the Internet—yet—you can find a lawyer when you need one. You can also get legal advice to help you through some troubled times.

Here's What You Need

All you need is access to the Internet.

Sites and Features

As we might expect, there are hundreds of places on the Internet to get legal information and advice. Most of the major law schools have Web sites, as do many legal firms.

Most of the sites include articles about various legal issues, links to legal sites, and often links to specific lawyers or a search engine to locate a lawyer near you.

The place I like to start for legal help, however, is DMS-Lawyer (www.dms-lawyer.com), sponsored by the firm of Dessen, Moses & Sheinoff in Philadelphia, PA, and shown in Figure 67.1. At this site, you can send an e-mail to a real-live lawyer and get a personal response in return (usually from one of the firm's partners, not just a legal assistant).

When you get to the site, click the Ask Us a Question link at the bottom of the page. This will launch your e-mail program so you can send DMS-Lawyer your question.

FIGURE 67.1   Online legal help from DMS-LAWYER.com

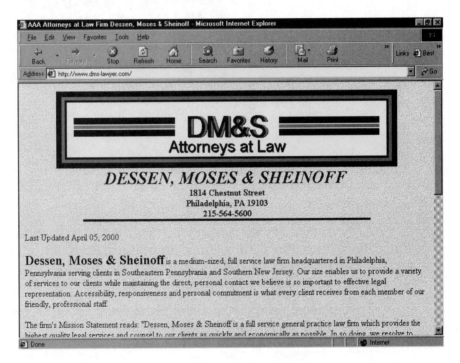

There are other links on this site that will let you access a library of legal resources and the Legal Article Wall, where you'll find articles on current legal issues.

Another place to try for legal information is www.freeadvice.com. As you can see in Figure 67.2, this site has links to legal information of all sorts, and a legal directory to help you find an attorney in your area.

FIGURE 67.2 **FreeAdvice legal help**

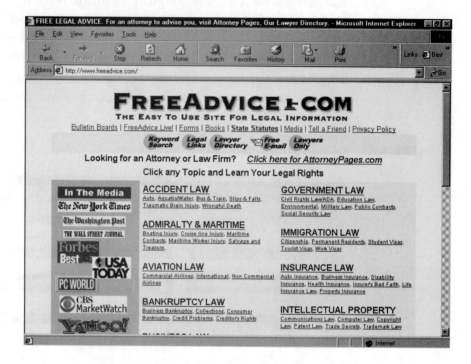

A similar site, www.lawyers.com, lets you find an attorney based on practice area and location. There are also links to all sorts of information, message boards, and chat rooms where you can get personal advice.

Now, as I said, there are hundreds of places on the Internet to get legal information and advice. Here are a few other sites that provide generalized legal help and links to additional sites:

◆ www.uslaw.com

◆ www.legalaccess.com.au/start.html

◆ www.alllaw.com

Some other interesting specialty sites include

`www.uni-sol.com/cca/index3.html` Provides help repairing damaged credit.

`www.divorcesupport.com` Helps with a divorce or with other marital problems.

`uscode.house.gov` Provides access to general and permanent laws of the United States.

`www.jurisline.com` Allows you to look up federal and state court cases, United States legal statutes, and other legal references.

Most of the legal support sites on the Internet are sponsored by legal firms or other organizations. Although altruistic in their offer of information and advice, their ultimate goal is to obtain clients. This does not diminish the usefulness or accuracy of the information they provide, but you should proceed with caution.

68 Finding Health and Medical Advice Online

If you have a medical emergency, don't start looking for information on the Internet. But for background and reference information, and details about the medications you're taking, the Web is the perfect place to explore.

Is There a Doctor in the House?

While the computer is no substitute for a good doctor, it contains a wealth of useful information that can help you in many ways. Information that you obtain on specific medications, for example, can prevent drug interaction and overdose accidents.

Here's What You Need

You'll need access to the Internet. For information about a medication, you'll need the name of the drug, its category of medication, and/or a sample of the medication to help identify it.

Sites and Features

Links for health and medical information are all over the Internet. You'll find them on ISP home pages and on all of the major search engines. For example, you can check out these search engine sites for information on specific conditions:

◆ dir.lycos.com/Health/Conditions_and_Diseases

◆ dir.yahoo.com/health/diseases_and_conditions

You can also look for the home pages of hospitals and medical centers, pharmaceutical companies, drugstore chains, and medical equipment manufacturers.

For current information on medications, medical tests, and procedures, consider consulting LaurusHealth at www.laurushealth.com.

If you want to research current literature for medical information, try Internet Grateful Med (igm.nlm.nih.gov/). This site, sponsored by the National Institutes of Health, offers research through these medical databases:

AIDSLINE	AIDSDRUGS	AIDSTRIALS	ETHICSLINE
DIRLINE	HealthSTAR	HSRPROJ	Medlne
POPLINE	SPACELINE	TOXLINE	HISTLINE
ChemID	OLDMEDLINE		

For information about your child's health, try these sites:

Your Kids Health (www.yourkidshealth.com) Specializes in pediatric information, including how to reduce Sudden Infant Death Syndrome (SIDS).

Dr. Paula (www.drpaula.com) Answers questions about your baby's health.

RxList and the Drug Information Database

For detailed information about medications, two great places to start are RxList (www.rxlist.com) and the Drug Information Database at Stayhealthy.com (www.infodrug.com).

At RxList, shown in Figure 68.1, you can search for drug information by the drug's name, by keyword, and by the ID number imprinted on most capsules and pills. You can also see a list of the top 200 drugs prescribed in the past six years.

FIGURE 68.1   **Get medication information at RxList**

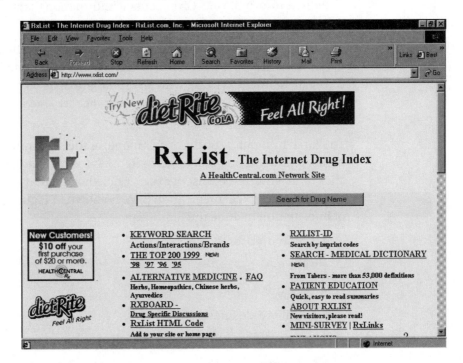

Once you locate the medication, you can get detailed information about it. The type of information available depends on the drug, but you'll usually find categories such as these:

Description   Explains the category of the medication, what the drug consists of, and other general information about it.

Clinical Pharmacology   Explains how the medication works.

Indications, Dosage, and Administration Details the conditions the medication is used to treat, the dosages it is available in, and how the medication should be taken.

Warnings, Contraindications, and Precautions Explains who should not take the medication.

Adverse Reactions and Drug Interactions Summarizes reported side effects of the medication and documented interactions with other medications.

Overdosage Details how to respond to an overdose.

Patient Information Gives general information that the user should be aware of.

The Drug Information Database, supplied by Stayhealthy.com, has similar options and information. You can search for the medication by entering its name or starting with an alphabetical list. To access the site, go to www.infodrug.com, or go to www.stayhealthy.com and click Drug Information.

To search by name, type the drug's name, or the beginning characters of its name, in the text box that appears in the Infodrug.com home page. Then click Find Now to see a list of drugs. Click the one that you want information about. A typical medication page is shown in Figure 68.2. Categories of information include the following:

◆ Common Uses

◆ How to Use

◆ Cautions

◆ Possible Side Effects

◆ Before Using

◆ Overdose

◆ Additional Information

The icon of a capsule next to one of the sources listed indicates that a detailed photograph of the medication is available by clicking the source.

You can also search for a drug by using an alphabetic index. You'll see buttons labeled A through Z on the Infodrug.com home page. Click the button for the letter that starts your medication to see several ranges of names,

FIGURE 68.2 **Sample of the Drug Information Database**

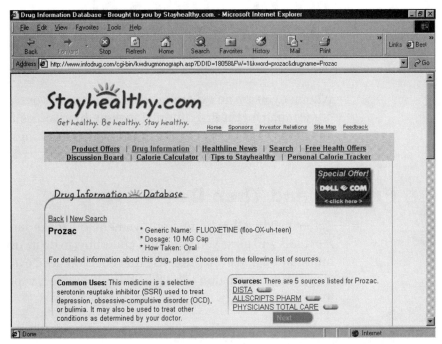

such as P–Panc, Pand–PE-C, and so on. Click the range in which your medication is listed. In the list of links that appears, click your medication to read its detailed description.

InfoDrug, by the way, is operated by the same company that offers Stayhealthy.com (`www.stayhealthy.com`), an excellent portal to health and fitness information of all types.

Now don't bet your life on the health and medical information you can get over the Internet. While most of it is accurate, much medical information needs to be interpreted by a physician in light of your symptoms. What you can get over the Internet is information to make you a wiser health consumer. This information may also fill in some answers that you did not get from your physician. Message boards and online support groups are wonderful resources for information, supportive words, and help in locating the proper medical care.

69 Fixing Things at Home

Whether you are an experienced do-it-yourselfer or trying your hand at home repair for the first time, fixing something yourself can be a rewarding and money-saving experience. But as with most things in life, it pays to be prepared.

Prepare and Then Do

Before tackling that home improvement job, make sure you have the correct tools and parts you need and know how to do it. You can get all of this information and even purchase the tools you need over the Internet. And if you find out you don't feel like doing it yourself, you can find someone to do it for you.

Here's What You Need

The only thing you need is an Internet connection.

Sites and Features

If you need some information about a specific product or tool, try the manufacturer. Some places to start are

www.andersenwindows.com Provides dimensions and information about doors and windows from Andersen.

www.blackanddecker.com Supplies information about using and selecting tools from Black & Decker.

www.dremel.com Allows access to the company catalog, parts pricing, and directions for ordering Dremel tools and accessories.

www.sears.com/craftsman Houses a catalog of Craftsman tools.

www.stanleyworks.com Provides information about tools, doors, hardware, and other products from Stanley.

Over at www.doityourself.com, shown in Figure 69.1, you can get information on projects of all sorts. You can also access bulletin boards to ask and answer questions about various subjects.

FIGURE 69.1 Look for "how-to information" at DoItYourself.com

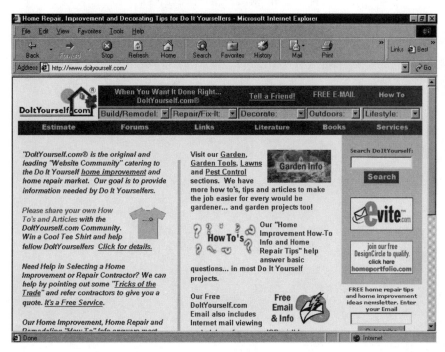

For links to manufacturers, builders, and other sources of information, try these links as well:

◆ www.build.com

◆ www.ehomeplans.com

◆ www.buildingonline.com

◆ www.buildnet.com

◆ www.buildernews.com

◆ www.buildtalk.com

Finally, if you need a special tool for that do-it-yourself project, check out any of the Internet shopping sites, or look at these locations that specialize in tools:

◆ www.toolcenter.com/

◆ www.highland-hardware.com/

◆ www.samallen.com/tool.html

◆ www.woodking.com/

◆ store.rlarson.com/

INDEX

Note to the Reader: Page numbers in **bold** indicate the principal discussion of a topic or the definition of a term. Page numbers in *italic* indicate illustrations.

About the CD

The CD packaged with this book contains over 80 programs that will make surfing the Internet faster, more interesting, and certainly more fun. Here's a sample of the programs you'll find—see the READ.ME file on the CD for a complete list of programs.

Internet Tool Pack   Some basic programs you'll need for your travels through the Internet

Microsoft Internet Explorer 5	BlackWindow
Webroot's Window Washer	ClipCache
Adobe Acrobat Reader	FileSpy
2bpop	Microsoft Dlls

See and Hear it Live   Enjoy multimedia, make your own CDs, watch the world go by, and communicate to the world from the comfort of your own chair.

RealPlayer   MP3 CD Maker   DJ Jukebox   PowWow   Active Worlds Browser

Searching The Unlimited Resource

Turbo Start

Get help finding all sorts of things over the Web.

ISearch	Shetty Search	Copernic 2000
MP3 Fiend	Search Master Demo	Generations Family Tree

It's About Time   Tracking your online time, telling time, and being on time!

EZE Clock	YATS32	CMDTime	AtomTime98	Online Time
TimeIt!	Total Timer	Worldclocks	Gtime	WorldTime

News and Mail   Be up on the latest news, don't miss any email ever again, avoid Spam, get free e-mail accounts, and pick up your e-mail from anywhere.

Headline Viewer	News Dart	EntryPoint	Mail Alert
Appload Notifiy	Active Names	V3 Mail	PureMail